Living in Christ

Christian Morality

Our Response to God's Love

Brian Singer-Towns

saint mary's press

The Subcommittee on the Catechism, United States Conference of Catholic Bishops, has found that this catechetical high school text, copyright 2012, is in conformity with the *Catechism of the Catholic Church* and that it fulfills the requirements of Course VI: "Life in Jesus Christ" of the *Doctrinal Elements of a Curriculum Framework for the Development of Catechetical Materials for Young People of High School Age.*

Nihil Obstat: Rev. William M. Becker, STD
               Censor Librorum
               October 11, 2011

Imprimatur: † Most Rev. John M. Quinn, DD
               Bishop of Winona
               October 11, 2011

The nihil obstat and imprimatur are official declarations that a book or pamphlet is free of doctrinal or moral error. No implication is contained therein that those who have granted the nihil obstat or imprimatur agree with the contents, opinions, or statements expressed, nor do they assume any legal responsibility associated with publication.

The publishing team included Gloria Shahin, editorial director; Brian Singer-Towns, development editor; Maura Thompson Hagarty, PhD, contributing editor and theological reviewer. Prepress and manufacturing coordinated by the production departments of Saint Mary's Press.

Printed in the United States of America

1150 (PO3417)

ISBN 978-1-59982-097-2, paper
ISBN 978-1-59982-118-4, e-book

Contents

Section 2: Honoring God

Section 3: Obedience, Honesty, and Justice

Section 5: Making Moral Choices

Introduction

God's Law is a tremendous gift for us—a reality I was reminded of once again while writing this textbook. Unfortunately, some people do not see it this way. They believe that Christian morality is only about rules, faithfully following do's and don'ts as sort of a divine test to pass to get into Heaven. But Divine Law is not a test. In his teaching Jesus Christ reveals that the real meaning of the moral law is more than just following rules. The "rules" only serve a greater purpose; they are not an end in themselves. God's Law is meant to be a teacher, teaching us how to truly love him, our neighbors, and ourselves.

In my own life, I have known the benefits of following God's Law. When I have been faithful to it, I have known love and happiness despite difficult times and challenging circumstances. In times when I have been unfaithful to it, my life has lacked true inner peace. This is a truth that many people need to learn: God doesn't require us to wait until Heaven to know his love and the true happiness it leads to. We can know it right now, here on earth, if we only strive to live holy lives and rely on the grace that he provides.

As you study this textbook, I hope you will come to see that Christian morality is more about being a loving person than about blindly following rules, that it is more about pursuing holiness than about avoiding sin. Living a moral life is the only way to achieve the happiness, health, and holiness that God desires for us.

The contributions of teens were invaluable to me in writing this text. In particular, I would like to thank the students at Cotter High School in Winona, Minnesota, and two of their teachers, Mary Hansel Parlin and William Crozier. These students provided me with personal stories about moral decisions they have faced and their reflections on living the Ten Commandments. I incorporated their wisdom and insights into many of the Live It! sidebars in this book. These gifted teens affirmed for me that God's grace is alive in the hearts and minds of young people.

Blessings,
Brian Singer-Towns

Foundational Principles for Christian Morality

Part 1

Moral Choices and God's Plan

A re you happy? I do not mean just the momentary feeling you get when someone pays you a compliment or when you eat your favorite ice cream on a hot day. But deep down are you at peace, a peace that lasts even if you lose your cell phone? Are you filled with a love and gratitude that stays with you even when life doesn't go your way? God made us to live in loving communion with him and with one another, and by doing so, we will experience true peace and happiness—but for many people these seem like unattainable goals.

Even though human beings lost the original state of perfect, loving communion that Adam and Eve enjoyed, God has been at work throughout history to restore that state to us. The life, death, Resurrection, and Ascension of Jesus Christ is the fulfillment of God's saving plan. When we make choices to follow Christ, we participate in God's saving plan and will know true peace and happiness, a peace and happiness that the world cannot give.

The articles in this part review topics you have studied before, if you have taken previous courses in this series. This review is important so that our study of moral topics and decision making is built on a solid foundation.

The articles in this part address the following topics:

9

Article 1
Created for Love and Happiness

God's Revelation made known to us through Scripture and Tradition is focused on one core truth: God created human beings to live in loving relationship with him. Stop and think about this for a moment; it is easy to take this amazing truth for granted. God, the Creator of the universe, the all-powerful, all-knowing Mystery who is beyond anything we can understand or imagine, wants to be in loving communion with us for all eternity. We should never take this lightly or for granted; it is the reason the Psalms are filled with praise and thanksgiving: "With my whole being I sing endless praise to you. \ O LORD, my God, forever will I give you thanks" (30:13).

Let's explore this fundamental truth further with a thought experiment. Let's think about how different things would be if God had a different purpose in creating human beings. For example, some ancient people believed that the gods (they often believed in more than one god) created human beings for the gods' amusement. Or they believed that human beings were created to feed the egos of the gods by worshipping them. If this were indeed the reason human beings were created, what would it mean for how we live? It could certainly mean some of the following things; you could probably come up with many other implications.

People in some cultures believed that they needed to keep their gods and goddesses happy through offerings and sacrifices.

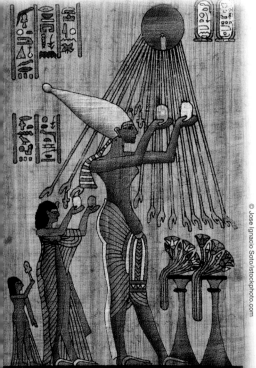

© Jose Ignacio Soto/istockphoto.com

- We would be at the mercy of the gods' changing whims and desires. An action that might please your god today could change tomorrow and leave you doing the wrong thing.

- Because the gods' value system is self-centered, focused on feeding their own egos and desires, then we human beings would imitate those values and would focus only on our own egos and desires.

- We would be in competition with other people for the gods' attention and rewards.

- Our understanding of love would be fundamentally changed. Rather than something that is freely given and freely received, love would be something that has to be earned. This would make love relationships open to manipulation and difficult to trust.

Living in such a world doesn't sound like much fun, does it? But some people reading this might say, "Wait, that's the world I live in!" The sad reality is that as a result of Original Sin, many people do not know the truth about God. And even when we know the truth, the effects of Original Sin make it difficult to live as God calls us to. We see this reflected in many of the false values present in the world: greed, dishonesty, revenge. This is why idolatry, the primary sin against the First Commandment, is probably the most prevalent sin in our world. Our lips confess belief in the one true God, but our actions indicate that we are living the values of false gods, gods that do not exist.

What are the most common things that keep human beings from seeing and appreciating the truths God reveals to us?

© tonobalaguerf/shutterstock.com

Created in God's Image and Likeness

Another fundamental truth revealed by God makes it clear what our relationship with him should be like. This truth is revealed in Genesis 1:26: "Then God said: 'Let us make man in our image, after our likeness.'" In making us in his image, God orders us to himself and destines us for eternal happiness. We are endowed with gifts that allow us to be in true, loving communion with him, both now and for all eternity. Let's look briefly at three of those gifts: our soul, our intellect, and our free will.

At our conception we are given a spiritual **soul**, a divine gift that is unique to human beings. Our soul is the innermost aspect of ourselves. It is immortal and it is what animates our bodies and makes us human. The soul and the body are not two different natures, however. Because the body and soul are completely united, they form a single nature— a human nature. Our soul will live on after our death until it is united with our resurrected body at the Last Judgment. Having a soul means that God has given us the

With God There Is No Coercion

Saint Irenaeus, a bishop and important theologian of the second century, wrote a five-volume set of books called Against Heresies. In the fourth volume, he affirms human freedom in beautiful and inspiring prose. Here is a sample of his writing.

God made human beings free from the beginning, possessing their own power, even as they possess their own soul, so that we obey the law of God voluntarily rather than because God compels us to do so. For there is no coercion with God. . . .

In human beings, as well as in angels, he has placed the power of choice (for angels are rational beings), so that those who have obeyed his law might justly possess what is good, given indeed by God but preserved by our freely chosen obedience. On the other hand, they who have not obeyed shall, with justice, not preserve for themselves what is good, and they shall receive punishment. For God did kindly bestow on them what was good; but they themselves did not choose to preserve it, nor deem it precious.

ability to be in communion with him in a way that is not limited by time or space.

God also gives every human person the gift of **intellect**. Intellect does not mean having a high IQ. Having intellect means that we have the ability to see and understand the order of things that God has established. Our intellect allows us to distinguish between what is truly good and what only appears to be good. Having an intellect means that God has given us the ability to understand how to be in communion with him.

The gift of **free will** makes it possible for us to choose the good that our reason enables us to understand. Because of human freedom, our actions are not predetermined by instinct or DNA (although these and other factors do impact our decision-making ability). Because we have free will, we are each individually responsible for our actions and will be held accountable for our moral choices. Having free will means that we have the ability to choose to be in loving communion with God or the opposite—that is, we can misuse our freedom and reject him. Our free will is a clear sign that God is not manipulative; he does not force us to love him. True freedom is a manifestation of the image of God present in every person.

Our soul, our intellect, and our free will give us a special dignity and a special place in God's plan. They orient us toward God and make it possible for us to be in a love relationship with him that is unique among all his creatures. But to paraphrase the comic-book hero Spiderman, "With great gifts comes great responsibility." Our intellect and free will also make it possible for us to turn away from God. Thus we now turn to the tragic side of salvation history, the reality of Original Sin and our separation from God. We must understand our history so that we can learn from it. ✝

soul

Our spiritual principle, it is immortal, and it is what makes us most like God. Our soul is created by God, and he unites it with our physical body at the moment of conception. The soul is the seat of human consciousness and freedom.

intellect

The divine gift that gives us the ability to see and understand the order of things that God places within creation and to know and understand God through the created order.

free will

The gift from God that allows human beings to choose from among various actions, for which we are held accountable. It is the basis for moral responsibility.

Article 2 The Freedom to Choose

Although God wants each of us to live in perfect communion with him, he doesn't force us to do so. Every person who has ever lived is free to accept or to reject God and his will for us. Adam and Eve, our first parents, exercised this freedom in the biblical account of the Garden of Eden (see

Original Sin
From the Latin *origo,* meaning "beginning" or "birth." The term has two meanings: (1) the sin of the first human beings, who disobeyed God's command by choosing to follow their own will and so lost their original holiness and became subject to death, (2) the fallen state of human nature that affects every person born into the world.

original holiness
The original state of human beings in their relationship with God, sharing in the divine life in full communion with him.

Genesis, chapter 3). They chose to go against God's plan for them to live in perfect communion with God, with each other, and with all of creation. Their decision to eat the forbidden fruit affects each of us, everyone who came before us, and all those who will come after us.

Human Freedom and Moral Choice

Adam and Eve experienced the same choice that all humans have had to face: whether to do good or to choose what is evil. And if Adam and Eve had a tough time resisting their forbidden fruit, how much more challenged are we by the world we live in. Every day we are surrounded by thousands of messages that tell us that true happiness is found in the number of friends we have, the kind of phone we use, what clothes we wear, and what our body looks like. The pursuit of popularity, pleasure, and wealth are temptations that distract us from the authentic happiness that comes from true, loving relationships with God and with one another.

But that's where our free will comes in. Unlike animals, whose instinct drives their actions, we can think about the moral aspects of our behavior both before and after we act. Our free will allows us to choose to act in ways that are consistent with God's revealed will. We can choose to ignore those temptations that lead us away from God because we are free to do so. Of course, freedom also means that we are

This image of Adam and Eve in the Garden of Eden is filled with symbolism. Why are Adam and Even naked? Why is Adam turned away from Eve? Why are they safe in the presence of a dangerous animal, the leopard?

© The Gallery Collection/Corbis

responsible for the choices we make, especially in religious and moral matters. Freedom and responsibility go hand in hand.

Although we are responsible for our actions, some factors may lessen the blame when we choose the wrong courses of action. For example, you might be ignorant of a rare side effect that a prescription drug will have on your behavior. Sometimes psychological factors such as fear can drive us to do things we would otherwise never think of doing. Likewise, strong social pressures may lessen the moral responsibility for some of our actions. These are not excuses for acting badly, but they are a recognition that we are not always acting with perfect freedom when we make moral decisions.

Although circumstances may weaken our ability to choose good over evil, our free will—and the responsibility that comes with it—cannot be taken away. God has built it into us; it is a basic human right that no one has the right to try to take from us. Our freedom to choose, however, does not give us the right to say or do anything we please. "If it feels good, do it" may make a clever slogan, but living that way is irresponsible and can lead to sinful choices that will hurt ourselves and others.

© Galushko Sergey/shutterstock.com

With freedom comes responsibility. The choices that human beings make can affect the entire planet for better or worse.

The Results of Original Sin

Making good moral choices is sometimes hard to do for another reason. We are all affected by Adam and Eve's disobedience of God's will, a condition we call **Original Sin**: "Adam and Eve transmitted to their descendants human nature wounded by their own first sin and hence deprived of original holiness and justice" (*Catechism of the Catholic Church [CCC]*, 417). Adam and Eve did not receive their state of **original holiness** for themselves alone but for all human nature. Thus when they sinned their sin did not

Has Original Sin Completely Corrupted Us?

Original Sin does not cause us to lose our goodness or make us completely spiritually corrupt. Some of the Protestant reformers taught that Original Sin had completely perverted human nature and destroyed our freedom to choose between right and wrong, and some Protestants today still hold that belief. In response, the Catholic Church more clearly articulated what God has revealed regarding Original Sin. Original Sin does not completely pervert human goodness, but it does weaken our natural powers for relating to God and for choosing to do good. It does not completely destroy our communion with God. It has damaged our communion with him and with one another. These effects of Original Sin can be overcome only by our faith in Christ and the grace that is given through the Sacraments.

concupiscence

The tendency of all human beings toward sin, as a result of Original Sin.

affect just themselves but affected their human nature, which was passed on to all their descendants.

Because of Original Sin, human nature is weakened. The loss of original holiness and justice makes things that should be natural to us harder and more challenging. Relationships with others that should naturally be good and loving are marked by tension and misunderstanding. We are more influenced by ignorance, suffering, and the knowledge of our own death. Moral decisions that should be easy and straightforward become more difficult and confusing; we are more inclined to sin. This inclination is called **concupiscence**.

Original Sin causes an even more serious loss. Our relationship with God is now clouded and hidden. We no longer naturally walk in the garden with God as with a close friend. Even though God desires to be just as close to us as he was to Adam and Eve, we struggle to find him. And there is the most serious loss of all: we now experience death. What God had warned Adam about has come true: "From that tree you shall not eat; the moment you eat from it you are surely doomed to die" (Genesis 2:17). ✝

God did not create human beings for death. How would you explain God's plan for humanity to someone who had never heard of Christ's saving work?

© Kratka Photography/shutterstock.com

Pray It!

Praying for the Desire to Change

Have you ever wanted to change a habit or characteristic you have but just couldn't find the willpower to do so? This happens when we have a long habit of acting in a certain way, when we suffer from an addiction, or when we are being greatly influenced by another person. Sometimes it seems like our free will isn't so free! An ancient spiritual wisdom says that when this happens we first have to ask God to give us the *desire* to change. When we ask God for the desire to change, we acknowledge that we are powerless to change on our own, without the help of his grace. We have to give up the illusion that we have control in order for God to work in our lives. Here's a short prayer you can say when you find yourself in this situation:

God, I've tried to change,

over and over again with the same results.

I end up in the same place I started

only more discouraged than before.

So I place myself in your loving hands

and acknowledge that I am powerless to change without your grace.

Give me the desire that I need to change my life

to turn away from sin and turn toward you.

For I trust that with your help all things are possible,

even the conversion of my stubborn heart.

All praise to you. Amen.

Article **3** New Life in Christ

If you have ever tried to make a positive change in your life, you probably discovered how hard it can be to do. Whether it is a commitment to spend more time in prayer, to work harder in school, or to get more physical exercise, the majority of people give up on such commitments within a month! The effort required to change seems too much for us and we give up.

Now think about God. After the Fall, he did not abandon humankind. Ever since Adam and Eve's sin, God has been working to get human beings to make a major change, to turn away from sin and to turn toward him. He called Abraham to be the father of a Chosen People. He formed a sacred covenant with his Chosen People and gave them Divine Law to teach them how to live as a holy people. He gave them rituals and the priesthood so they could unite with him and with one another in prayerful worship. When they fell away, he called judges, kings, and prophets to lead them back to him. Sadly, when we study these biblical accounts, we find that the human response to God's initiatives was lacking throughout salvation history. At first the people would get excited and committed, but within a generation or less they would go back to their old ways of ignoring the covenant God had formed with them. If anyone has reason to give up on us, surely it is God.

This is a painting from the Church of the Transfiguration on the top of Mount Tabor in Israel. The tablet that Moses is holding and the light around his forehead symbolize the divine truth provided by God's Law.

© Brian Singer-Towns/Saint Mary's Press

But God never gives up on humanity, both corporately and individually. You have studied **salvation history** and the **Paschal Mystery** in other courses. You know how God the Father sent his only begotten Son as his ultimate saving act. You know how Jesus Christ saves us from sin and death through his suffering, death, Resurrection, and Ascension. You know that those who believe in Christ have new life in the Holy Spirit. The battle against sin and death has been won. In light of this reality, every person in the world faces a question only he or she can answer: Will you answer Christ's call to place your faith in him?

Called to Beatitude

In calling us to place our faith in him, Christ calls us to an entirely new vision of life. This vision is expressed in the Beatitudes. You will find these in Matthew 5:3–12 and Luke 6:20–26. If you haven't read them in a while, look them up and read them again. They present a vision of life that is rad-ically different from the vision of life held by many people, both in Jesus' time and in our time. Just consider the mean-ing of the first beatitude in Matthew: "Blessed are the poor in spirit, for theirs is the kingdom of Heaven." Being poor in spirit is the opposite of being self-centered or egotistical. It means putting other people's needs before our own. It means trusting in God for what we need and not just in ourselves. And living this way comes with a promise, that we shall be citizens of the Kingdom of Heaven, both in this life and for all eternity with God in Heaven.

The other seven beatitudes are just as radical in their implications. They illustrate the paradoxes of God's wisdom. It is only in looking to other people's needs that our deepest needs will be met. It is only in letting ourselves feel grief that we shall know God's comfort. It is only in being persecuted for doing what is right that we shall be worthy of Heaven. As we begin to understand the meaning of the individual Beati-tudes we start to see the big picture that Christ calls us to as his disciples. That big picture we might call a life of **beatitude**.

The Beatitudes teach us our vocation as Christians, the goal of our existence. We call this goal by different names: coming into the Kingdom of God, the beatific vision, enter-ing into the joy of the Lord, being adoptive children of God (also called divine filiation), or entering into God's rest. By

salvation history
The pattern of specific salvific events in human history that reveal God's presence and saving actions.

Paschal Mystery
The work of salvation accomplished by Jesus Christ mainly through his life, Pas-sion, death, Resurrec-tion, and Ascension.

beatitude
Our vocation as Christians, the goal of our existence. It is true blessedness or happiness that we experience partially here on earth and perfectly in Heaven.

Comparing Matthew and Luke's Beatitudes

Beatitudes in Matthew 5:3–12	Beatitudes in Luke 6:20–23
Blessed are the poor in spirit, for theirs is the kingdom of heaven.	Blessed are you who are poor, for the kingdom of God is yours.
Blessed are they who mourn, for they will be comforted.	
Blessed are the meek, for they will inherit the land.	
Blessed are they who hunger and thirst for righteousness, for they will be satisfied.	Blessed are you who are now hungry, for you will be satisfied. Blessed are you who are now weeping, for you will laugh.
Blessed are the merciful, for they will be shown mercy.	
Blessed are the clean of heart, for they will see God.	
Blessed are the peacemakers, for they will be called children of God.	
Blessed are they who are persecuted for the sake of righteousness, for theirs is the kingdom of heaven.	
Blessed are you when they insult you and persecute you and utter every kind of evil against you (falsely) because of me. Rejoice and be glad, for your reward will be great in heaven.	Blessed are you when people hate you, and when they exclude and insult you, and denounce your name as evil on account of the Son of Man. Rejoice and leap for joy on that day! Behold, your reward will be great in heaven.

living the Beatitudes, we begin to experience on earth the happiness that God has wanted human beings to know from the beginning of creation. A life of beatitude purifies our hearts and prepares us for the eternal happiness and joy that will come when we enter into perfect communion with the Holy Trinity in Heaven.

Living the Beatitudes brings meaning to our moral choices. For example, the Beatitudes promise that we will know happiness by embracing the hardships of life, not by avoiding those hardships. They promise that we will know true joy by pursuing righteousness (or justice) and peace, not by pursuing wealth, fame, or power. Finally, the Beatitudes do not promise that we will fully know the joy God intends for us during our earthly life, only that we shall know it partially now and completely in Heaven. So the moral choices we make to live a life of beatitude purify our hearts and remove our vices in preparation for the perfect joy and happiness we will know in Heaven.

The Holy Trinity, Our Compass and Our Strength

Through our Baptism we are already on our way to living a life of beatitude. Through the Sacrament of Baptism, Original Sin and all personal sin are washed away, removing our separation from God. We die to sin and the false promises of Satan, which lead only to unhappiness and eternal death. We are reborn to a new life in Christ, which leads to true happiness and eternal life. As baptized people we trust God to do for us what we cannot do by ourselves.

God provides us with what we need to live the Beatitudes. Through Scripture and Tradition, he provides the compass, showing us the way to live as disciples. Through the graces given in Baptism, the Eucharist, and the other Sacraments, we are provided with the strength we need.

Live It!

Inspired to Live the Beatitudes

What gives you inspiration for living a life of beatitude? Many students report that respected peers and authority figures inspire them to make good moral choices. One student tells about having behavioral problems in middle school: "My teacher, Mr. S., understood that what I needed was some discipline in order to break my habit of disrespect. He helped me to realize that the easy road in life is often the one that can ruin us. But the hard road is the one that gives us the most happiness."

Another student reported getting her inspiration from the Word of God. She struggled with getting her homework done on time and with helping with family chores willingly. Then one Sunday at Mass she heard the Beatitudes proclaimed in the Gospel reading. The priest's homily was about making good moral decisions. The Gospel reading and the priest's homily helped her to realize she had been making some bad decisions and inspired her to make some changes. She stopped procrastinating on homework assignments and started helping at home cheerfully.

Where do you find your inspiration to live the Beatitudes?

© Sorin Popa/shutterstock.com

Scripture and Tradition provide the divine compass that shows us the way to live a life of beatitude.

Called by God the Father, empowered by the Holy Spirit, and guided by the teaching and example of Jesus Christ, the Son of God, we constantly grow closer to the Holy Trinity through our moral choices. God alone reveals to us that he is Father, Son, and Holy Spirit. The mystery of the Holy Trinity is the central truth of the Christian faith. Through grace, we move toward the goal of Christian life, which is union with the Holy Trinity in Heaven.

Living the Beatitudes isn't the easiest way to live. Jesus himself acknowledges this. "Enter through the narrow gate; for the gate is wide and the road broad that leads to destruction, and those who enter through it are many. How narrow the gate and constricted the road that leads to life. And those who find it are few" (Matthew 7:13–14). At times it will be tempting to give up trying to live a moral life. We can come up with a thousand reasons to justify a decision we know deep down is wrong. But even if we give in to temptation, God never gives up on us. Since Adam and Eve's sin, God has been at work, gently calling us to true happiness and joy. Put your faith in Jesus Christ and never stop asking God to be your compass and your strength. ☩

Article 4 Justification and Sanctification

Why should we be good? Or to put it another way, what is the purpose of aligning our moral choices with God's plan? Do you do good things so that you can win the reward of Heaven? Or is being good a result of putting your faith in Jesus? Maybe you've had discussions on this question with someone who has asked whether you believe we are saved by our faith or by our (good) works?

In past centuries these questions have been the cause of angry disagreement between some Christians. Thankfully, ecumenical discussions in the last decades have resulted in greater clarity about these questions and wider recognition of the truth that God has revealed. And what has been revealed to us is this: we are saved through God's work, not our own efforts. Our primary goal in Christian morality is to collaborate with God's grace, not to try to earn our way into Heaven.

Justified by Faith in Christ

The process by which God's grace frees us from sin and sanctifies us (makes us holy) is called **justification**. Think of it this way: through our faith in Christ and the Sacrament of Baptism, we become a new person, an adopted son or daughter of God who shares in Christ's righteousness. Through Christ's Passion and the sanctifying grace received at Baptism, Original Sin is erased. Though the consequences of Original Sin remain, the restoration of our original holiness and **original justice**—which was lost through Original Sin—is made possible. Without the separation caused by sin, harmony with ourselves, with God, and with one another is again possible. God grants us this wonderful gift through Baptism because it is through our Baptism that we unite ourselves to Christ's Passion and share in his death and Resurrection.

justification
The process by which God frees us from sin and sanctifies us.

original justice
The state of complete harmony that our first parents had with their inner self, with each other, and with all of creation.

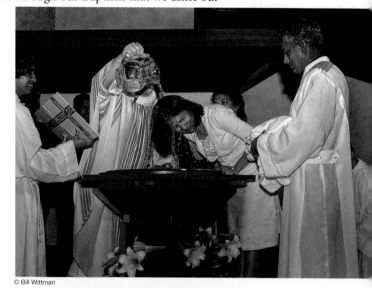

How is Baptism related to the process of justification? Why is it such a joyful Sacrament?

© Bill Wittman

Catholic Wisdom

Justification Is God's Greatest Work

Saint Augustine explains why the justification of the sinner is God's greatest and most excellent work in his commentary on John 14:12, "Whoever believes in me will do the works that I do, and will do greater ones than these."

> The justification of the wicked is a greater work than the creation of heaven and earth [because] heaven and earth will pass away but the salvation and justification of the elect . . . will not pass away.[1] (*CCC*, 1994)

Our justification begins and ends with God's work. It starts with conversion. Prompted by the grace of the Holy Spirit, we realize that we need to turn to God and away from sin. We accept God's gifts of forgiveness and righteousness. As the process of justification continues, we become increasingly freed from the tyranny of sin and healed from its effects. We become reconciled with God, and the desire to become more and more like him grows inside us. Nourished by grace through celebrations of the Eucharist and the other Sacraments, we want our every decision to reflect what God desires. As the process of justification reaches its end, we become **sanctified**, that is, we become a holy person, a saint. Through sanctification we give glory to God here on earth; after our death we shall continue to give him glory in Heaven.

Making these ideas a little more concrete might be helpful. Consider the life of Saint Ignatius of Loyola (1491–1556), the founder of the Jesuit order. In his early life, Ignatius was determined to become a distinguished nobleman, and he was not considered to be particularly religious. He enjoyed the pursuits of young nobles: gambling, sword fighting, and chasing women. But at the age of thirty, all his noble pursuits came to a halt when he was struck by a cannonball and injured in both legs. This turned out to be an occasion for a special grace in his life.

God's grace was active in Saint Ignatius of Loyola's life long before he was aware of it. Saint Ignatius allowed God's gifts of forgiveness and righteousness to bear great fruit in his life.

© Gene Plaisted

During his long recuperation, Ignatius began reading about the life of Christ and the lives of the saints. Thus began his conversion. Ignatius came to believe that modeling one's life on the example of Christ was a worthy goal and eventually became convinced that such a life would be more satisfying than life in a royal court. He repented of his previous sins and was determined to change. A series of fortunate events led him to spend ten months living in simple circumstances while praying and studying the spiritual life. God had begun the process of justification in Ignatius's life. The rest of his life would be marked by the desire to discover God's will and to do it, despite numerous challenges and setbacks. Sanctified through the grace of God, Ignatius achieved true holiness. He was declared a saint in 1622. You can find more about the life of Saint Ignatius in a lives of the saints book or by asking a Jesuit priest or brother about him.

sanctify, sanctification
To make something holy. Sanctification is the process of becoming closer to God and growing in holiness, taking on the righteousness of Jesus Christ with the gift of sanctifying grace.

God's Work and Our Collaboration

The theological concept of **merit** is sometimes used to describe our standing in the eyes of God. In general, "merit" refers to the compensation owed by a community or to a community for the actions of its members. Merit can be a reward, or it can be a punishment. In the theological sense, having merit means that God sees us as justified persons, free from sin and sanctified by his grace. Or it can mean that God sees us in need of merit, that we have not accepted his forgiveness and grace.

merit
God's reward to those who love him and follow Christ's Law of Love. To have merit is to be justified in the sight of God, free from sin and sanctified by his grace. We do not earn merit on our own; it is a free gift from God due to the grace of Christ in us.

It should be clear from all you have learned so far that there is nothing that we can do to earn merit in God's sight. God just doesn't need anything that we can give; everything that we are and everything that we have is already a gift from God. God has taken the initiative by freely choosing to share his love, his grace, and his forgiveness with us. God first initiates and then we respond. If our response is the response of faith in Jesus Christ, we become collaborators in God's saving work. So the merit we have in the sight of God is first and foremost God's free gift to us and then, secondly, our acceptance of his gift and our participation in his saving plan.

This brings us back to the original question: Why should we be good? We should be good because that is how God made us. We should be good because God has given us a share in his life and his love. We should be good because God has given us his grace to justify us and sanctify us so that we can live in perfect communion with him and all the saints for all eternity. Any other reasons, such as trying to impress others, trying to gain social status, or even to trying to earn our way into Heaven, will eventually backfire on us because they put *us* at the center of our moral choices rather than putting God at the center. ✝

Justification and Divinization

God reveals that it is possible for us to be a true image of him. Jesus teaches us this in the Sermon on the Mount when he commands his disciples to "Be perfect, just as your heavenly Father is perfect" (Matthew 5:48). And in addressing this question, Saint Athanasius of Alexandria wrote, "The Son of God became man that we might become god."

Eastern Catholics describe three stages in the process of justification:

1. The first stage is *katharsis*, or purification. In this stage we remove sin from our lives so that we can focus on God.

2. The second stage is *theoria*, or illumination. In this stage we come to know and experience what it means to be fully human through our communion with Jesus Christ.

3. The last stage of the process, *theosis*, comes from a Greek word meaning "divinization." As we put into perfect practice the teachings of Jesus Christ, we achieve *theosis*. We become saints who are in the fullest communion with God that is possible in this life.

Divinization is not something we can do on our own; it is possible only through the power of God's sanctifying grace imparted through the Sacrament of Baptism. Divinization will be fully realized only with our own resurrection.

Review

1. Why are human beings unique among all of God's creation?

2. Briefly describe the three God-given gifts that allow us to live in true, loving communion with God.

3. What are some factors that can diminish our freedom and lessen the moral responsibility of our resulting actions?

4. What is concupiscence?

5. Describe what it means to live the Beatitudes.

6. How does God provide us with the direction and the strength to live a life of beatitude?

7. Define *justification*.

8. How do we gain merit in the sight of God?

Part 2

The Law of God

God has a law. Or to say it more accurately, God is the source of all true law. Our loving Creator placed in his creation an order that is a reflection of himself. This is why law and order go together naturally. God's Law governs the universe and directs it to its ultimate purpose. Everything God created obeys the order he established in creation. Well, almost everything.

Just as physical laws govern the physical universe (for example, what comes up must come down—the law of gravity), moral laws govern the relationships human beings have with God and with one another (for example, treat others as you would want them to treat you). Human beings are unique in that God has given us the gift of free will. We alone, among all of God's creatures, can choose to act in ways that disrupt the natural order and bring chaos, pain, and suffering into creation. But we can also choose to act in ways that support and strengthen the natural order and bring greater love and healing into creation.

Through the use of our reason and by studying Revelation, we are able to discover and understand God's Eternal Law. This is a necessary step in living a moral life.

The articles in this part address the following topics:

Article 5 Eternal Law

Let's say one day you wake up and decide that you are going to walk backward for the rest of your life. At first it is pretty rough going. You trip a lot, run into things, and maybe get a lot of people confused and even upset. But with practice you get pretty good at it. You can get places just about as fast as everyone else, and you rarely trip or fall over. People even get used to it and stop commenting on how strange you are. So you think you've proven there is nothing natural about walking forward. Except . . . a few years later, your knees start to hurt and you have constant headaches. Your doctor tells you it is from the unnatural stress you have placed on your knee joints from walking backward and on your neck from constantly looking over your shoulder. Sooner or later, he says, you are going to require knee replacements if you keep walking backward. There is a price to pay for going against God's natural order.

Let's put this in a moral context. You wake up one day and decide to tell at least one lie every day—usually something that will benefit you. At first it is pretty rough going. You aren't very good at it; people often catch you doing it and get upset. But over time you get more polished. People catch you less often, and when they do, they just shrug it off because they are used to it. You think you have proven that there is nothing natural about telling the truth and few consequences for not doing so. Except . . . a few years later, you are engaged to the person of your dreams. As you grow nearer your wedding date, your fiancé catches you telling a lie, and then another, and another. Your fiancé breaks off the engagement, announcing the decision to you by simply saying, "I cannot spend my life with a person I cannot trust." There is always a price to pay for going against God's natural order.

There are consequences to pay if we go against the order God establishes in creation. These consequences can be physical, relational, and spiritual.

© Tatiana Morozova/shutterstock.com

Types of Moral Law

We have many different expressions of moral law to discuss in the articles in this part. They include the following:

- natural moral law
- moral law revealed in the Old Testament (the Old Law)
- moral law revealed by Christ in the New Testament (the New Law)
- the Precepts of the Church
- canon law

These other kinds of law are true because they express the truth of God's Eternal Law.

Eternal Law
The order in creation that reflects God's will and purpose; it is eternal because it is always true and never changes. All other types of law have their basis in Eternal Law and are only true if they reflect the truth of Eternal Law.

moral law
The moral law is established by God and is a rational expression of Eternal Law. Moral law reflects God's wisdom; it is the teaching that leads us to the blessed life he wants for us.

Eternal Law and the Moral Law

These two stories are simple examples of the order in creation—an order that reflects God's will and purpose. We sometimes call this order Divine Law or **Eternal Law**. It is eternal because it is always true and never changes. Every part of creation finds its purpose, its true end, in Eternal Law. And God has given human beings the gift of intellect by which we can understand and appreciate Eternal Law, even if only partially. We do this by using reason (reason is the application of our intellect) and by listening to God's revealed truth.

In studying Christian morality, we discuss many different kinds of law. In general, law is a rule of behavior that is made by a competent authority for the sake of the common good. In particular, the **moral law** comes from God and is a rational expression of Eternal Law. Moral law reflects God's wisdom and love. It is the guidance and teaching he gives us that leads to the blessed life he wants for every person. Everyone can know the moral law through the gift of our conscience. As a parent guides a child away from the dangers of the world, so God's moral law prevents us from falling prey to evil and urges us to do what is good. If we listen to our conscience and follow the moral law, we will live in loving communion with God now and forever. This is why every person is obliged to follow the moral law. ✝

This seedling can symbolize the order God has established in creation. How many natural laws can you name that govern the growth of this seedling and that are true for all seedlings?

© WendellandCarolyn/istockphoto.com

Live It!

If I'm Free, Why Must I Follow the Moral Law?

Some people might ask, if God created me with the gift of freedom, aren't I free to decide what is right or wrong for me? This question shows a misunderstanding of human freedom. We are free to choose to do what is right or what is wrong. But we are not free to decide what is right and what is wrong, because we would have to be as wise as God to do so! Moral truth is objective truth; it is not subjective. It is based in God's Eternal Law. We simply cannot decide on our own that something is good when in God's created order it is evil.

Still someone might ask why we need to follow laws that were created thousands of years ago. If this is referring to the Ten Commandments and the New Law taught by Jesus, then these laws were not created thousands of years ago. They were created at the beginning of time. They are based in Eternal Law, which is true forever. Yes, it is true that the moral law needs to be applied to new historical situations and new scientific advances. But this is the work of the entire Church, not just one person by himself or herself.

One final thing to remember about this question: Obeying the moral law actually makes us more free, and disobeying the moral law makes us less free. Think about the example of telling lies given at the beginning of this article. People who are recovering from chronic dishonesty will tell you that staying on top of whom they told which lies to eventually occupied their entire attention. They became totally controlled by their fear of being discovered. They were trapped and imprisoned by their immoral behavior.

Article 6 Natural Moral Law

natural law
The moral law that can be understood through the use of reason. It is our God-given ability to understand what it means to be in right relationship with God, other people, the world, and ourselves. The basis for natural law is our participation in God's wisdom and goodness because we are created in the divine likeness.

The Declaration of Independence appeals to natural law: "We hold these truths to be self-evident, that all men are created equal, that they are endowed by their Creator with certain unalienable Rights, . . ."

Every person is born with an awareness of good and evil, of right and wrong. Through the gift of reason, every person, Christian or not, can follow the moral law and live a life pleasing to God. We call the moral law that can be understood through our intellect and the use of reason **natural law**, because it is part of our human nature. Saint Thomas Aquinas describes natural law as "nothing other than the light of understanding placed in us by God; through it we know what we must do and what we must avoid"[2] (*Catechism of the Catholic Church [CCC]*, 1955). Because we are made in God's image, the natural moral law enables us to participate in God's wisdom and goodness.

This ability to use our reason to do good and avoid evil is universal. Every human being is equipped with this ability; it does not depend on any religion. The founders of the United States acknowledged this in the Declaration of Independence, which proclaims that certain moral truths are self-evident. We just know them. It goes further to say that all human beings have fundamental rights and duties that cannot be taken away, including the pursuit of true happiness.

The Golden Rule is a good example of a natural moral law. Call it common sense or basic moral sense, but natural law dictates that we should treat people the way we want to be treated. Jesus reminds us of the wisdom of the Golden Rule (see Matthew 7:12), but Christians have no monopoly on it. Other great world religions, including Judaism, Islam, Buddhism, Hinduism, and Taoism, espouse it as well, although they may have a different way of saying it. Even many people who profess no belief in God adhere to the Golden Rule.

Because natural moral law is an expression of God's Eternal Law, it does not change with time. Regardless of the culture or religious belief, common principles bind us together and form the basis for all other moral rules and civil laws. Any community that wishes to embody justice and goodness will develop civil laws that reflect—and do not contradict—natural law.

© Paul McKenna

To summarize, natural law is part of our humanity—part of our nature. To be moral is to be fully human. The phrase "man's inhumanity to man" and the word *inhumane* express what happens when we do not live morally—that is, when we are no longer acting as human beings.

Natural Moral Law and the Church

Greek philosophy, particularly the teachings of the philosopher Aristotle, was one of the earliest expressions of natural law. Greek philosophy distinguished between laws that were customs and laws that were based in nature. Laws based in custom were true in a particular place and time, but laws based in nature, natural laws, were true everywhere and for everyone. Greek philosophy had a strong influence in the Roman Empire, so the early Christians were familiar with it and even made use of the natural law teaching. We can see evidence of this in the New Testament. In the first chapter of the Letter to the Romans, Saint Paul explains why every person is responsible for the consequences of their sins.

> For what can be known about God is evident. . . . Ever since the creation of the world, his invisible attributes of eternal power and divinity have been able to be understood and perceived in what he has made. . . . And since they did not see fit to acknowledge God, God handed them over to their undiscerning mind to do what is improper. . . . Although they know the just decree of God that all who practice such things deserve death, they not only do them but give approval to those who practice them. (1:19–20,28,32)

Essentially Paul is saying that knowledge of God and of the moral law is evident to every person through creation. So if we fail to acknowledge this and thus do not follow the natural moral law, we deserve God's just punishment.

Centuries later, Saint Augustine also appeals to the natural moral law to explain how all people, Christian or not, know in their hearts what is right. He uses the image of a king stamping his ring with the royal seal into wax as a metaphor for the way God stamps the seal of his Law into our hearts.

> Where indeed are these rules written, wherein even the unrighteous recognizes what is righteous, wherein he discerns that he ought to have what he himself has not? Where, then,

are they written, unless in the book of that Light which is called Truth? Whence every righteous law is copied and transferred (not by migrating to it, but by being as it were impressed upon it) to the heart of the man that works righteousness; as the impression from a ring passes into the wax, yet does not leave the ring. ("On the Trinity," Book XIV) ☩

The Importance of Natural Moral Law

Because each of us is born with the natural moral law stamped on our hearts, we all have a natural orientation to live a moral life. A person does not have to be a baptized Christian to live a life pleasing to God. A person who has never heard God's Revelation through Scripture and Tradition still has the possibility of being saved if she or he lives according to the natural moral law implanted in her or his heart.

Natural law also serves another important function. It allows for the development of civil laws that everyone can agree to regardless of their faith, religion, or culture. Pope Benedict XVI in his encyclical *God Is Love* (*Deus Caritas Est*, 2005), reminds us that we shape just civil policies and laws by appealing to reason and natural law.

> The Church's social teaching argues on the basis of reason and natural law, namely, on the basis of what is in accord with the nature of every human being. It recognizes that it is not the Church's responsibility to make this teaching prevail in political life. Rather, the Church wishes to help form consciences in political life and to stimulate greater insight into the authentic requirements of justice as well as greater readiness to act accordingly, even when this might involve conflict with situations of personal interest. (28)

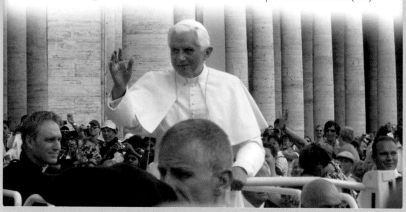

Article 7 Law and the Original Covenant

Imagine that the bishop of your diocese called people from all the parishes of the diocese together for a special, once-in-a-lifetime gathering. So many people were attending that the gathering had to be held outdoors at a huge stadium. People began gathering hours before the event was to start. Suddenly, before everything was scheduled to start, something dramatic happened. Clouds gathered in the sky, and brilliant flashes of lightning and loud peals of thunder filled the air. While this was happening, a small earthquake shook the ground, causing people to lean on one another to stay upright. Then just as suddenly as it began, all the noise and commotion came to a stop. As the bishop ascended the stage to begin the event, people turned to one another and said, "We better pay attention!"

Why is natural law not sufficient for human beings to live moral lives? Why is it necessary for God to reveal his Law through Scripture and Tradition?

© Sybille Yates/shutterstock.com

This is close to what happened when God gave the Israelites the Ten Commandments. Take a look at Exodus 19:16–25. After the people arrived at Mount Sinai, they experienced a spectacular display of God's glory: thunder, lightning, trumpet blasts, earthquakes, and even an erupting volcano. It is the most dramatic appearance of God in the Bible, and it immediately precedes the proclamation of the Ten Commandments. Through these events God was saying, "Pay attention, for these commandments are very, very important."

Natural Moral Law Is Not Enough

If you read the news headlines every day, it is painfully clear that not everyone obeys natural moral law. The presence of so much suffering caused by immoral human actions is a testimony that since Adam and Eve, natural moral law has not been an adequate guide for our moral decisions. Public debates by well-intentioned people on the morality of everything from stem-cell research to same-sex marriages point out that there is significant disagreement about what is moral. This is in large part owing to the effect of Original Sin, which clouds our intellect's ability to know and understand natural moral law.

It is for this reason that God has revealed his moral law to us through Scripture and Tradition. This first takes place in the Old Testament of the Bible. The Law of Moses, also called the **Old Law**, was the first stage of God's Revelation to us about how we are to live as people made in his image. This Old Law is summarized in the Ten Commandments that God revealed to Moses on Mount Sinai (see Exodus 20:1–17). The Ten Commandments are also referred to as the **Decalogue**. They are a special expression of natural law, making perfectly clear through God's Revelation what he had already placed in the human heart.

The Ten Commandments and the Original Covenant

The Ten Commandments are found in the Book of Exodus (see 20:2–17) and the Book of Deuteronomy (see 5:6–21). They are part of the sacred Covenant that God made with the Israelites, his Chosen People, at Mount Sinai. To under-

Old Law
Divine Law revealed in the Old Testament, summarized in the Ten Commandments. Also called the Law of Moses. It contrasts with the New Law of the Gospels.

Decalogue
The Ten Commandments.

Other Laws in the Torah

The Jewish name for the first five books of the Bible is the Torah. The Hebrew word *torah* is sometimes translated as "law," but it is better translated as "instruction." This helps us to remember that the primary purpose of the Old Law is to teach us how to live in right relationship with God and with one another. These are some of the kinds of laws you will find in the Torah:

- *The Covenant Code* (see Exodus 20:22—23:33) This set of laws immediately follows the Ten Commandments and is considered to be part of the Sinai Covenant in Exodus. The laws address slavery, personal injury, property damage, money, religious practices, and a few other topics. Many of them describe the punishment for breaking the law.
- *The Priestly Code* (see Leviticus, chapters 1–7 and 11–26) In general, these laws deal primarily with religious concerns, including instructions for proper worship.
- *The Holiness Code* (see Leviticus, chapters 17–26) This distinct section of the Priestly Code may have originally been for priests and later applied to all the people. The central theme of this set of laws is "Be holy, for I, the LORD, your God, am holy (19:2).

Keep in mind that all these laws must be interpreted in light of the New Law modeled and taught by Jesus Christ.

stand the purpose of the Ten Commandments, we must first understand the purpose of the Sinai Covenant. We sometimes call this the Old Covenant to distinguish it from the New Covenant. But we might better call it the Original Covenant because it is not "old" in the sense of being outdated. It is "old" in the sense that it was the Original Covenant God made with a special people. Jesus did not do away with this Covenant, rather he fulfilled it.

First and foremost, the Covenant was a relationship of love between God and his Chosen People. God tells Moses to tell the Israelites, "If you hearken to my voice and keep my covenant, you shall be my special possession, dearer to me than all other people, though all the earth is mine" (Exodus 19:5). Through the Covenant, God sought to restore the loving communion that was lost through Original Sin, starting with the Israelites and then extending to all the people of the earth. As part of the Covenant, the Ten Commandments taught the Israelites how to live in loving relationship with God and with one another. They summarized the many particular laws that follow in the books of Exodus and Deuteronomy, and they actually make up only a small percentage of the laws in the **Pentateuch**. Although many of these particular laws are no longer applicable to our culture, the moral principles expressed in the Ten Commandments are true in all places and all times.

Christians have always acknowledged the importance and significance of the Ten Commandments. Strictly speaking, the Commandments address serious moral issues: idolatry, murder, theft, adultery. But they also embody moral principles that help us to address all the moral issues we face, including less serious issues that we still have an obligation to address morally. For this reason, many **catechisms** throughout the Church's history have used the Ten Commandments as the framework for teaching Christian morality. The *Catechism of the Catholic Church* uses this approach, as does this student book.

Pentateuch

A Greek word meaning "five books," referring to the first five books of the Old Testament.

catechism

A popular summary, usually in book form, of Catholic doctrine about faith and morals and commonly intended for use within formal programs of catechesis.

Pray It!

The Torah Psalms

One category of psalms in the Book of Psalms is called the Torah psalms. These psalms praise God for giving us his Law and proclaim that following God's Law brings true happiness, and that the wise person knows this, but the foolish person does not. Examples of Torah psalms are Psalms 1, 19, and 119. Psalm 119 is the longest psalm in the Bible; at 176 verses it is almost like reading ten psalms! It is a beautiful psalm to meditate on and pray with. Here's a sample.

> Lord, teach me the ways of your laws;
>> I shall observe then with care.
> Give me insight to observe your teaching,
>> to keep it with all my heart.
> Lead me in the path of your commands,
>> for that is my delight.
> Direct my heart toward your decrees
>> and away from unjust gain.
> Avert my eyes from what is worthless;
>> by your way give me life.
>> (Verses 33–37)

Scripture teaches that our loving Father gives us his Law to lead us to a life of eternal happiness and to keep us from sin and evil. But as holy, spiritual, and good as the Old Law is, it was not enough to restore humanity's original holiness. The Ten Commandments show what must be done, but they do not give us the strength, or the grace of the Holy Spirit, to do it. The Old Law is the first stage on the way to the Kingdom of God, preparing us for conversion and faith in Jesus. In this way the Old Law is a preparation for the Gospel. ✝

1. I am the LORD your God; you shall not have strange gods before me.

2. You shall not take the name of the LORD your God in vain.

3. Remember to keep holy the LORD's day.

4. Honor your father and your mother.

5. You shall not kill.

6. You shall not commit adultery.

7. You shall not steal.

8. You shall not bear false witness against your neighbor.

9. You shall not covet your neighbor's wife.

10. You shall not covet your neighbor's goods.

Article 8 Law and the New Covenant

God's Old Covenant with humanity is impossible to separate from the Old Law. So it should come as no surprise that when Jesus established the New Covenant he also taught a **New Law**, which fulfilled and completed the Old Law. This New Law, also called the Law of the Gospel, is the perfection of God's moral law, both natural and revealed. The New Law challenges us to be perfect in love by following the example of Jesus himself.

The Sermon on the Mount

Although Jesus' New Law is found in many different places throughout the Gospels, he taught the core of it in his Sermon on the Mount (see Matthew 5:1—7:29; see also Luke 6:20–49). The location where this teaching took place is important because it makes connections between Moses and Jesus, between the Old Law and the New Law. Just as Moses delivered the Old Law to the people from a mountain as part of the Old Covenant, Jesus taught the New Law from a mountain (see Matthew 5:1) as part of the New Covenant.

The Sermon on the Mount starts with Jesus' proclaiming the Beatitudes. This is no accident. The values of the Beatitudes—poverty of spirit, meekness, mercifulness, righteousness, purity of heart, peacemaking, willingness to suffer for what is right—are the values we need to live a moral life and to satisfy the desire for happiness that God has placed in our hearts. God's original promises in the Old Covenant find their fulfillment in the Beatitudes. By embracing the Beatitudes and living them out, we become citizens of the Kingdom of God. (The meaning of the Beatitudes is described in more detail in student book article 3, "New Life in Christ.")

In the Sermon on the Mount, directly following the Beatitudes, Jesus teaches us an important purpose of living the New Law. He says that his followers should be the salt of the earth and the light of the world (see Matthew 5:13–14). These two metaphors emphasize that by living according to Christ's New Law, we can show others the way to true happiness and joy. We live by Christ's Law not only to bring ourselves into communion with God but also to show others the way to that communion.

Jesus then gives a series of teachings on topics such as avoiding anger, lust, revenge, and violence; loving our enemies; avoiding hypocrisy; giving generously; and trusting in God. Many of these teachings begin with Jesus' saying "You have heard that it was said . . ." after which he quotes a law from the Old Testament. Jesus then teaches the true meaning of that law. With this formula, Jesus is showing us that his New Law does not abolish or devalue the Old Law but instead releases its full potential. Let's consider one example:

> You have heard that it was said, "An eye for an eye and a tooth for a tooth." But I say to you, offer no resistance to one who is evil. When someone strikes you on [your] right cheek, turn

New Law
Divine Law revealed in the New Testament through the life and teaching of Jesus Christ and through the witness and teaching of the Apostles. The New Law perfects the Old Law and brings it to fulfillment. Also called the Law of Love.

Great Commandments
Jesus' summary of the entire divine Law as the love of God and the love of neighbor.

Jesus' teaching attracted great crowds of people. Why is his teaching so inspiring when it is also so challenging to follow?

the other one to him as well. If anyone wants to go to law with you over your tunic, hand him your cloak as well. Should anyone press you into service for one mile, go with him for two miles. (Matthew 5:38–41)

Does this strike you as a little crazy? What was Jesus saying here? Well, first he reminded his listeners that the Old Law limited the revenge you could take on someone who had hurt you. If someone put out your eye, the most you could do was put out his or her eye; you could not kill the person. But the New Law taught by Jesus is about love. Rather than exacting revenge (even if it was limited revenge), the morality of the New Law witnesses to others the love of God through forgiveness, patience, and even outrageous generosity. Who can live this way? Only the kind of people Jesus describes in the Beatitudes—people who are meek, pure in heart, merciful, and willing to suffer for righteousness' sake.

The Great Commandments: The Law of Love

An even shorter summary of the New Law is found in all three synoptic Gospels. In Mark it is told like this:

> One of the scribes . . . asked him, "Which is the first of all the commandments?" Jesus replied, "The first is this: 'Hear, O Israel! The Lord our God is Lord alone! You shall love the Lord your God with all your heart, with all your soul, with all your mind, and with all your strength.' The second is this: 'You shall love your neighbor as yourself.' There is no other commandment greater than these." (12:28–31)

The two **Great Commandments** emphasize that the heart of the New Law is love. These two Commandments were not new;

they were part of the Old Law (see Deuteronomy 6:4–5 and Leviticus 19:18). In fact, you have probably noticed that the first Great Commandment, "Love God with all your heart, with all your soul, with all your mind, and with all your strength," is a pretty good summary of the first three Commandments of the Decalogue. And the second Great Commandment, "Love your neighbor as yourself," summarizes the last seven Commandments of the Decalogue. What is new about the Great Commandments is that Jesus pulls them out, highlights them, and says that these two are the first and the greatest of all the Commandments. This is why the New Law is also called the Law of Love. The Law of Love is the basis for properly understanding and interpreting all other moral laws. Christ's Law of Love fulfills the Old Law by going beyond the letter of the Old Law. Jesus challenges us to live the deeper moral truths the Old Law is intended to teach us, thus revealing its true meaning. Through his Paschal Mystery, Jesus redeems us from all our sins against the Old Law. The New Law is the reason we treat sinners with mercy rather than with vengeance—the reason, for example, we no longer put people to death for cursing their parents (see Exodus 21:17)

Other New Testament Moral Teachings

Besides Jesus' teachings in the Gospels, many of the letters, or epistles, of the New Testament contain moral teaching too. Often the letters address a particular moral situation, as the Apostles apply Jesus' New Law to their moral situations. Here are some examples.

Passage	Moral Teaching
Romans 12:9–21	general guidelines for moral living
Romans 13:1–7	respecting civil authority
Romans 14:13–23	whether to eat meat sacrificed to idols
1 Corinthians, chapter 13	defining what true love is
Ephesians 4:17—5:5	what it means to live according to the New Law
Ephesians 5:21—6:4 and Colossians 3:18–21	guidelines for family life
Colossians 3:5–17	vices to avoid and virtues to practice
Philemon	slavery

Love God with all your heart, with all your soul, with all your mind, and with all your strength.

Love your neighbor as yourself.

or for adultery (see Leviticus 20:10) or for the many other sins that in the Old Law required the death penalty.

To correctly understand the two Great Commandments, we must properly understand what Jesus means by *love*. Jesus isn't talking about a do-whatever-feels-good-to-you kind of love. He is talking about a love that is based in God's Eternal Law. It is a love that is forgiving but also expects that we are working hard at being holy people. It is a sacrificial love that puts the good of others before our own comfort, just as we hope others would do for us. The Law of Love means that we hold ourselves to a high standard of moral living—God's standard.

Jeremiah describes in beautiful language the promise of the New Law, the Law of Love: "I will make a new covenant with the house of Israel. . . . I will place my law within them, and write it upon their hearts; I will be their God,

Catholic Wisdom

Pope Benedict XVI on the Greatest Commandments

In his encyclical *God Is Love*, Pope Benedict discusses the two Great Commandments and emphasizes that you cannot have one without the other.

> If I have no contact whatsoever with God in my life, then I cannot see in the other [my neighbor] anything more than the other, and I am incapable of seeing in him the image of God. But if in my life I fail completely to heed others, solely out of a desire to be "devout" and to perform my "religious duties," then my relationship with God will also grow arid. It becomes merely "proper," but loveless. Only my readiness to encounter my neighbour and to show him love makes me sensitive to God as well. . . . Love of God and love of neighbour are thus inseparable, they form a single commandment. But both live from the love of God who has loved us first. (18)

and they shall be my people" (Jeremiah 31:31–33). It is truly amazing that God wrote the natural law into the hearts and minds of all people, made it even clearer in the Ten Commandments, and when we still didn't get it, the Father sent his Son, who became one of us to reveal the perfection of the divine Law. Now through our faith in Christ, we receive the grace of the Holy Spirit, which enables us to live the two Great Commandments. And each time we receive the Sacraments, we receive further grace, nurturing us to love God and to share his love with others. ✝

Article 9 Moral Law and the Church

"He's a Christian, but I know he goes out drinking most weekends." "She belongs to that big church in town, but she's the worst gossip in school." "They read the Bible every day, but they've never reached out to anyone with a helping hand."

Unfortunately, some people love to point out the flaws of others but seem more than willing to overlook their own shortcomings. Rather than sitting in judgment of others, we should reflect on how we can live more fully as Christ taught. None of us is perfect and without sin (see Romans 3:9–10), yet being Christian means we must strive to live a life of holiness and to be models of holiness for others, leading them to God. Saint Paul uses the concept of imitation to describe this: "So be imitators of God, as beloved children, and live in love" (Ephesians 5:1–2). "Join with others in being imitators of me" (Philippians 3:17). "You became imitators of us and of the Lord . . . so that you became a model for all the believers" (1 Thessalonians 1:6–7).

The Law of Love, embodied in Christ's two Great Commandments, calls us to put our faith into loving action.

© Bill Wittman

Precepts of the Church

Sometimes called the commandments of the Church, these are basic obligations for all Catholics that are dictated by the laws of the Church.

canon law

The name given to the official body of laws that provide good order in the visible body of the Church.

To help us to be imitators of Christ, the Church's teaching authority guides us, and the Sacraments strengthen us.

Two Types of Church Law

With Christ as our head, the Church is the visible Body of Christ. Christ has given the Church the responsibility of being a light to the world and a model of his New Law. The Church does this through the witness of her members and by teaching the world Christ's Law of Love. In addition, the Church has her own laws to guide her members. The **Precepts of the Church** provide us with general guidance in living a Christian life, and the Church's **canon law** provides specific rules to maintain good order within the visible society of the Church.

The most basic of Church laws are called the precepts of the Church. You will find these laws listed in the sidebar on page 47. As you read them, you will notice that they primarily ask us to participate in the sacramental life of the Church and to participate in the Church's mission in the world. They are meant to be the minimum disciplines that we must practice to ensure that we grow in love of God and neighbor. For example, they require us to receive the Sacrament of Penance and Reconciliation only once a year (but hopefully we would receive it more often than that).

Catholics are obligated to follow these precepts. Rather than seeing them as a burden, we should approach them as helpful reminders about how to live our faith in a deep and enriching way. They are really minimum requirements for being Catholic, asking us to participate in the rich faith life of the Church to receive the nourishment we need to live morally and to fulfill what it means to be a Christian. The last part of this book will return to these precepts in discussing the gifts and guides that God provides for us for making moral choices.

Canon law is the law of the Church. *Canon* comes from the Greek word for "rule." Each individual law of the Church is called a canon. The canons are collected in a large book called *The Code of Canon Law*. Trained experts in canon law are called canonists or canon lawyers. These people often teach in seminaries and universities and work for bishops in diocesan offices.

Canon law is concerned with the relationships among different members of the Church and with matters that affect the Church's mission. It governs such things as norms for the celebration of the Sacraments and public worship, norms for Catholic education, regulations for the administration of Church property, the rights and responsibilities of bishops, priests, deacons, consecrated religious, and the laity, and how to resolve conflicts among members of the Church. Canon law even gives penalties that apply when certain canons are broken. Canon law is of course based in Eternal Law and applies the truths of Eternal Law to life within the Church community.

The Precepts of the Church

The following are the Precepts of the Church as articulated by the bishops of the United States:

1. To keep holy the day of the Lord's Resurrection; to worship God by participating in Mass every Sunday and on the holy days of obligation; to avoid those activities that would hinder renewal of the soul and body on the Sabbath (for example, needless work or unnecessary shopping).

2. To lead a sacramental life; to receive Holy Communion frequently and the Sacrament of Penance and Reconciliation regularly—minimally, to receive the Sacrament of Penance and Reconciliation at least once a year (annual confession is obligatory only if serious sin is involved); minimally also, to receive Holy Communion at least once a year between the first Sunday of Lent and Trinity Sunday.

3. To study Catholic teaching in preparation for the Sacrament of Confirmation, to be confirmed, and then to continue to study and advance the cause of Christ.

4. To observe the marriage laws of the Church; to give religious training, by example and word, to one's children; to use parish schools and catechetical programs.

5. To strengthen and support the Church—one's own parish community and parish priests, the worldwide Church, and the Pope.

6. To do penance, including abstaining from meat and fasting from food on the appointed days.

7. To join in the missionary spirit and apostolate (work) of the Church.

The Magisterium and Moral Teaching

The moral guidance of the Church goes beyond the Precepts of the Church and canon law. God has given the **Magisterium**—the bishops of the world united with the Pope—the responsibility for passing on and teaching his revealed truth. Revelation includes moral truth of course, and so the Magisterium has the responsibility for teaching the fullness of the New Law of Christ first to the Church and secondly to the entire world.

The Magisterium is always applying Christ's moral teaching to modern situations. In recent times they have given moral direction on such issues as genetic testing, the use of embryos in medical research, abortion, the death penalty, and welfare laws. When speaking on these issues, they apply natural law and reason to appeal to people of diverse faiths and beliefs. The people who make civil law do not always accept the moral truth spoken by the Pope and the bishops, but the Church's voice must be an important part of the dialogue when people make important decisions about moral issues.

Catholics always have a special obligation to listen carefully to what the Pope and bishops say about moral matters. When they speak to us, they are the "living, teaching office of the Church, whose task it is to give an authentic interpretation of the word of God, whether in its written form (Sacred Scripture), or in the form of Tradition" (*CCC*, page 887). The Magisterium ensures that we stay faithful to the teaching of the Apostles in matters of faith and morals.

The bishops of the Church, united with the Pope, have the responsibility for passing on and teaching God's revealed truth.

© Bettmann/CORBIS

When the Pope and the bishops agree on a matter of faith and morals, they speak with infallible authority. This means that the Holy Spirit guides them to teach the truths, or doctrines, of our faith without error.

Infallibility is a great gift God has given to the Church; it means we can rely on the Church's teaching as being true. Thus we as Catholics are obliged to accept the doctrine of the Church. The gift of infallibility applies to all doctrine, including moral doctrine, that is necessary for our salvation. The role of the Magisterium is to see that these truths of the faith are preserved, explained, and observed. To be clear, not every statement of every Pope or every bishop is an infallible statement; however, the Magisterium speaks with infallibility when teaching doctrine of faith and morals clearly revealed in Scripture and Tradition. Because of this special charism, we must take seriously all the Magisterium's teachings.

Magisterium
The Church's living teaching office, which consists of all bishops, in communion with the Pope.

infallibility
The Gift of the Holy Spirit to the whole Church by which the leaders of the Church—the Pope and the bishops in union with him—are protected from fundamental error when formulating a specific teaching on a matter of faith and morals.

Can the Church Impose Her Moral Views on Others?

Some people have a concern that the Catholic Church imposes her morality on people who are not members of the Church. Their concern is that in a free society people should be free to make their own moral decisions. Should you ever face this argument from someone, here are some important points to make in response.

- The moral law taught by the Church is not her invention but is God's universal law meant for all people. All people have the ability to know the universal Divine Law, as it is written on our hearts and can be understood by using our intellect. The majority of the Church's moral teaching is something most reasonable people of all faiths and traditions readily agree with.

- The Catholic Church does not try to impose her moral teaching on anyone, but part of the Church's mission is to share with all people the moral law revealed by God. Even though the Church does this as publicly as possible, she respects each person's right to accept or reject this truth.

- The Catholic Church has a responsibility to influence public opinion to create laws and build social structures that support and defend the moral truths revealed by God. This is true in free societies, but it is even truer in dictatorships and other societies with limited freedoms. The Church's moral teaching is crucial for the common good. Imagine the chaos and suffering that would result if every person lived only by his or her own personal moral code. And remember the suffering and evil that happens in the world when states enact laws that are contrary to divine Law.

- The Church does not seek to take over the responsibilities of the state or to make Church law the law of the land. Catholics recognize the important distinction between the Church and the state and the dangers that come when one of these institutions tries to take over the responsibilities of the other. ✝

Review

1. Why is every person obliged to follow moral law?

2. Name five different types or expressions of moral law.

3. Describe the natural law.

4. Why is natural moral law important?

5. What law do the Ten Commandments summarize? What is another name for the Ten Commandments?

6. Why is the New Law called "New"?

7. Give an overview of the content of the Sermon on the Mount.

8. Describe the two types of Church law.

9. What is infallibility?

Part 3

Sin and Its Consequences

The first two parts of this introductory section have painted a pretty positive picture of God's moral law. We described it as the path to beatitude, to living a life of true happiness in union with God in this life and in the next. Yet if God's moral law is in fact a path to happiness, why are so many people in the world unhappy, including many Christians? The main reason for this discrepancy is the reality of sin.

Is the word *sin* a part of your vocabulary? Sin is real. It is deliberately choosing to act in a way that is contrary to God's will. There are small sins and big sins, sins that mostly harm ourselves (but never only ourselves) and sins that cause harm to thousands or maybe even millions of people. Because of the sin of our first parents, we are all born under the influence of Original Sin. This unfortunately makes it easier for us to commit other sins. Every human being ever born except Mary is guilty of sin.

The result of every sin is that we are further alienated from God, from other people, and from our true self. We become less and less the holy people we know deep in our hearts we should be. We become unhappy because we are alienated from God and others, and we are ashamed because we know we should be better than we are. The ultimate consequence of sin is death. But sin does not have the final word; God the Father sent his Son to save us from our sin.

The articles in this part address the following topics:

51

Article 10 Sin in the Old Testament

Some people claim that the awareness of sin is disappearing from our society. Annual Gallup polls taken since 2010 indicate that 76 percent or more of the United States' population believe the country's moral values are getting worse. You could view this statistic as encouraging news because it means the majority of people in this country care enough about morality to notice that it needs improving. Or you could view it as discouraging news because it means that even though a majority of people believe the country's moral values are declining, it doesn't seem to be making any difference!

Regardless of how aware our society is about sin, in the Bible sin is a prominent topic. The word *sin* and its variations occur 915 times in the New American Bible translation. The central focus of salvation history is how God saves us from sin and death. Sin entered the world through the sin of Adam and Eve. And with sin came death. Sin and death were not part of God's plan for human beings. Throughout history he has worked to save us from our slavery to sin and death. Starting with his Covenants with Noah, Abraham, and the Israelites, continuing through the preaching of the prophets, and culminating in the Paschal Mystery, the Bible tells how the miraculous power of God's saving love defeats sin and death once and for all.

Previous courses in the Living in Christ series have covered the story of salvation history and the Paschal Mystery in depth. In this article and the next one, we focus on key ideas about sin that are revealed in Scripture.

Rebelling against God

One key idea about sin, especially in the Old Testament, is that sin is rebelling against God. This happens at the beginning of salvation history when Adam and Eve disobey God's direct command not to eat the fruit from the tree of the knowledge of good and evil (see Genesis 2:1–6). It is also a common theme in Exodus. The Israelites openly rebel against God by grumbling against him in the desert (see Exodus 16:2) and by creating and worshipping a golden calf (see chapter 32). At the end of his life, Moses even says:

Take this scroll of the law and put it beside the ark of the covenant of the Lord, your God, that there it may be a witness against you. For I already know how rebellious and stiff-necked you will be. Why, even now, while I am alive among you, you have been rebels against the Lord! (Deuteronomy 31:26–27)

The prophets spoke frequently about sin as a rebellious attitude toward God:

Woe to the rebellious children,
    says the Lord,
Who carry out plans that are not mine,
    who weave webs that are not inspired by me,
    adding sin upon sin.

(Isaiah 30:1)

Old Testament Understanding of the Consequences of Sin

The Old Testament contains no teaching about Heaven or Hell. The ancient Israelites believed that you would be punished for your sins or rewarded for your virtues in this life, not in an afterlife. Although there are exceptions, the Old Testament teaches that these were some of the consequences of sin:

- *Sin affects people's children and the people in their community.* "The Lord is slow to anger and rich in kindness, forgiving wickedness and crime; yet not declaring the guilty guiltless, but punishing children to the third and fourth generation for their fathers' wickedness" (Numbers 14:18). This belief is also the reason that so many sins carried the penalty of death: to remove the sinner so his or her sin could not infect the rest of the community.

- *God punishes people directly for their sin.* Many Old Testament passages teach that God directly punished people for their sins. See Psalm 99:8, Jeremiah 23:2, Ezekiel 5:8, 2 Maccabees 1:17.

- *God withdraws his favor as a consequence of sin.* This understanding is strong during the time of the judges and the kings of Israel. Repeatedly the Israelites would fail to follow the Law of the Covenant and as a result they experienced God's withdrawing his favor from them, allowing them to fall under the power of other kings and nations. See Judges 3:7,12 and 2 Kings 17:1–18, 24:19–20.

These Old Testament understandings of the consequences of sin contain important insights but are incomplete. We must interpret them in light of the teaching of Jesus Christ, who fulfills and completes the Old Law.

The Israelites rebelled against God because they grew tired of waiting for Moses to return from the holy mountain. What are some reasons people rebel against God's Law today?

© Scala/Art Resource, NY

> But this people's heart is stubborn and rebellious;
> they turn and go away,
> And say not in their hearts,
> "Let us fear the LORD, our God."
> (Jeremiah 5:23–24)

> Son of man, you live in the midst of a rebellious house; they have eyes to see but do not see, and ears to hear but do not hear, for they are a rebellious house. (Ezekiel 12:2)

The Hebrew word most often used to express this idea is *pesha',* which is translated as "transgression" or "rebellion" or "sin." Why do we rebel against God? People rebel because they want life to be different than it is, and ultimately they want God to be different than he is; we want to be "in control." But when you give it some thought, rebelling against God is kind of like rebelling against the air or against the sun. God is love and truth and life; we have no existence outside of him. Why rebel against that which makes life possible? Living a moral life means accepting God's Eternal Law as it is and not as we want it to be and accepting God as he is and not as we want him to be. This is what Jesus meant when he said that we must have a childlike faith in the Kingdom of God (see Mark 10:14); we must trust that God loves us even more than we love ourselves.

Missing the Mark

The Hebrew word in the Old Testament most commonly translated as sin is *chatâ*, a word that literally means "to miss," as in an archer missing his target. This concept points us to another key understanding of sin, that sin is missing the goal of living a life that is in harmony with God's Eternal Law. This understanding of sin is slightly different than seeing sin only as active rebellion against God because *chatâ* indicates a desire to live according to God's will but failing in some of our attempts to do so. Some reasons for this failure are a lack of commitment, not setting our moral standards high enough, letting outside forces influence us—this list could go on and on.

Sin as an occasion of missing the mark happens throughout salvation history. In fact, many of Israel's greatest heroes were guilty of this. Here are just a few of the instances recorded:

- After God gives Gideon victories in battle, Gideon makes a golden idol, breaking the First Commandment (Judges 8:27).

- The mighty judge Samson breaks the Law repeatedly: he marries a foreign woman, touches a dead lion's carcass, takes outrageous revenge, visits prostitutes, and reveals the secret of his divine power to another foreign woman (see Judges 14:1—16:19).

- The sons of the wise judge, priest, and prophet Samuel "sought illicit gain and accepted bribes, perverting justice" (see 1 Samuel 8:3).

- King David, known for his great faith in God, committed adultery and then arranged for the husband of the woman he got pregnant to be killed in battle (see 2 Samuel, chapter 11).

- King Solomon, known as one of the wisest men in the Bible, had many foreign wives and joined them in worshipping their foreign gods and goddesses (see 1 Kings 11:1–10).

The understanding that sin is missing the mark points out a reality that Saint Paul names in one of his letters: "What I do, I do not understand. For I do not do what I want, but I do what I hate" (Romans 7:15). Sometimes sin seems to have its own life within us; even when we want to do what is right, something in us makes us act wrongly. But realizing our inclination to act in this way can actually be an occasion of grace, because missing the mark should make it clear to us that we cannot overcome sin on our own power. We must ask for and trust in the grace of Christ given to us through the power of the Holy Spirit. We can find encouragement in these further words of Paul: "The Spirit too comes to the aid of our weakness. . . . We know that all things work for good for those who love God" (Romans 8:26,28). ✝

Pray It!

Psalm 51

The most famous prayer about sin in the Bible is Psalm 51. It is attributed to King David, who would have written it to acknowledge his guilt and to ask for forgiveness after committing adultery with Bathsheba (see 2 Samuel, chapter 11). You can pray this Psalm whenever you feel the weight of sin upon your heart.

Have mercy on me, God, in your goodness;
    in your abundant compassion blot out my offense.
Wash away all my guilt;
    from my sin cleanse me.
For I know my offense;
    my sin is always before me.
Against you alone have I sinned;
    I have done such evil in your sight. . . .
Cleanse me with hyssop, that I may be pure;
    wash me, make me whiter than snow.
Let me hear sounds of joy and gladness;
    let the bones you have crushed rejoice.
Turn away your face from my sins;
    blot out all my guilt.
A clean heart create for me, God;
    renew in me a steadfast spirit. . . .
My sacrifice, God, is a broken spirit;
    God, do not spurn a broken, humbled heart.
                (Verses 3–6,9–12,19)

Article 11 Sin in the New Testament

Hamartia is the most common Greek word used for sin in the New Testament. It literally means "falling short" and is essentially equivalent to the Hebrew word *chatâ'*. So the understanding of sin as missing the moral mark continues to be important in the New Testament.

Other Greek words associated with sin in the New Testament are *paraptoma* and *parabasis,* which can be translated as "trespass" or "transgression" (see Matthew 6:14–15 and Galatians 6:1), and *anomia,* which is usually translated as "lawlessness" (see 1 John 3:4). When we consider the meaning of these Greek words, an expanded understanding of sin emerges. Sin is not only missing the goal of living in accordance with God's will but also crossing a boundary established by God and breaking the natural law that is written on every human heart (see Romans 2:14–16). The result is that human beings live in lawless communities that do not reflect God's plan for humanity. Although these concepts can be found in the Old Testament, the New Testament provides some new teaching that deepens our understanding of the reality of sin.

One result of sin is that it can lead to lawless situations or lawless communities that endanger human life and dignity.

© Carlos Cazalis/Corbis

Everyone Has Sinned

A truth about sin made clear in the New Testament is that everyone, except Jesus and his mother, Mary, is affected by Original Sin and is subject to death and a weakened nature prone to evil because of this. This truth is implied in the Gospels, but it is made explicit in the writings of Saint Paul. For example, John the Baptist proclaims "a baptism of repentance for the forgiveness of sins" (Mark 1:4). Jesus implies that people in all nations have sinned when he charges the Apostles to continue his mission, saying, "Thus it is written that the Messiah would suffer and rise from the dead on the third day and that repentance, for the forgiveness of sins, would be preached in his name to all the nations" (Luke 24:46–47).

Saint Paul directly addresses this in his Letter to the Romans. Paul speaks at length about sin, its effects, and how we are freed from it. He teaches that Jews and Greeks (meaning all non-Jews) are "all under the domination of sin" (3:9). A few verses later he says, "All have sinned and are deprived of the glory of God" (3:23). A few chapters later he makes the point again: "Therefore, just as through one person sin entered the world, and through sin, death, and thus death came to all, inasmuch as all sinned" (5:12). Paul is teaching the Romans and all believers that we are all in need of the salvation that comes through faith in Jesus Christ.

Light and Truth versus Darkness and Lies

In the Gospel of John, Jesus says this in response to some questions from the Pharisee Nicodemus:

> And this is the verdict, that the light came into the world, but people preferred darkness to light, because their works were evil. For everyone who does wicked things hates the light and does not come toward the light, so that his works might not be exposed. But whoever lives the truth comes to the light, so that his works may be clearly seen as done in God. (3:19–21)

Jesus is revealing an important insight about sin: every sin is a lie against the truth, a lie about what truly brings God's saving love and joy into the world. People sin because they have fooled themselves into believing that a sinful action will make them happy or fulfilled. They tell themselves that this little bit of cheating, this act of revenge, this physical pleasure, or this act of stealing will make them happy. And maybe it will for a while, but the feeling of happiness that comes from sin is not lasting, because sin does not lead to beatitude, the true and lasting happiness that comes from union with God.

This brings us to the second insight about sin in Jesus' statement, which is that sinful acts are done in darkness—not literal darkness, of course, but metaphorical darkness. You will meet some people who brag about their sinful actions, but these people are the exception. Most people keep their sins secret because they are ashamed of them, because deep in their hearts they know that their actions are lies against God's truth and are wrong.

Jesus says "I am the light of the world" (John 8:12) and "I am the way and the truth and the life" (John 14:6). To escape the lies and darkness of sin, we must accept and follow Jesus Christ, the light and the truth.

Forgiveness

The Old Testament speaks in several passages about God's forgiveness. But these times are outnumbered by the more numerous passages about God's judgment and God's punishment. In the New Testament, the exact opposite is true. Jesus' teachings about God's judgment are outnumbered by his teachings about God's forgiveness. Connected to this, Jesus makes it abundantly clear that we also need to practice generous forgiveness.

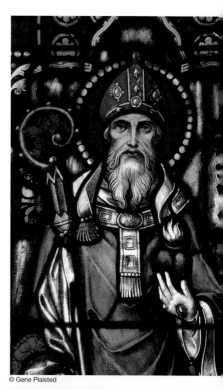

© Gene Plaisted

Catholic Wisdom

Every Sin Is a Lie

Human beings were made upright, that they might live not according to themselves, but according to God who made them; in other words, that human beings might do God's will and not their own. Not to live as we were made to live, that is a lie. . . . It is truly said that all sin is a lie. (Saint Augustine, *The City of God*)

Jesus is concerned about sin. He uses hyperbole to teach how serious sin is: "If your right eye causes you to sin, tear it out and throw it away. It is better for you to lose one of your members than to have your whole body thrown into Gehenna" (Matthew 5:29). But what Jesus emphasizes even more is that he has come to reach out to sinners and to forgive sin. Jesus proclaims, "I did not come to call the righteous but sinners" (9:13). He goes to the homes of people stigmatized as public sinners and dines with them (9:10). He forgives the sins of the paralytic (see Luke 5:20), the sinful woman who washes his feet (see 7:48), and the woman caught in adultery (see John 8:11). He tells many stories—the Parable of the Lost Sheep (see Matthew 18:10–14), the Parable of the Unforgiving Servant (see 18:21–35), the Parable of the Prodigal Son (see Luke 15:11–32)—that emphasize the importance of forgiveness.

The New Testament places great emphasis on God's forgiveness. The Church continues Christ's ministry of forgiveness through the Sacrament of Penance and Reconciliation.

Jesus also emphasizes how critical it is that his followers practice loving forgiveness. In the Sermon on the Mount, he teaches, "As you judge, so will you be judged" (Matthew 7:2). In giving us the Lord's Prayer, he emphasizes this: "forgive us our debts, as we forgive our debtors" (6:12). When Peter asks how many times we should be willing to forgive someone who sins against us, Jesus tells Peter we must forgive not seven times, as Peter suggests, but seventy-seven times (see Matthew 18:21)—meaning an unlimited number. Jesus shared the power to forgive sins in God's name with his Apostles (see John 20:22–23). This wonderful gift in which sins are forgiven in God's name is still with the Church today in the Sacrament of Penance and Reconciliation.

This emphasis on forgiving sin is the heart of the New Law, the Law of Love. Christ teaches us that God is primarily waiting to forgive us, not to condemn us. God loves us so much that he wants us to be free from the burden of sin, from the shame, the isolation, the hungers that are never satisfied. This freedom can happen only if we accept God's forgiveness and die to sin through Baptism. Then we will be given the grace to forgive ourselves. After that we will be given the grace to forgive others, as hard as that may be to do at times.

The Consequences of Sin

The New Testament is clear about the ultimate consequences of sin: In his Letter to the Romans, Paul says, "For the wages of sin is death, but the gift of God is eternal life in Christ Jesus our Lord" (6:23). Paul is confirming the teaching of the Old Testament—sin leads to death. We have all sinned and we all will die. But Paul adds something new: Death is not the end! Because of his obedient, loving sacrifice, Jesus Christ opened up the doors to life after death, eternal life in Heaven for all who believe in him.

Jesus' work of salvation does not mean that Heaven is guaranteed for all people. In the Parable of the Last Judgment, Jesus teaches that the penalty for those who fail to live the Law of Love is the "eternal fire prepared for the devil and his angels" (Matthew 25:41). For those who live a life of unrepented sin, Hell is the ultimate consequence.

In his earthly teaching, Jesus corrects some misunderstandings about the consequences of sin, such as God causes bad things to happen to people who sin. When his disciples ask him, "Who sinned, this man or his parents, that he was born blind?" Jesus replies, "Neither he nor his parents sinned" (John 9:2–3). In another place Jesus says about some Galileans who were killed by Pilate: "Do you think that because these Galileans suffered in this way they were greater sinners than all other Galileans? By no means!" (Luke 13:2–3). From passages like this, we learn that God does not directly punish people for their sins, and he does not directly punish people's children for their parents' sins.

Similarly, Jesus teaches that just because some people are blessed with material wealth does not mean that they are living a life pleasing to God. In the Parable of the Rich Man and Lazarus (see Luke 16:19–31) and the Parable of the Rich Fool (see 12:16–21), Jesus makes it clear that being materially blessed in this life does not necessarily mean you will be rewarded in the next. ✝

^{Article}
12 Requirements for Sin

To truly understand a concept, it often helps to start with a definition of the words associated with that concept. Definitions force us to be clear and consistent about what we believe. They provide a common language and a common understanding so that we can intelligently discuss abstract concepts and complex realities. Sin is one of those complex realities. Sin can be about serious matters and less serious matters. Some actions almost everyone agrees are sinful in all circumstances, and other actions may or may not be sinful depending on the circumstances and the intention of the person doing them. All this makes it challenging to define sin in a single, clear statement.

Fortunately, God guides the Church to truth and clarity, and the Church guides us in our understanding of sin and what is sinful.

A Definition of Sin

The glossary of the *Catechism of the Catholic Church* gives this definition for sin:

> [Sin is] an offense against God as well as a fault against reason, truth, and right conscience. Sin is a deliberate thought, word, or deed, or omission contrary to the Eternal Law of God. In judging the gravity of sin, it is customary to distinguish between mortal and venial sins. (Page 999)

The first part of this definition sums up almost everything we have discussed to this point. Sin is a primarily an offense against God; it is rebellion against God's will and his desire that we live in loving communion with him and with one another. It is a rejection of God's love for us. When we sin we put our will before God's will, our desires before God's desires. We make ourselves the center of the universe. This is the exact opposite of the obedience of Jesus Christ, who "humbled himself, becoming obedient to death" (Philippians 2:8).

Sin is also an offense against the truth of God's Eternal Law and against the gift of reason that we use to understand natural law. It is a betrayal of right conscience, which is the sure knowledge of what is right and wrong that we are working to develop within our hearts. Sin is a rejection of the gifts that God has provided us to live a life pleasing to him, a life devoted to his Law of Love. Sin leaves us wounded in body, mind, and soul and wounded in our relationships with God and others.

The *Catechism's* definition also makes clear what kind of things can be sins. Sin can be a deed or act, of course. But sin can also be a word. Words can be used to reject God, to tell lies, or to hurt other people through gossip, libel, or cruel remarks. Thoughts can also be sins—not the thoughts that enter our heads unbidden and we quickly dismiss, but the thoughts of revenge, lust, envy, or domination that we dwell upon and keep alive. These thoughts are real, they are in our control, and they negatively affect our relationships with God and with one another. The *Catechism's* definition is clear that thoughts and actions must be deliberate to be sinful; they cannot be accidental or unintended.

New Testament Lists of Sins

Several New Testament passages list sins that were common at the time the New Testament was written. How are these sins part of our culture? What other sins would you add to these lists?

Matthew 15:19	"For from the heart come evil thoughts, murder, adultery, unchastity, theft, false witness, blasphemy."
Romans 1:29–31	"They are filled with every form of wickedness, evil, greed, and malice; full of envy, murder, rivalry, treachery, and spite. They are gossips and scandalmongers and they hate God. They are insolent, haughty, boastful, ingenious in their wickedness, and rebellious toward their parents. They are senseless, faithless, heartless, ruthless."
Galatians 5:19–21	"Now the works of the flesh are obvious: immorality, impurity, licentiousness, idolatry, sorcery, hatreds, rivalry, jealousy, outbursts of fury, acts of selfishness, dissensions, factions, occasions of envy, drinking bouts, orgies, and the like."

Sin is the result of a deliberate thought, word, or deed. The hurt caused by sinful words can be just as damaging as a physical attack.

© oliveromg/Shutterstock.com

We will consider more closely the different kinds of sin mentioned in the *Catechism*'s definition—sins of commission (deliberate), sins of omission, mortal sins, and venial sins—in the next article.

What Makes Something a Sin?

Three elements determine the morality of any human act: (1) the **object**, that is, the specific thing the person is choosing to do, (2) the **intention** of the person doing the action, and (3) the **circumstances** surrounding the act. In determining whether a human act is morally good or morally bad, we must consider all three elements together. For an act to be morally good, both the object and the person's intention must be good. The circumstances play a secondary role, as they can affect the person's moral freedom or determine how good or bad the act actually is.

Consider a situation in which Jill is organizing a fund-raiser to help earthquake victims. Jill wants to keep everyone's focus on the suffering people, so she stays in the background, not making a big deal about the work she is doing. In this case Jill's act is morally good because both the object (raising money for charity) and the intention (helping people who are in need) are good.

On the other hand, let's say Jack is also organizing a fund-raiser to help earthquake victims. Unlike Jill, Jack's only reason for doing this is to draw attention to himself. He uses every opportunity to get his picture in the news and to talk about himself. The object of Jack's act (raising money for

object

In moral decision making, the object is the specific thing—an act, word, or thought—that is being chosen.

intention

The intended outcome or goal of the person choosing the object when making a moral decision.

circumstances

The specific conditions or facts affecting a moral decision. Circumstances can increase or decrease the goodness or evil of an action.

charity) is good, but the intention (Jack's pride) is bad. This makes Jack's actions sinful. Doing the right thing for the wrong reasons will not make your actions morally good.

The circumstances surrounding a situation can affect how good or bad an act is. For example, let's say Jill's friends are pressuring her to take more credit for her fund-raising work. Under these circumstances the goodness of Jill's actions is even greater because she is resisting that pressure.

© TOBIAS SCHWARZ/Reuters/Corbis

Sophia Thomalla

How could a person doing an objectively good act, such as raising money in a telethon, still be guilty of a personal sin?

Live It!

Why Can't I Make Up My Own Mind about Sin?

All this explanation about what is required for a sin makes some people say: "I'll just make up my own mind about what is right and wrong; why do I need help from anyone? God gave me a free will to control my own destiny." There is a lot of truth in this attitude but also some misconception. God has given us the freedom to make up our own mind about our actions and to determine our eternal destiny. The key is whether our moral decisions are based on an informed conscience, and we need help to have an informed conscience.

All human beings, no matter how experienced or how well educated, have a limited perspective. We cannot possibly know all there is to know about all the moral decisions we need to make. We need God's help to make the best decisions about our actions. Through the Church, God has revealed the guidance we need, at least when it comes to religious truths and moral law. The Church is not trying to make people's moral decisions for them. The Church only desires to share the truth human beings need to make the best possible moral choices, which is the truth revealed by God.

Should we require proof about the need people have for help in making good moral decisions, we just need to look at the world around us. The many abuses and tragic conflicts occurring in the world testify to our inability to make good moral choices using only our own knowledge and power.

sin of commission
A sin that is the direct result of a freely chosen thought, word, or deed.

sin of omission
A sin that is the result of a failure to do something required by God's moral Law.

A final consideration is that some actions are evil in themselves, and they are always wrong to choose. Good intentions or special circumstances can never make these action morally good. Put simply, you cannot do evil so that good can come from it. Rape would be one example of an action that is always wrong. Circumstances such as being drunk or being pressured by peers to commit this act will never make such a choice morally right. Other examples of actions that are always morally wrong are adultery, murder, and blasphemy. These things are never morally right—ever. ✝

Article 13 Types of Sin

In the previous article, we began examining the meaning of this definition of sin from the *Catechism*:

> [Sin is] an offense against God as well as a fault against reason, truth, and right conscience. Sin is a deliberate thought, word, or deed, or omission contrary to the Eternal Law of God.
> In judging the gravity of sin, it is customary to distinguish between mortal and venial sins. (Page 899)

In this article we look at the four types of sin mentioned or implied in this definition: sins of commission, sins of omission, mortal sins, and venial sins.

Sins of Commission and Omission

Some people fall into the trap of believing that we are only responsible for the sins we directly commit, sins that are the direct result of our deliberate thoughts, words, or deeds. We call this type of sin **sins of commission**. But the *Catechism* also talks about **sins of omission**. A sin of omission occurs when we fail to do something that is required by God's moral law.

For example, let's say you witness a classmate stealing a lawn ornament from the neighbor's yard. Later your neighbor comes over and asks your family if they saw anything suspicious. You say nothing because you do not want to get your classmate into trouble. You did not directly tell a lie, so are you guilty of a sin? Yes, you are guilty of a sin of omission because you are required by the Eighth Commandment to tell the truth and instead you withheld it.

© Amma Cat/shutterstock.com

Mortal Sin and Venial Sin

Sins can have different degrees of severity (or what the *Catechism* calls "gravity"). The most basic distinction in this regard is between mortal sins and venial sins. A **mortal sin** is a serious offense against God, one that destroys within us the virtue of charity, which helps us to love God and our neighbor. A mortal sin involves serious immoral acts, or what the Church calls "grave matter." The Ten Commandments specify the issues that constitute grave matter. Jesus referred to the Ten Commandments when he spoke to the rich young man who asked him how to inherit eternal life (see Mark 10:19). Jesus implied to the young man that sins against the Ten Commandments, if unrepented, would keep us from eternal life. This is the reason they are called mortal sins; *mortal* means "death," and these sins have the power to cause eternal death—that is, eternal separation from God.

For a sin to be a mortal sin, the person committing it must have full knowledge of the immorality of the act and give her or his complete consent to doing it. She or he must know how wrong an action is and then deliberately and freely choose to do it. A person cannot unintentionally commit a mortal sin. Accidentally seeing a few answers on your classmate's test paper is not a mortal sin. But making specific plans to try to move ahead in class rank by consistently cheating on your exams, knowing that it's wrong, and then doing so anyway, is a mortal sin against the Seventh Commandment: You shall not steal.

Venial sins are less serious than mortal sins because they do not destroy our relationship with God and our ability to love. But they do damage it. Venial sins involve a lesser

mortal sin

An action so contrary to the will of God that it results in a complete separation from God and his grace. As a consequence of that separation, the person is condemned to eternal death. For a sin to be a mortal sin, three conditions must be met: the act must involve grave matter, the person must have full knowledge of the evil of the act, and the person must give his or her full consent in committing the act.

When might cheating on a test be a venial sin? When might it be a mortal sin?

© Lise Gagne/istockphoto.com

degree of evil, or they may be seriously wrong acts committed without full knowledge of just how wrong they are. Or a venial sin may involve a seriously wrong act, such as failing to attend Mass on Sunday (a sin against the Third Commandment), which is lessened by some circumstance, such as your alarm failing to go off. With God's grace, charity can repair the damage to our relationship with God caused by venial sins.

Venial sins are closely associated with **vices**. Vices are the opposite of **virtues**, which are habits of good actions. When we keep repeating sins, even venial ones, we are in

The Seven Deadly Sins

Church doctrine identifies and cautions against seven particularly harmful sins. They are sometimes referred to as **capital sins**—meaning "most serious or influential"—because they lead to and reinforce all sorts of other sinful actions, thoughts, and omissions. The capital sins, all of which are sins against God, are deadly in that they increase our tendency to sin and cause us to turn away more and more from God. For example, the capital sin of envy can lead to spreading rumors about people who have more than you do or to lying or stealing to get the things you want. Here is a list of the seven deadly sins with present-day definitions:

- *Pride* Believing you are better than others, often resulting in despising or disrespecting other people. Pride is the root of all sins, including those of disobedience committed by Satan and Adam and Eve.
- *Greed (covetousness)* Greediness; hoarding money and things
- *Envy* Resentment that we direct at others who have some success, thing, or privilege that we want for ourselves
- *Anger (wrath)* Strong anger that makes us want to seek revenge and prevents reconciliation
- *Lust* Undisciplined, unchecked desire for self-enjoyment, especially of a sexual nature
- *Gluttony* Excessive eating or drinking
- *Sloth* Habitual laziness; failing to put forth effort and take action

Do you struggle with any of these sins? Have you noticed in your own experience that these seven sins make it hard to resist other sins? One way to overcome the struggle against sin is through the practice of the human virtues. By choosing to do what is good, we grow in virtue and become increasingly disposed to choose what pleases God and to seek communion with him. (See articles 49 and 50 for more on virtues.)

danger of forming bad habits, called vices. The danger of developing a vice is that it makes it easier to commit sin without seriously thinking about it. Ultimately, this makes it easier to commit mortal sin. Let's return to the example of cheating on a test. Let's say that one day you just don't have time to study properly, and you "accidentally" see an answer on someone else's test for a question you aren't sure of, and you use it. This approach turns out to be so simple and effective that you repeat this sin by copying an answer or two on other tests. You are developing a vice for cheating. Then one day someone offers you a complete test with all the answers, stolen from a teacher's file. This is clearly a serious sin, but the vice you have developed for cheating makes it hard to resist the temptation.

If instead of developing vices we develop virtues, it is easier for us to resist temptation. Virtues are firm attitudes, stable dispositions, and the habitual perfection of our intellect and our will that guide our actions according to reason and faith. The human virtues develop in us through practice. Practice helps us harness the power of grace within us, and the more we practice, the easier it is to make good moral decisions and achieve our God-given potential. (For more on virtues, see articles 49 and 50.)

Christian morality, then, is being the person God created you to be—a person who chooses to be good. You grow into a moral person by choosing good acts, carefully examining your motives to be sure your intentions are good, and avoiding circumstances that lessen your ability to choose freely. Choosing to act morally and avoiding sin have many benefits, including greater self-esteem, healthier relationships with others, and a deeper sense of the love of God coming through loud and clear in your life. ✟

venial sin

A less serious offense against the will of God that diminishes one's personal character and weakens but does not rupture one's relationship with God.

vice

A practice or habit that leads a person to sin.

virtue

A habitual and firm disposition to do good.

capital sins

Seven sins that are particularly harmful because they lead to and reinforce other sins and vices. The seven are traditionally called pride, covetousness (greed), envy, anger (wrath), gluttony, lust, and sloth.

Article 14 Social Sin

Some sins seem to infect societies, sins that become accepted as normal attitudes or actions by a significant number of people in that society. One modern example is the acceptance of abortion in the United States and other countries around the world. We could also point to the widespread acceptance of slavery in the not-too-distant past.

social sin
The collective effect of many personal sins over time, which corrupts society and its institutions by creating "structures of sin."

social justice
The defense of human dignity by ensuring that essential human needs are met and that essential human rights are protected; to fight against social sin.

state
The word used in Church documents to indicate a political authority, for example, a kingdom, a nation, a country, or a state within a country.

common good
Social conditions that allow for all citizens of the earth, individuals and families, to meet basic needs and achieve fulfillment.

And there is the long history of prejudicial attitudes and genocidal actions against Jewish people, against indigenous populations in the Americas and Australia, and the horrible atrocities that occurred in the ethnic conflicts of Bosnia, Rwanda, and Darfur. These are just some of the better known examples; many others could be listed.

Connected to this are injustices that seem to be the result of social structures that allow and support the causes of the injustice. Examples include people without jobs when some people are overworked, people without homes when there could easily be enough homes for everyone, people who go hungry when there are supermarkets full of food. You could probably add many more examples.

These sins fall under a category called **social sin**. Social sin is connected to the Gospel teaching on **social justice**. This article introduces the main concepts, and later articles speak to some specific issues of social justice.

Human Dignity and the Common Good

Every person is created in the image of God. Therefore every human being has infinite worth and dignity because we all share God's worth and dignity. No other thing, no amount of money, no building project, no scientific discovery, no new technology is more important than preserving the life and dignity of a single person. Every group, every culture, every nation—if it wants to be just—must make preserving the dignity of each person the highest priority in its planning, its laws, and its organizational structure.

It is an essential part of human nature that we live in societies. God did not create man and woman to live alone and isolated. The community of the family and community of the **state** are an important part of God's plan. The

Every community or group must respect and protect the rights and dignity of every person.

doctrine of the Trinity can help us to understand this. Recall that God is a communion of Three Divine Persons, living in perfect love and harmony. Because we have been created in God's image, our human communities should reflect the love and harmony of the Holy Trinity. Human communities must support our spiritual life and orient us toward, or at a minimum not get in the way of, our ultimate goal: eternal communion with God in Heaven. Communities do this by being attentive to what the Church calls the **common good**.

The *Pastoral Constitution on the Church in the Modern World* (*Gaudium et Spes,* 1965) gives excellent guidance on

Encyclicals on Social Sin

Since the late 1800s, popes have addressed social justice and the reality of social sin through teaching letters called encyclicals. Here are three important ones.

Encyclical	Pope	Major Themes
On the Condition of Labor (Rerum Novarum)	Pope Leo XIII, 1891	Addresses the Church's right to speak on social issues and the rights and duties of workers and employers. Supports unions and the just wage.
On Christianity and Social Progress (Mater et Magistra)	Pope John XXIII, 1961	Says modern society is becoming more complex and interdependent. The gap between rich and poor nations threatens society, as does spending on nuclear weapons. When necessary, governments must act on these problems to protect the common good.
The Gospel of Life (Evangelium Vitae)	Pope John Paul II, 1995	Warns that society is increasingly influenced by a "culture of death," in which people focus on their own wants and needs and fail to respect the dignity of human life. Abortion, infanticide, capital punishment, and euthanasia are symptoms of the culture of death. Proposes a "culture of life" in which Christian love leads people to actively protect and care for one another.

this topic. It defines the common good as "the sum of those conditions of social life which allow social groups and their individual members relatively thorough and ready access to their own fulfillment (26)." In other words, we ensure the common good by making sure that all persons' basic needs are met and their human rights are respected.

Every person is equal in her or his God-given dignity and has the same God-given rights. The *Church in the Modern World* goes on to say what some of the needs and rights are that must be made available to all people: "everything necessary for leading a life truly human, such as food, clothing, and shelter; the right to choose a state of life freely and to found a family, the right to education, to employment, to a good reputation, to respect, to appropriate information, to activity in accord with the upright norm of one's own conscience, to protection of privacy and rightful freedom even in matters religious" (26).

Notice that the common good does not require any specific religious beliefs or practices; rather it specifies that individuals be allowed the freedom to pursue their own religion. It might be tempting to think that mandating Christianity as the state religion would be a good thing, but mandating any religion, including Christianity, would be a violation of the common good. God does not violate the individual's right to choose his or her religious belief, and neither should human beings.

Although each individual and every community group has a responsibility to create and support institutions that improve the quality of human life, the political community has a specific responsibility to do so. States have the authority and responsibility to defend and promote the common good; it is the primary reason they exist. This authority comes from God.

A concept related to the common good is social justice. Social justice is the defense of human dignity by ensuring that essential human needs are met and that essential human rights are protected. A society that preserves the common good is practicing social justice.

Defining Social Sin

We are now ready to define *social sin.* Social sin is not one person's individual sin, but it is rooted in personal sin. Social sin is the collective effect of many people's personal sin. So if one employer pays a woman less than he pays a man for doing the same job, this is his personal sin. But if many employers in a city, state, or country pay women less than they pay men for doing the same jobs they have created a situation of social sin. They are each guilty of personal sin, but they have produced a social condition in which an injustice is accepted and tolerated. This is why many of the "isms"—racism, sexism, ageism—are often also instances of social sin.

© Bettmann/CORBIS

Social sin happens when a sinful attitude or action becomes so commonly accepted that it goes unchallenged by most people. An example of this could be when a country's resources are concentrated in the hands of a few wealthy people while large numbers of people have barely enough to survive. Social sin can actually become a part of society's law. For example, in the last century some states had laws mandating separate schools, separate bathrooms,

What responsibility do we have for fighting social sin? How can we fight social sins such as racism, poverty, and abortion?

Catholic Wisdom

Social Sin and Personal Conversion

In addressing members of Catholic Charities in 1987, Pope John Paul II clearly made the connections between personal sin and social sin.

> In the final analysis, however, we must realize that social injustice and unjust social structures exist only because individuals and groups of individuals deliberately maintain or tolerate them. It is these *personal choices*, operating through structures, that breed and propagate situations of poverty, oppression and misery. For this reason, overcoming "social" sin and reforming the social order itself must begin with *the conversion of our hearts*. (6)

and separate seating on public transportation for black Americans and white Americans. Such established norms or laws are sometimes called structural sin or institutional sin, indicating that a sinful practice or attitude has become part of the fundamental attitudes, laws, and practices that make up the structure of society. ✝

Review

1. Briefly describe two key understandings of sin found in the Old Testament.

2. What are some of the consequences of sin taught in the Old Testament?

3. Why does Jesus say that sin is about lies and darkness?

4. Name three things that Jesus teaches about forgiveness.

5. Give a definition of *sin.*

6. What three things determine whether a human act is a sin?

7. What is the difference between a mortal sin and a venial sin?

8. What is the relationship between personal sin and social sin?

9. Give three examples of social sin.

Honoring God

Part 1

The First Commandment: Faith, Not Idolatry

The first three Commandments all have a common theme: loving and honoring God. Jesus, who is himself God, summed them up with the first of his Great Commandments: "Hear, O Israel! The Lord our God is Lord alone! You shall love the Lord your God with all your heart, with all your soul, with all your mind, and with all your strength" (Mark 12:29–30).

The First Commandment, "I am the Lord, your God: you shall not have strange Gods before me," is the starting point of our moral life. It calls us to put our faith in God alone. There is no other god, no other creature, no other thing that is worthy of our complete faith and adoration. There is no one and nothing else that can save us from sin and death. The opposite of placing our faith in God is idolatry, which is placing our faith, hope, and love in something that is not God.

We face a great many temptations to sin against the First Commandment, more than you might think. Our culture is filled with messages that promise certain things will bring us true happiness and fulfillment. Experiences and substances provide temporary highs. It is tempting to chase after these things, to make them the center of our lives. We may not worship idols made in the image of Baal and Asherah, but idolatry is alive and well in our time.

The articles in this part address the following topics:

Article 15 Living the First Commandment

A politician who was Christian gave an interview on the challenges he faced in integrating his faith and his political positions. He supported legislation that provided help for immigrants and people in poverty, legislation that protected the environment, and legislation providing health care for all people. He also opposed capital punishment, legalized abortion, and legalized euthanasia. He maintained these positions despite the criticism he received from people within his own political party. When asked why he did this, he answered simply, "My first and primary commitment is to God and his Law."

This politician was being faithful to the First Commandment, "I am the Lord, your God: you shall not have strange Gods before me." The First Commandment is first because it is the primary foundation for our life and happiness. All the other Commandments depend on the First Commandment. For example, why would you keep holy the Sabbath if you really didn't believe in God? Why would you always speak the truth if you didn't believe it was part of God's Eternal Law? Why would you not have as much sex as you want with whomever you want if you didn't believe that God established sacramental Marriage as the only proper place for sexual intimacy?

The First Commandment is a summons—a call for us to have faith in God, to put our hope in him, and to love him completely, without holding back anything. Obeying the First Commandment is not for the indecisive and weak-hearted; it is an exciting journey that requires a complete commitment of heart, soul, and mind. You cannot say you believe in God and then trust a horoscope to guide your future. You cannot say you put your complete hope and trust in God and then live as

What responsibility do we have for fighting social sin? How can we fight social sins such as racism, poverty, and abortion?

theological virtues
The name for the God-given virtues of faith, hope, and love. These virtues enable us to know God as God and lead us to union with him in mind and heart.

heresy
The conscious and deliberate rejection of a dogma of the Church.

though the only thing that matters in life is being the best athlete or having the highest grade point no matter what the cost. You cannot say you love God absolutely and not follow the guidance of the Church he established as his Body on earth.

Sins against Faith, Hope, and Love

Living the First Commandment is a natural expression of the **theological virtues** of faith, hope, and love. If God is the unchanging source of all life and goodness, faithful in all his promises, how can we not put our faith in him? After Jesus Christ has shown us the depth of his Father's forgiveness and humility, how can we not place our hope in him? Knowing God's unconditional, saving love for us revealed in the Paschal Mystery, how can we not love him in return? These virtues are indeed gifts from God, gifts that we are called to embrace and live out. Failure to do so leads to various sins against the First Commandment.

Putting our faith in God calls us to accept all the truths of faith revealed by him through Scripture and Tradition and taught by the Church's Magisterium. Failure to do so can lead to the sin of doubt, which is to either disregard the truths of faith or to question them without seeking to further understand them. This can lead even further to **heresy**, which is to deny an essential truth of our faith or even apostasy, which is complete rejection of the Christian faith.

Placing our hope in God means to confidently expect his blessing in this life and the reward of Heaven in the next. We must avoid the sin of despair, which is to stop believing that God cares for us and that he will fulfill his promises to us. It also means that we must avoid the sin of presumption, which means believing that we can be saved by our own efforts or that God will save us even if we are not fully committed to reforming our lives and following his will.

Loving God above everything else might seem quite obvious. But we should never think that love is easy or happens without struggle, even loving God. We can fail in many ways to return God's love, such as through indifference, ingratitude, and refusing to fully commit to loving him (sometimes called lukewarmness, see Revelation 3:15–16). The sin most contrary to the love of God is hatred of God, a sin of pride that involves the denial of God's goodness. This sin presumes that we are somehow knowledgeable enough to judge God and find him deserving of our hatred.

Undoubtedly you desire to put your faith, hope, and love in God and make him the most important thing in your life. The Church identifies these sins as warnings to not let down your guard and take the First Commandment for granted. We must regularly and intentionally nurture our relationship with God. This is an important key to living a moral life and why the gift of the Church is essential to our moral life.

Religious Freedom

Some people might ask, "If true religion is so important to our life with God, wouldn't the Church want to require the Catholic faith as the religion for all people?" The answer is absolutely not. The Catholic Church is strongly against any state-mandated religion. We follow the example of God, who honors each person's free decision to accept God's gift of faith. If God does not force people into accepting faith, than certainly it would be wrong for us to do so.

This means several things for believers. First, we must continually work to guard and promote religious freedom in all nations and states. All people, no matter where they live, must be free to choose how to live out their relationship with God. Second, we have a responsibility to share and promote the truths of the Catholic faith with the world. Although we respect other religions and the truth they may share with us, only the Catholic Church has the fullness of truth, which has been revealed by God. How can people of other faiths know this and choose it if we do not share it with them as clearly and confidently and humbly as possible?

Nurturing Your Relationship with God

God does not want us to develop our relationship with him in isolation. Participating in the Sacraments and in the life of the Church is the best way to nurture and enrich our relationship with God. The virtues of faith, hope, and love help us to live our faith in the following ways as members of the Body of Christ.

Adoration To adore God is to acknowledge him as our Creator, as our Savior, as never ending Love, as the gift giver who provides everything we need for salvation. When we

The First Commandment requires that we nurture our relationship with God. What are some of your practices for growing in your relationship with God?

© Bill Wittman

tithe

A commitment to donate a tenth or some other percentage of our income to the Church and other charitable causes.

evangelical counsels

The call to go beyond the minimum rules of life required by God (such as the Ten Commandments and the Precepts of the Church) and strive for spiritual perfection through a life marked by a commitment to chastity, poverty, and obedience.

adore God, we acknowledge that all life, all holiness comes from him alone, and that we are humble creatures who wholly depend on his love and mercy. We offer adoration to God in all the Church's liturgies, especially in the Sacrament of the Eucharist.

Prayer Prayer is the primary means through which we strengthen our relationship with God. It must be a constant in our lives; Saint Paul directs us to "Pray without ceasing" (1 Thessalonians 5:17). Adoration is only the beginning of prayer; it focuses our attention on God. Prayer must also include praise and thanksgiving, intercession and petition, meditation and contemplation. We experience all these forms of prayer in the liturgy of the Church.

Sacrifice Following Christ's example, we are called to lives of sacrificial love. We make sacrifices in many ways—by following the Church's guidelines for abstinence and fasting, by spending time with family and friends even when it is inconvenient, by accepting sickness and suffering with dignity and courage. In the Eucharist we unite our sacrifice with Christ's perfect sacrifice and grow closer to him.

Promises and Vows Just as God keeps his promises to us, we must keep our promises to him. For example, in the Sacraments we make promises to God, such as promising to believe in him and to reject Satan, and promising to love, cherish, and be faithful to our spouse until death. We can also make personal promises to God, such as a promise to pray daily or to **tithe**. Deacons, priests, and bishops promise to obey their superiors and serve the People of God. God also calls some people to take vows to live the **evangelical counsels** and live as consecrated religious. Our faith community supports us in keeping the promises and commitments we make to God. ✝

Live It!

Teens Reflect on Modern Idols

If you were asked, "What things do people idolize and put at the center of their lives instead of God?" how would you answer? When we asked some teens this question, their most common answers were money, video games, sports, celebrities, and television. Other things were mentioned too, but each of these five was named by 20 percent or more of the teens in the group we surveyed. Overall they seemed to agree that in our society we are tempted to idolize things that should not be nearly as important as our love for God.

The majority of the teens believed that money is the most common thing people idolize. Many say the reason for this is simple practicality. "You can't live without money," said one teen, "and people find more comfort in something tangible than they find in God, who is intangible." Another important reason mentioned was societal values. A teen put it like this: "Our society is very materialistic. The media consistently portray that having money and things brings happiness. God is almost never mentioned as the source of happiness."

Video gaming was the next most frequently mentioned potential idolatry. The teens felt that societal values are also a big factor in people's obsession with video games, but they also identified forgetting about life's problems and adding excitement to life as reasons for idolizing video games. "People play video games because they are a way to forget about the bad things that are happening in your life," observed one student. Another student said, "All the action in video games is very exciting and makes you feel like you are doing something more interesting than normal life."

For some people money can be an idol and a distraction from God; for others it might be video gaming. These are just two of many things that can keep us from focusing on what truly matters in our lives: our relationship with God. What distractions keep you from growing in your relationship with God?

Article 16 Idolatry, Ancient and Modern

One of the most popular television shows in the last decade is *American Idol*. Over several months, talented (and some not-so-talented) people pursue their dreams of being voted the top amateur performer of the year. Many people find the show fun to watch and, at times, even inspirational as people overcome various challenges to advance in the competition.

But have you ever wondered about the title? Why are the final contestants American "idols"? The label "idol" signifies a person who is greatly admired or loved, even to excess. But an idol can also signify a person or object worshipped as a god, which is the biblical meaning of the word. Are the two definitions connected?

© Sara De Boer/Retna Ltd./Corbis

Is there a connection between pop culture "idols" and the sin of idolatry? If so, how would you describe it?

Original Meaning of the First Commandment

The full text of the First Commandment from the Book of Exodus reads like this: "I, the Lord, am your God, who brought you out of the land of Egypt, that place of slavery. You shall not have other gods besides me. You shall not carve idols for yourselves in the shape of anything in the sky above or on the earth below or in the waters beneath the earth; you shall not bow down before them or worship them" (20:2–5). In its original context, the First Commandment focused on the sin of **idolatry**, which is the literal worship of gods and goddesses other than Yahweh. For the ancient Israelites, idolatry was a real and concrete thing. They had just come from slavery in Egypt, a kingdom that worshipped many different gods and goddesses. They were settling in a land where the native people, the Canaanites, worshipped many different gods and goddesses too. It would only be natural for them to also believe in a **pantheon** of divine beings.

The record of the Old Testament reveals how difficult it was for Israelites to worship Yahweh alone. Yes, they offered sacrifice to Yahweh in the Temple, but they often fell into

old practices of worshipping gods like **Baal** and **Asherah** (also called Ashtaroth). Here's one example from Judges:

> The Israelites again offended the LORD, serving the Baals and Ashtaroths, the gods of Aram, the gods of Sidon, the gods of Moab, the gods of the Ammonites, and the gods of the Philistines. Since they had abandoned the LORD and would not serve him, the LORD became angry with Israel and allowed them to fall into the power of (the Philistines and) the Ammonites. (10:6–7)

It seems that throughout their history the Israelites struggled with **monotheism**. Yahweh might be their God, but the gods and goddesses of the people around must have seemed just as real. So to protect themselves from the possibility that following Yahweh was the wrong choice, they also worshipped Baal, Asherah, and other gods and goddesses. Some of these gods and goddesses were worshipped in sacred places in which people prayed and offered sacrifice. Carved statues of these gods and goddesses would be placed on home altars for prayer and protection—thus the prohibition against carven images in the Commandment.

Some worship practices were particularly offensive, but they must have occurred because they are mentioned in Scripture. The worship of Asherah included having sex with temple prostitutes to ensure good harvests (see 1 Kings 15:11–12). The worship of Molech seemed to involve child sacrifice (see Leviticus 18:21).

God had to remind the Israelites again and again, with painful consequences, that he is all-powerful and the only God. Eventually they learned their lesson. After the Exile and certainly by the time of Jesus, Jews had come to the conclusion that there is only one God and that the gods and goddesses of other peoples were only myths. But is that the end of idolatry?

© Gianni Dagli Orti/CORBIS

In the Old Testament, idolatry was literally the worship of gods or goddesses other than Yahweh. The Old Testament's books record that the Israelites frequently fell into this sin.

idolatry
The worship of other beings, creatures, or material goods in a way that is fitting for God alone. It is a violation of the First Commandment.

pantheon
A group of gods and goddesses worshipped by a particular people or religion.

Baal
The Canaanite god of rain and vegetation, often represented by a bull and worshipped in the "high places." He was considered a false god by the Israelites but worshipped by them when they fell away from the one true God.

Asherah (also called Astarte or Ashtoreth)
The Canaanite goddess of love and fertility, often represented by a serpent and worshipped in sacred groves. She was considered a false god by the Israelites but also worshipped by them when they fell away from the one true God.

monotheism
The belief in and worship of only one God.

Do Catholics Worship Graven Images?

Although the First Commandment forbids us to worship images, like the golden calf, it is permissible, and indeed good, to use images like crucifixes, statues, pictures, or icons to symbolically represent the sacred and holy. If you have been in other Christian churches, particularly Protestant churches, you may have noticed that they are different from Catholic churches. Most have no statues, no vigil lights, no stations of the cross. Catholics have sometimes been criticized for the images in our churches because of the mistaken understanding that we worship these things. But we do not worship or adore these objects. We **venerate**, or give respect and honor to, saints, sacred objects, and images. Veneration is different from worship and adoration, which is for God alone. It is based on the mystery of the Incarnation and does not violate the First Commandment.

Idolatry in Today's World

Judaism, Islam, and Christianity are all monotheistic faiths. Today no devout Christian, Jew, or Muslim would have a statue of Baal in their room or secretly worship Asherah. So is the sin of idolatry a thing of the past? Not according to Jesus. Recall the Sermon on the Mount. In it Jesus teaches: "No one can serve two masters. He will either hate one and love the other, or be devoted to one and despise the other. You cannot serve God and mammon" (Matthew 6:24). In this teaching Jesus is broadening our understanding of idolatry. *Mammon* means wealth and riches. Idolatry is not just worshipping pagan gods and goddesses, it is letting something like money take the place that God should have in our lives.

Jesus focuses on money because that is the thing that people of his time thought would bring them security and happiness. That is certainly true in our time too. But money isn't the only thing we idolize. No doubt you have heard this said or have thought of it before. For example, the pursuit of success and fame can be a form of idolatry whether through sports, academics, or the arts. A good example would be a person who takes illegal performance enhancing drugs or sabotages a competitor in order to win. That person has crossed the line from healthy competition and made winning and fame a god in his or her life.

Entertainment can also be a form of idolatry. Think of people who spend so much time in role-playing games or watching television or on social networking sites that they neglect their family and friends, their grades, and even their health. Have those people made entertainment a god in their lives? Another form of idolatry is the pursuit of "things." Have you ever known someone who was obsessed with getting the latest phone, or a particular car, certain clothes, or any other material thing?

Idolatry has a strong connection to the complex issue of addictions and obsessive behaviors. Our society has all kinds of recognized addictions—to alcohol, to narcotics, to sex, to gambling, to food, even to shopping. People with addictions have learned to turn to their addictive behavior when bored or stressed or hurting rather than to turn to God. This is the common thread in all these examples of modern idolatries: we turn to something that is not God to try and find the happiness and fulfillment that can only come from God.

So what are the signs that you have crossed the line from having a normal and healthy interest in something to making it an idol in your life? Here are some questions to consider:

- Has your focus on the thing in question (for example, sports, academics, game playing, popularity, alcohol) affected your relationship with God? Has it caused you to spend less time in prayer, to miss Mass, to feel uncomfortable around members of your faith community?

- Has the thing in question affected your relationships with family and friends in unhealthy ways? Are you spending less quality time with them? Is it causing you to keep secrets?

venerate

An action that shows deep reverence for something sacred. For example, on Good Friday, individuals in the assembly venerate the cross by bowing before it or kissing it.

Catholic Wisdom

Saint Augustine on Idolatry

"Idolatry is worshipping anything that ought to be used, or using anything that is meant to be worshipped." (Saint Augustine)

© Chen Fei/XinHua/Xinhua Press/Corbis

Many people believe that our culture's preoccupation with possessing material things is a form of idolatry. What would be the arguments for such a viewpoint?

- Is the thing in question taking over God's role in your life? Are you relying on it for your happiness more than you are relying on God for your happiness? Are you making your life choices based on its influence rather than making your life choices based on God's calling?

If your answers to some of these questions make you uncomfortable, it may be a sign that you need to assess your spiritual priorities and make some changes in your life. You can start by talking to a spiritual adviser such as a priest or other minister in your church and by making a renewed commitment to put God first in your life. ✝

Article 17 Other Sins against the First Commandment

The previous two articles discussed some of the most common sins against the First Commandment. Other sins against the First Commandment are less likely to be committed by the Christian faithful, but have been widely practiced throughout human history. They fall generally into two categories: (1) sinful excesses of religion, which can be thought of as irrational and irresponsible religion, and (2) irreligion, which can be thought of as the absence or rejection of the virtue of religion.

Sinful Excesses of Religion

Superstition is the practice of assigning magical power to certain practices or objects, such as charms or omens. When items like crystals or good-luck charms become more than

just decorations and are seen as having the power to bring about a particular outcome, there is the danger of superstition. Even the worship of the one true God can become a form of superstition. This happens when religious symbols or rituals are used in superstitious ways, with the belief that they can influence God. Although expressing your desires to God through prayer is good, believing he will fix the outcome of a game because you made the Sign of the Cross or prayed three Our Fathers is wrong. In all ages we find people who have turned worship of the true God into a superstition.

Hobbies and games that lead individuals to believe in **magic** or the occult can be sinful. They too are not compatible with true Christian belief and worship of God. Believing in creatures, devices, or objects as if they had divine power is a serious sin. Satanism, astrology, palm reading, and attempts to call up the dead or see the future are all forms of the sin of **divination**. They are wrong because "they contradict the honor, respect, and loving fear that we owe to God alone" (*Catechism of the Catholic Church*, 2116).

superstition

Attributing to someone or something else a power that belongs to God alone and relying on such powers rather than trusting in God; a sin against the First Commandment.

magic

The belief in supernatural power that comes from a source other than God; a sin against the First Commandment.

divination

The practice of seeking power or knowledge through supernatural means apart from the one true God; a sin against the First Commandment.

sacrilege

An offense against God. It is the abuse of a person, place, or thing dedicated to God and the worship of him.

© Anyka/shutterstock.com

Why are palm reading and other forms of divination sins against the First Commandment?

Sins of Irreligion

One of the sins that falls under the category of irreligion is **sacrilege**, or the abuse of the Sacraments, persons, things, or places that are consecrated to God. Some movies, TV shows, and celebrities poke fun at objects or actions that are specifically Catholic. There is nothing funny about belittling the symbols and rituals of the faith.

simony
Buying or selling
something spiritual,
such as a grace, a
Sacrament, or a relic.
It violates the honor
of God.

atheist; atheism
One who denies the
existence of God; the
denial of the existence
of God.

Simony is another sin of irreligion. Simony describes the practice of buying and selling spiritual things and favors, and is another sin against the First Commandment. A modern example of simony would be a television preacher's promising people miraculous cures if they only send in a certain amount of money. Although it is permissible to expect a contribution for goods and services so that the ministers of God can earn a living, someone who tries to buy or sell spiritual power, or con unsuspecting people with promises of God's favor, is guilty of sin.

Atheism is a serious and common problem of our time. Atheism is the denial of God's existence and is the ultimate violation of the First Commandment, which assures us of God's loving and ongoing presence in our lives. Atheism

Pray It!

Praying for Those Who Do Not Believe in God

In recent years a number of books have been published that promote atheism and claim that the Church has done more harm than good. These claims do not hold up to any close scrutiny. It is easy to be angry at these vocal atheists for their denial of God and criticism of the Church, but God calls us to be compassionate toward all. Often people who deny God have been hurt in some way. They cannot believe in a God that would allow their pain. During the Good Friday Liturgy, we pray for those people specifically, but they should be regularly in our prayers.

>Let us pray also for those who do not acknowledge God,
>that, following what is right in sincerity of heart,
>they may find the way to God himself.
>Almighty ever-living God,
>who created all people
>to seek you always by desiring you
>and, by finding you, come to rest,
>grant, we pray,
>that, despite every harmful obstacle,
>all may recognize the signs of your fatherly love
>and the witness of the good works
>done by those who believe in you,
>and so in gladness confess you,
>the one true God and father of our human race.
>We ask this through Christ our Lord. Amen.
>
>*(Roman Missal)*

can have many faces, including the belief that humans aren't dependent on God. Atheistic political systems, like Communism, deny the existence of God and blame religion for the economic and social oppression of people. Agnosticism is a cousin to atheism. Instead of declaring that there is no God, agnostics claim that it is impossible to prove God's existence. Thus agnostics believe that one cannot know anything about God or his nature. ✝

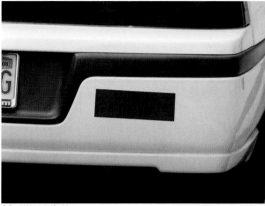

© David Howells/Corbis

Atheists deny the existence of God, a serious sin against the First Commandment.

Review

1. What is the heart of the First Commandment? How do we keep it?

2. What are two ways that we sin against the call to place our hope in God?

3. What is the original meaning of the First Commandment?

4. List some modern examples of the sin of idolatry.

5. Describe three ways that people practice sinful excesses of religion.

6. What is atheism?

Part 2

The Second Commandment: Reverence, Not Profanity

Is there someone in your life that you cannot ever imagine disrespecting? Maybe it is a grandparent or an aunt or an uncle who has always loved and accepted you, or maybe it is a teacher or a coach or a priest or a youth minister who has always been wise, kind, and honest with you. You honor these people by always speaking respectfully about them. You would never think to use these people's names as a curse or to involve them in some lie or wrongdoing.

So if you hold this level of respect for people in your life, is it not just as important to treat God and his name with the same or even greater honor? God deserves our complete respect, and we should honor him in our every thought, word, and deed. This is what the Second Commandment, "You shall not take the name of the Lord your God in vain," is all about. Some people think it is just a command against swearing, but it is so much more than that. The Second Commandment calls us to revere God by our every word and action, especially by keeping his name holy and by keeping our promises.

The articles in this part address the following topics:

- Article 18: Reverence, Responding to the Sacredness of God (page 91)

- Article 19: Keeping Sacred Commitments (page 94)

- Article 20: Other Sins against the Second Commandment (page 99)

Article 18 Reverence, Responding to the Sacredness of God

A young person went to Mass regularly with his grandmother. The grandmother was advanced in years, and it was getting harder and harder for her to get around. Every week the young man watched his grandmother enter the church and painfully genuflect toward the tabernacle before entering the pew. When Mass was over, she would genuflect again and then go to the tabernacle, where she would painfully kneel for a few minutes of prayer. One day he asked his grandmother: "Grandma, why do you always genuflect and kneel in church? Surely, God sees how hard it is for you and doesn't need you to do that." His grandmother answered: "Of course God doesn't need me to do it. But I need to do it for God. Every time I genuflect or kneel in reverence to him, I remind myself of his love and care for me, and I remind myself of all he has done for me."

© Voronin76/shutterstock.com

sacred
The quality of being holy, worthy of respect and reverence.

Reverence versus Profanity

Showing reverence for God and his **sacred** name is the proper response of true faith. How else would we respond to the One who is the creator of all that is, to the one who is faithful in all his promises, to the One who is perfect love, to the One who suffered death on the cross to save us from sin and death? When we reverence God, we recognize that he is sacred, that he is not ordinary, that he is holy and just, and that he is worthy of our praise and adoration. We practice this reverence especially in sacred places, such as churches and shrines, and at sacred times, such as during the Eucharist or our private prayer.

But showing God reverence should not happen only at Mass once a week or when we take time to pray. We must also show reverence for God in all the words and actions

profanity

Speaking disrespectfully about something that is sacred or treating it with disrespect.

of our daily life. We can do this by having reverence for creation because creation reveals to us the wonder of God. We can also do this by treating all people reverently because every person is made in God's image and likeness.

The opposite of reverence is **profanity**. Profanity is more than just swearing or vulgar language. It means to treat something that is sacred as if it were ordinary or meaningless. To treat God profanely or to live your life profanely is to miss the mark. (Remember the Bible's definition of *sin*?) It is a failure to live up to the high calling that we have as children of God: to love and honor all people and all things, and most especially God. Speaking profanely and living profanely is to settle for less than the best, to accept a second-rate way of life. It brings dishonor to God and to ourselves.

The Name of God

The people of the Bible placed great value on names. A person's name usually indicated something special about a person, maybe something about her or his character or family. A person and her or his name were closely connected— to misuse a person's name was literally seen as causing injury to the person. Because of this ancient belief, people would not give their names casually to a stranger. This is why God's Revelation of his personal name, Yahweh, to Moses (see Exodus 3:14) is a big deal. It indicated God's trust in Moses and his Chosen People that they would not abuse his name. Jesus emphasized the importance of keeping his Father's name holy in teaching his disciples to pray: "Our Father in heaven, hallowed (holy) be your name" (Matthew 6:9). Still today many Jewish people will not say the personal name for God aloud out of respect for the sacredness of his name.

© David Lees/CORBIS

In the Book of Exodus, God reveals his sacred name to Moses. Why is this such an important event in salvation history?

It is in this context that we should understand the Second Commandment, "You shall not take the name of the Lord your God in vain." To use God's name in vain means to use it for dishonorable or profane purposes. It is treating or using his name, which is holy and worthy of the greatest respect, as something ordinary, or even worse, for evil purposes. The people of the Bible would have seen this as not only dishonoring God's name but also dishonoring God himself. We should see it the same way.

If you were to listen carefully to your own speech, the conversations of others, and the spoken media for an entire day, how many times do you think you would hear God's name? How many of those times do you think it would be used respectfully? All too often we hear people use the expressions "Oh, God!" "Jesus Christ!" or even "Holy Mother of God!" as a way to express humor, surprise, or anger. Rarely is it used in a situation where people really intend to call on our God and Savior! Using the name of God profanely is a sin and a sign that we are losing the awe and respect due to him.

The sinfulness of abusing God's name also extends to other names. Using the name of the Virgin Mary or the name of any of the saints in vain is also wrong. God calls us each by name, and so our names have great value. Every person's name is sacred in the sight of God. ✝

Catholic Wisdom

Baptism and Confirmation Names

Catholics experience the sacredness of names in choosing Baptism and Confirmation names. Because most Catholics are baptized as infants, the parents choose the child's Baptism name. When it comes time for Confirmation, many dioceses encourage people to keep their Baptism name as their Confirmation name. Some dioceses, however, allow Confirmation candidates to choose a different name for their Confirmation name.

People often pick the name of a saint (or someone close to them) who has holy qualities they wish to emulate when choosing a name for Baptism and Confirmation. What is the meaning behind your Baptism and Confirmation name or names?

The Names of God in the Old Testament

The Hebrew names of God in the Old Testament have several different forms. Here are some of the variations.

Hebrew	Literal Translation	Name Used in English Bible Translations
El or Elohim	"God" or "gods"	God
El Shaddai	"God, the One of the Mountains"	God Almighty
El Elyon	"God Most High"	God Most High
Yahweh	"I am who am"	LORD (with small caps)
Yahweh Sabaoth	"Lord of Hosts"	Lord Almighty

Article

19 Keeping Sacred Commitments

One of the most interesting paradoxes of the spiritual life is that we are the most free after we have made a major commitment. Some people think of freedom as the ability to do whatever you want, whenever you want, with whomever you want. But the reality of trying to live that way is that people become trapped by having too many choices. They are always moving on to new experiences or relationships, always leaving their options open. Unfortunately, people who live this way almost always end up not accomplishing anything that has lasting significance, and they rarely have relationships of real depth and meaning. Living life like this actually makes a person less free when it comes to loving and being loved and when it comes to making a meaningful difference in the world.

Only someone who fully commits—to a cause, to a particular work or ministry, or to a particular person or group—is truly free to live the full life God intends for us. When you think of people who are admired for their contributions to family life, sports, society, or the Church, what do they all have in common? Almost always these people have been faithful to the commitments they have made. By making a complete commitment to a specific person, group, or cause, they are not distracted by other things. This leaves them freer to focus on being true to the person, the ministry, or the cause that God has called them to as their primary commitment.

How is this related to the Second Commandment? The Second Commandment's original focus was on the importance of being true to vows or commitments made in God's name. This article looks at what that meant for the ancient Israelites and what it means for us today.

covenant
A solemn agreement between human beings or between God and a human being in which mutual commitments are made.

Vows Made in God's Name

In the world of the ancient Israelites, individuals swore oaths to one another, and tribes or nations made **covenants** with one another. Today we would probably call these agreements contracts and treaties. It is characteristic of these oaths and covenants that they were made in the name of the gods the people believed in. They called upon these gods to witness their agreement, and they believed that their gods would enforce these sacred promises and would bring punishment upon anyone who broke his or her oath or covenant agreement.

We see examples of this type of oath frequently in the Bible. When Jacob and his Uncle Laban made a peace agreement, they concluded by saying, "May the God of Abraham and the god of Nahor (their ancestral deities) maintain justice between us!" (Genesis 31:53). When King Saul finally understood that David would succeed him as king, he asked David to make an oath to spare his family: "Swear to me by the LORD that you will not destroy my descendants and that you will not blot out my name and family" (1 Samuel 24:22).

Making an oath on the Bible emphasizes the importance of keeping sacred commitments.

© jim pruitt/istockphoto.com

The Saints on Commitments to God

"What does it profit you to give God one thing if he asks of you another? Consider what it is God wants, and then do it." (Saint John of the Cross)

"Obedience is the only virtue that implants the other virtues in the heart and preserves them after they start growing." (Pope Gregory the Great)

"You must refuse nothing you recognize to be God's will." (Jane Frances de Chantal)

The original meaning of the Second Commandment was to protect these sacred oaths and covenants the Israelites made in the name of God. The Second Commandment warned them not to make these promises "in vain." That is, it warned them not to make a sacred oath or covenant about something trivial. And if they made a sacred oath or covenant, they better fully intend to keep that promise. The second part of the Commandment warns: "For the LORD will not leave unpunished him who takes his name in vain" (Exodus 20:7). As was discussed in the previous article, invoking God's name was serious business, and people had better be serious when they did it.

In the Sermon on the Mount, Jesus reinforces the importance of keeping commitments:

> Again you have heard that it was said to your ancestors, "Do not take a false oath, but make good to the Lord all that you vow." But I say to you, do not swear at all; not by heaven, for it is God's throne; nor by the earth, for it is his footstool; nor by Jerusalem, for it is the city of the great King. Do not swear by your head, for you cannot make a single hair white or black. Let your "Yes" mean "Yes," and your "No" mean "No." Anything more is from the evil one. (Matthew 5:33–37)

Jesus is saying that we should be so honest in everything we do and say that there is no need to use God's name in making an oath. It should be assumed that as his disciples we will tell the truth and keep our important commitments.

Sacred Commitments Today

The practice of making sacred oaths in the name of God isn't just an ancient practice. It is part of public life in the United States and many other countries. Politicians swear to fulfill their public duties with their hand on the Bible while calling upon God's help. Judges swear to uphold the law of the land in the same way. Defendants in a courtroom usually swear to tell the truth "so help me God." These are all sacred oaths, and to break these oaths is a serious sin. Because we make them publicly in God's name, breaking them implicates God in our failure or lie.

We make sacred oaths in the context of liturgy and prayer also, but we usually call them promises or vows. Often these are associated with one of the Sacraments. In the Sacraments of Baptism and Confirmation, we promise to reject Satan and all his works and empty promises. In the Sacrament of Matrimony, the bride and bridegroom promise to be true to each other until death no matter what happens to them. In the Sacrament of Holy Orders, a man being ordained to the priesthood makes promises of celibacy and obedience to his bishop. Men and women who enter the consecrated life commit to the evangelical counsels by taking vows of chastity, poverty, and obedience. These are all sacred promises made in God's name, and breaking them is a serious sin. People should make these vows only after a time of prayerful discernment, being as sure as is humanly possible that God is calling them to this particular vocation and commitment.

What sacred promises do we make in the Sacraments of Baptism and Confirmation?

© Bill Wittman

Besides these major vows we make during our lives, many people also make less serious promises to God. Often these promises are commitments to some kind of spiritual practice. For example, you might promise to watch less television during Lent. Or you might pledge to give a certain amount of money to charity every month or every year. Or you might commit to a regular time of prayer every day. These types of promises are important commitments to growing in our relationship with God, and we should do our best to keep them. But breaking them is generally a less serious sin than breaking a sacramental vow or a vow to a religious vocation. ✝

Live It!

Keeping Your Commitments to God

Personal prayer, regularly receiving the Sacraments of the Eucharist and Penance and Reconciliation, spiritual reading, and attending retreats are examples of spiritual practices that nurture and deepen our relationship with God. Maintaining these practices is a type of sacred commitment. Here are some suggestions from experienced leaders on keeping spiritual commitments.

1. **Start with some nonnegotiables.** Make a list of the practices that you know you must do no matter what. The Precepts of the Church are a good place to start. These are the minimal requirements for living a Christian life (see student book article 9, "Moral Law and the Church"). Do not let anything get in the way of these nonnegotiable commitments.

2. **Be realistic.** Some people become overenthusiastic in making new spiritual commitments. Instead of trying one new thing, they want to try six. Unless you join a monastery, it is unlikely that you can fit a lot of new spiritual commitments into your life all at the same time. If you are feeling the need to grow in your relationship with God by adding new spiritual practices to your nonnegotiables, make a commitment to try one new spiritual practice at a time.

3. **Make a commitment to try a new practice for forty days.** Forty is an important symbolic number in the Bible. One reason is that forty is the number of days and nights Jesus spent in the desert fasting and praying (see Matthew 4:1–2). If you decide to try a new spiritual practice, such as reading a chapter of the Bible a day, make a commitment to do it for forty days. Decide on the time and place and stick to it. It takes forty days for a new spiritual practice to start to become a habit and for us to be able to evaluate the difference it is making in our relationship with God.

Article 20 Other Sins against the Second Commandment

The previous two articles discussed some of the most common sins against the Second Commandment. Blasphemy and perjury are sins against the Second Commandment that are less likely to be committed by the Christian faithful but have been widely practiced throughout human history.

Blasphemy and Perjury

Far worse than a casual curse is using the name of God, of Jesus Christ, of the Virgin Mary, or of the saints in an intentionally offensive way. This is called **blasphemy**. Blasphemy could be expressing hatred of God or defiance against him either publically or privately. It is like saying, "I know better than God." Blasphemy could also be using God's name as an excuse to cover up a crime or to excuse some sin you have committed. For example, some so-called Christian militia organizations say that God wants them to commit acts of terrorism against elected officials or public institutions.

Blasphemy is a grave sin. In Jesus' time blasphemy was considered so serious that a person could be put to death as punishment. Jesus' claim to be the Messiah and the Son of God was considered blasphemous by those who wanted to kill him. Although in our society today we would not put someone to death for blasphemy, perhaps we have become too used to the offensive use of God's name.

blasphemy

Speaking, acting, or thinking about God, Jesus Christ, the Virgin Mary, or the saints in a way that is irreverent, mocking, or offensive. It is a sin against the Second Commandment.

To attack, destroy, or deface a sacred object or holy place is a sin against the holiness of God, protected by the Second Commandment.

© ATEF HASSAN/Reuters/Corbis

perjury

The sin of lying while under an oath to tell the truth. It is a sin against the Second Commandment.

examination of conscience

Prayerful reflection on, and assessment of, one's words, attitudes, and actions in light of the Gospel of Jesus; more specifically, the conscious moral evaluation of one's life in preparation for reception of the Sacrament of Penance and Reconciliation.

As mentioned in student book article 19, "Keeping Sacred Commitments," a time when we publicly use God's name in a reverential manner is when someone takes an oath promising to uphold the law or to tell the truth in court and ends by saying, "So help me, God." This oath is a sacred promise because it is asking God to be a witness to the truth of a person's commitment or testimony. A false oath calls on God to be witness to a lie. That is why the crime of **perjury**, lying under oath, is a serious sin against the Lord, who is always faithful to his promises. If we can't trust individuals who swear to tell the truth, then the law and order of our community is threatened.

People have a deep desire to be connected to the sacred, a connection to the holiness that is God. Yet so much of popular culture seems to poke fun at anything that is sacred and often belittles people who treasure God and holy things. The Second Commandment is all about keeping holy things holy. Keeping the Second Commandment requires a conscious effort not to give in to the many subtle ways God's name and holy symbols are belittled. God wants us to use his name only for good purposes: to bless, praise, and glorify it. ✝

Pray It!

A Second Commandment Examination of Conscience

A good practice is to make a regular **examination of conscience** part of your prayer life. Some people do this daily, some monthly, some before receiving the Sacrament of Penance and Reconciliation. Here are some questions connected to the Second Commandment that you can use for an examination of conscience:

- Have I used vulgar, suggestive, or obscene speech?
- Have I used the name of God in cursing or swearing?
- Have I spoken about God, the Church, the saints, or sacred things with irreverence, hatred, or defiance?
- Have I talked disrespectfully about other people or myself?
- Have I behaved disrespectfully in Church?
- Have I failed to keep vows or promises that I have made to God?
- Have I sworn by God's name either falsely (perjury) or rashly?

© Pascal Rossignol/Reuters/Corbis

Review

1. What does it mean to say that something is sacred? How do we show respect for the sacredness of God?

2. How did people in biblical times understand the importance of names?

3. Why did ancient people make oaths and covenants in the name of their god(s)?

4. Name some of the ways we continue to make sacred vows today.

5. Define *blasphemy*.

6. Why is perjury a serious sin?

Part 3

The Third Commandment: Preserving Holiness

Ask your grandparents sometime to tell you what Sundays were like when they were children. It is quite possible that they will tell you that on Sundays most stores and businesses were closed and people worked at essential jobs only. There were no professional sports games on Sundays let alone high school games and practices. Just about every Christian attended church and afterward spent the day visiting family, enjoying a special meal, maybe playing games. Sunday, a day reserved for prayer and rest, was noticeably different from the other six days of the week.

Sundays today differ dramatically. Most stores and businesses are open, many people have to work, and many do not attend any religious service. You and your peers may have sporting events to play in, or practices, or meetings that cut into family time and time for rest and prayer. These changes make some people wonder if we have completely lost our understanding of the Third Commandment: "Remember to keep holy the Sabbath Day." The Sabbath Day, a day God set aside for rest and for worship of him, is very important. It is God's will that we keep the Sabbath Day holy.

The articles in this part address the following topics:

Article 21 Observing the Sabbath

A married couple tells the story about how they started taking the Third Commandment more seriously. "It just seemed like our lives were rush, rush, rush," said the wife. "Even on Sundays. Sure we went to Mass, but then afterward we would go grocery shopping, do the laundry, maybe one of us would go into work for a while. By the time we went to work on Mondays, we were exhausted. We hardly saw the kids because after Mass they would head upstairs to do homework or go over to a friend's house for the afternoon."

"One day we just said to ourselves, 'This is crazy,'" continued the husband. "So we sat down and after talking about it made an agreement as a family to do a better job at keeping the Sabbath. We decided to go to the later Mass on Sunday morning so we could sleep in if we wished or spend the early morning reading or meditating. After Mass everyone would stay home for the afternoon unless we planned to visit friends or relatives together. We would not do any shopping or home chores. We would play games as a family and read the Bible, pray, and take naps. The television, cell phones, and computers stayed off until after dinner. We would all eat a nice home-cooked dinner together that everyone helped prepare. It wasn't until after dinner that the kids would spend time with friends or go to youth group."

Keeping Sunday holy includes resting from work, attending Mass, and spending quality time with family. How does your family keep Sunday holy?

"After a few weeks, I couldn't believe what a difference it made," said the wife. "Of course, there were some sacrifices, but my husband and I felt more relaxed, more in touch with God, even during the rest of the week. I think even the kids would secretly say that they appreciated having a reason to tell their friends that they would be offline for most of Sunday. I don't think God intended us to live at the pace that we were living without a break."

© Catherine Yeulet/istockphoto.com

The Origin of the Sabbath

Sabbath

In the Old Testament, the "seventh day" on which God rested after the work of Creation was completed. In the Old Law, the weekly day of rest to remember God's work through private prayer and communal worship. For Catholics, Sunday, the day on which Jesus was raised, which we are to observe with participation in the Eucharist in fulfillment of the Third Commandment.

The Bible traces the origin of the **Sabbath** back to the creation of the world.

> Since on the seventh day God was finished with the work he had been doing, he rested on the seventh day from all the work he had undertaken. So God blessed the seventh day and made it holy, because on it he rested from all the work he had done in creation. (Genesis 2:2–3)

Of course, this passage doesn't mean that God got physically or mentally tired and had to rest. Rather it indicates that he was setting an example of a balanced life. Human beings were not created just for work. We need the Sabbath to refresh and renew ourselves. We need the Sabbath to strengthen our relationship with God through prayer and worship. We need the Sabbath to remind ourselves that there is something more important than making another dollar. Jesus affirms that we have been given the Sabbath for our physical and spiritual well-being when he tells the Pharisees, "The Sabbath was made for man, not man for the Sabbath" (Mark 2:27).

Keeping the Sabbath is a reminder of God's saving power. The Israelites were commanded to keep the Sabbath in remembrance of their liberation from slavery in Egypt: "For remember that you too were once slaves in Egypt, and the LORD, your God, brought you from there with his strong hand and outstretched arm. That is why the LORD, your God, has commanded you to observe the Sabbath day" (Deuteronomy 5:15). Jesus intentionally healed people on the Sabbath as a sign that the Kingdom of God had arrived, bringing salvation to all who believed (see Mark 3:1–5). He even declared, "That is why the Son of Man is lord even of the Sabbath" (Mark 2:28), connecting his role as Savior with the keeping of the Sabbath.

Keeping the Sabbath is also a reminder of the sacred Covenant. Because the Commandment to keep the Sabbath is part of the Law of the Old Covenant, keeping the Sabbath is a regular reminder of the Covenant and God's faithfulness. God says to the Israelites, "Take care to keep my Sabbaths, for that is to be the token between you and me throughout the generations, to show that it is I, the LORD, who make you holy" (Exodus 31:13).

To sum up: God is the origin of the Sabbath, giving it to us for our well-being. When we keep the Sabbath, we remind ourselves of God's saving love and his covenantal faithfulness. Our natural response is to praise and thank God in prayer and worship.

Other Applications of the Sabbath in Scripture

The Bible applies the concept of the Sabbath as a day of renewal to a variety of practices. Here are a few.

Practice	Passage
Work of Slaves, Animals, and Foreigners	"The seventh day is the Sabbath of the LORD, your God. No work may be done then either by you, or your son or daughter, or your male or female slave, or your beast, or by the alien who lives with you." (Exodus 20:10)
The Keeping of Slaves	"When you purchase a Hebrew slave, he is to serve you for six years, but in the seventh year he shall be given his freedom without cost." (Exodus 21:2)
Rest for the Land	"When you enter the land that I am giving you, let the land, too, keep a Sabbath for the LORD. For six years you may sow your field, and for six years prune your vineyard, gathering in their produce. But during the seventh year the land shall have a complete rest, a Sabbath for the LORD, when you may neither sow your field nor prune your vineyard." (Leviticus 25:2–4)
Jubilee Year	"Seven weeks of years shall you count—seven times seven years—so that the seven cycles amount to forty-nine years. . . . This fiftieth year you shall make sacred by proclaiming liberty in the land for all its inhabitants. It shall be a jubilee for you, when every one of you shall return to his own property, every one to his own family estate." (Leviticus 25:8,10)

Observing the Sabbath

The Pharisees of Jesus' time had restrictive rules for observing the Sabbath and even challenged Jesus and his disciples for breaking some of these rules. Jesus challenged them for focusing on the letter of the law rather than on the Commandment's true, intended meaning (see Matthew 12:1–13). This same challenge holds true for us today. The Church provides for us basic laws for keeping the Sabbath holy, but we must determine how to follow these laws in our circumstances.

Here is a summary of the basic laws:

- Every Catholic is expected to keep the Sabbath by attending Mass on Sundays and other holy days of obligation. This is one of the Precepts of the Church and is a serious obligation.

- We are to abstain from working on Sundays and other holy days of obligation, especially work that would keep us from

The sacred liturgy renews us spiritually and strengthens us to live as disciples of Christ throughout the week.

© andres balcazar/istockphoto.com

Catholic Wisdom

The Greatest Action on Earth

"To me nothing is so consoling, so piercing, so thrilling, so overcoming, as the Mass. . . . It is not a mere form of words—it is the great action, the greatest action on earth. It is, not the invocation merely, but, if I dare use the word, the evocation of the Eternal." (John Henry Cardinal Newman)

attending Mass or work that keeps us from the relaxation and enjoyment the Sabbath is meant to provide.

- We should devote time on Sundays to rest and leisure, to works of service and charity, to spending quality time with our families, and to spiritual reading, silence, and prayer.

Student book article 23, "Keeping Sunday Holy," discusses these in greater detail. Remember, failing to attend Mass on Sundays and other holy days of obligation is a sin against the Third Commandment. So try to keep holy the Lord's Day by abstaining from work if at all possible and using the time for rest, prayer, and works of charity. ✝

Article 22 The Sabbath and Sunday: A Short History

People familiar with both the Jewish and the Christian faiths know that the celebration of the Sabbath and the celebration of the Lord's Day fall on two different days of the week— Saturday for Jews, Sunday for Christians. In fact, even the wording of the Third Commandment is different for the two religions, "Remember to keep holy the Sabbath day" for Jews, versus "Remember to keep holy the Lord's Day" for Christians. So how did this shift in names and days of the week come about? You probably would not be surprised to know that the reason is the glorious triumph of Christ's Resurrection.

Observance of the Sabbath

Jewish observance of the Sabbath begins at sundown on Friday and continues through sundown on Saturday. In their religious observances, Jews follow the practice that the day begins and ends at sundown because the first account of Creation says, "Thus evening came, and morning followed— the first day" (Genesis 1:5), implying that a day begins in the evening.

The first account of Creation also determines the day on which the Sabbath is celebrated. "Since on the seventh day God was finished with the work he had been doing, he rested on the seventh day from all the work he had undertaken. So God blessed the seventh day and made it holy,

© Anyka/shutterstock.com

because on it he rested from all the work he had done in creation" (Genesis 2:2–3). Following God's lead the Sabbath falls on the last day of the week—Saturday for both Christians and Jews. The Jewish Sabbath is typically celebrated with a special meal on Friday night, Sabbath services at a synagogue on Friday night and Saturday morning, Torah study, and leisure activities with family and friends.

The Jewish Sabbath begins at sundown on Friday and is celebrated with a special meal, synagogue services, and leisure activities with family and friends.

The Beginning of the Lord's Day

As faithful Jews, Jesus and his disciples would have carefully observed the Sabbath. So why did the first Jewish Christians break from their tradition and begin to observe their holy day on Sunday? The reason is Jesus Christ's Resurrection. The Gospels carefully record that the Resurrection occurred sometime after the Sabbath day ended and by dawn on Sunday: "After the sabbath, as the first day of the week was dawning, Mary Magdalene and the other Mary came to see the tomb" (Matthew 28:1).

Because of Christ's Resurrection, Jesus' followers came to see Sunday not only as the first day of God's creation of the world but also as the symbolic "first day" of the new creation that begins with Christ's Resurrection. They began meeting on Sundays to celebrate the Eucharist in honor of Christ's command to "Do this in memory of me." Thus the first Christians moved the observance of the Sabbath from Saturday, the last day of the week, to Sunday, the day of the Resurrection, the first day of the new creation.

© Bill Wittman

Christians have moved the celebration of the Sabbath to Sunday, the Lord's Day, in honor of the Resurrection of Jesus Christ.

Thus, we call Sunday the Lord's Day in honor of our Lord and Savior, Jesus Christ. Christians also sometimes call Sunday the "eighth day," in recognition that with the Resurrection everything was changed, God had ushered in a new beginning in the history of salvation. ✝

Pray It!

A Lord's Day Prayer

This is a prayer that you can pray every Sunday.

> God our Father, creator of all,
> today is the day of Easter joy.
> This is the morning on which the Lord appeared to men
> who had begun to lose hope
> and opened their eyes to what the scriptures foretold:
> that first he must die, and then he would rise
> and ascend into his Father's glorious presence.
> May the risen Lord
> breathe on our minds and open our eyes
> that we may know him in the breaking of bread,
> and follow him in his risen life.
> Grant this through Christ our Lord. Amen!
>
> (Roman Missal)

The Early Church's Sunday Eucharist

Here is a description of an early celebration of the Eucharist from the writings of Saint Justin the Martyr. It was written around AD 150, nearly nineteen centuries ago. See if you can match his descriptions with the parts of the Mass today.

And on the day called Sunday, all who live in cities or in the country gather together in one place, and the memoirs of the apostles or the writings of the prophets are read, as long as time permits. When the reader has ceased, the president verbally instructs, and exhorts to the imitation of these good things. Then we all rise and pray, and . . . when our prayer is ended, bread and wine and water are brought, and the president in like manner offers prayers and thanksgivings, according to his ability, and the people assent, saying Amen. There is a distribution [of the Eucharistic elements] to each person . . . and to those who are absent a portion is sent by the deacons.

And they who are well to do and willing, give what each thinks fit; and what is collected . . . is used to aid orphans and widows and those who, through sickness or an other cause, are in want.

Sunday is the day on which we hold our common assembly, because it is the first day on which God, having worked a change in the darkness and matter, made the world; and Jesus Christ our Savior on the same day rose from the dead. (*First Apology*, 67)

Article 23 Keeping Sunday Holy

As the Sabbath evolved into the Lord's Day, Christians preserved God's original command to us: "Remember to keep holy the Lord's Day." We keep holy the Lord's Day by celebrating the Eucharist, performing works of service and charity, and taking time for relaxation and prayer. This article looks more closely at specific ways we can do these things.

Attending Mass

You might ask, "Why is missing Mass on Sundays a sin?" One reason is that the practice dates back to the days of the Apostles. The Letter to the Hebrews reminds the faithful to "not stay away from our assembly" (10:25). A few centuries later, Saint John Chrysostom was asked why not just pray in the privacy of our home or in some other place that is sacred to us. He replied:

> You cannot pray at home as at church, where there is a great multitude, where exclamations are cried out to God as from one great heart, and where there is something more: the union of minds, the accord of souls, the bond of charity, the prayers of the priests.[1] (*CCC*, 2179)

Saint John's language may seem dated, and yet the reasons he gives make sense today. You can and should still pray in the privacy of your home, outside in nature, or in some special place that helps you to communicate with God. But the Sunday Eucharist (also celebrated on Saturday evening)

Live It!

Choosing to Keep the Lord's Day Holy

The young adult years are often the time when teens face an important moral choice: whether to attend Mass on Sundays and holy days willingly, to attend under protest, or to stop attending all together. Students report that the motivation to attend Mass willingly typically comes from the example of others and a personal commitment to follow God's will.

For some students the example of their parents' attending Mass provides an important inspiration. One young man says his parents' decision to take him to Mass every Sunday since birth has greatly affected him: "I have grown so accustomed to going to Church that Sunday feels weird and incomplete even if I miss Mass because I'm sick or snowed in."

Other students talk about their relationship with God as an important motivation. One student says: "I keep the Sabbath holy even when other important commitments are in conflict. I've missed soccer practices scheduled for Sunday in order to go to Mass or to be with my family. And I finish my homework early, on Friday or Saturday, so I don't have to worry about it on Sunday. My commitment to keeping the Sabbath helps me to stay close to God." By following the example of other believers and staying focused on their relationship with God, many young adults find the motivation to keep Sunday holy.

is the opportunity to praise God through song, prayer, and Scripture, and to receive the Body and Blood of Christ with the whole community on the day of rest that God set aside for us.

Another reason to participate in the Mass on Sunday is that it is important to gather with other members of the Church on a regular basis. God insists that his people set aside Sunday so that nothing else gets in the way of that date with one another and with God. We should arrange the rest of our lives—our work, study, leisure, and business—so we can be available for Mass and for time to properly relax our minds and bodies.

The most important reason for attending Mass on Sunday, though, is because the Eucharist is the ultimate source of our spiritual nourishment. In the Eucharist Jesus feeds our heart and soul with his sacred Word and with his holy Body and Blood. Jesus' sacrifice is made present for us as we celebrate the Paschal Mystery. Fed by the Eucharist, we are strengthened to be Christ for others in the week ahead.

What works of service and charity could be part of your Sunday celebration?

Works of Service and Charity

We can certainly perform works of service and charity on other days besides Sunday. But when we keep Sunday free of work and unnecessary commitments, we have time for other people that we do not have during the rest of the week. You could use this time to do activities like these:

- Take someone to church who needs a ride or who needs a friend to go with.
- Visit an elderly family member, friend, or neighbor. If you cannot visit in person, make a phone call.
- Volunteer to help serve a meal to those in need or invite someone who is lonely to share a meal with your family.

© Lisa F. Young/shutterstock.com

- Visit someone who is in the hospital or nursing home. Sunday afternoons are a good time to visit.
- Write e-mails to your legislators encouraging them to take a strong moral stance on a social concern.

These might seem like obvious things, but they are important and we often do not make time for them. And you do not have to look far from home to find these works of service. Start by looking at the needs in your own family and neighborhood.

Sunday Rest

We should not forget that the original primary obligation of the Third Commandment is to rest from the week's work. The Old Law saw this as more than just a suggestion; it was an obligation: "Therefore, you must keep the sabbath as something sacred. Whoever desecrates it shall be put to death. If anyone does work on that day, he must be rooted out of his people. Six days there are for doing work, but the seventh day is the sabbath of complete rest, sacred to the LORD" (Exodus 31:14–15). Christians no longer follow the Old Law with its severe penalties, of course. But the seriousness of the moral obligation not to work on the Lord's Day should give us pause, especially if we have not questioned the need to work on Sundays. If you have a job that absolutely requires that you work on Sundays, be creative. See if you can work reduced hours. If that doesn't work, try keeping your Sabbath on another day of the week, like Saturday, or even start looking for another job.

You can rest and renew yourself in many ways on Sundays. Some people take an afternoon nap. Others use the time for spiritual and recreational reading. Watching an uplifting movie or playing games or taking a walk alone or with family and friends can be fun and relaxing. Just be sure it is something that is positive and uplifting.

As Christians we should pause and think of ways we can change the way we do business. We should never make demands on others that would keep them from observing the Lord's Day. When stores and restaurants are open around the clock, including Sundays, it is easy to lose respect for the Third Commandment. Truett Cathy, the owner of a successful chain of fast-food restaurants, lives out his Christian faith

© Chris Kocek/istockphoto.com

by intentionally closing all his stores on Sunday. He truly honors the Lord's Day by giving his workers the day off to worship and be with their families.

Reclaiming Sunday as the Lord's Day by participating in the celebration of the Eucharist and taking the time for rest and recreation helps us to remember God's original blessing in creation. We need to "recreate," so we can be the people God calls us to be. We know this is a blessing—something that is good for us. It is one of those laws written on our hearts and minds, as well as in stone. ☦

The Great Sabbath Rest

There is also an **eschatological** dimension, that is, a life-after-death dimension, to the Third Commandment. The Sabbath rest, the worship of God, and the peace and joy that we experience on Sundays is a foreshadowing of the eternal rest and joy that we will know in Heaven. Pope John Paul II explained this in one of his homilies in the Holy Land:

> The Resurrection of Jesus is the definitive seal of all God's promises, the birth-place of a new, risen humanity, the pledge of a history marked by the Messianic gifts of peace and spiritual joy. At the dawn of a new millennium, Christians can and ought to look to the future with steadfast trust in the glorious power of the Risen One to make all things new (see Revelation 21:5). He is the One who frees all creation from its bondage to futility (see Romans 8:20). By his Resurrection he opens the way to the great Sabbath rest, the Eighth Day, when mankind's pilgrimage will come to its end and God will be all in all (1 Corinthians 15:28). ("Mass in the Church of the Holy Sepulchre," 4)

Review

1. What is the biblical basis for keeping the Sabbath Day holy?

2. What are three principal ways that Christians are called to observe the Sabbath?

3. Why did the keeping of the Third Commandment move from being observed on Saturday to being observed on Sunday?

4. Why is Sunday sometimes called the "eighth day"?

5. Give three reasons that it is important to attend Mass on Sundays and holy days of obligation.

6. What are some good ways to seek rest and personal renewal on Sundays?

eschatology

The area of Christian faith having to do with the last things: the Last Judgment, the particular judgment, the resurrection of the body, Heaven, Hell, and Purgatory.

Obedience, Honesty, and Justice

Part 1

The Fourth Commandment: Respecting Authority

Beginning with this section, we make the transition from the first three Commandments with their focus on the love of God to the final seven Commandments with their emphasis on the love of our neighbor. The Fourth Commandment is the first in this group, and it is focused on those closest to us, our family. Unlike the last six Commandments, the Fourth Commandment is a positive Commandment; it tells us what to do rather than what not to do.

As is true with all the Commandments, the scope of the Fourth Commandment is broader than it first appears. It isn't limited to just the relationship between children and parents. It applies to our relationships with all authorities: teachers, coaches, law officers, civil authorities, and so on. By focusing on the responsibilities and duties that family members have toward one another, the Fourth Commandment teaches us how we are to act toward all people. Jesus taught us that all people are children of his heavenly Father and so are in a spiritual sense our brothers and sisters. Thus the Fourth Commandment acts like a bridge between the love of God taught in the first three Commandments and the love of neighbor taught in the final six Commandments.

The articles in this part address the following topics:

Article 24 The Importance of Families in God's Plan

Have you noticed how many TV shows are centered on family life? These media families portray funny, touching, and sometimes troubling stories that may or may not be similar to your own experience of family life. The popularity of families in the entertainment media says something about the importance of families in God's plan.

© Catherine Yeulet/istockphoto.com

The family is the central social institution in God's plan of salvation. All other forms of community are built upon the family, which is why family life must be nourished and protected by society.

Student book article 14, "Social Sin" discussed how human communities should reflect the love and harmony of the Holy Trinity. In God' plan, families are the most basic building block of communal life. The family is intended to be and usually is the first place where people come to know God's love through the love of parents and grandparents, brothers and sisters, aunts and uncles, and anyone else who is part of their extended family. The family should also be the first place where people learn how to love God and one another as Jesus Christ taught us to love. Families should be places where the Beatitudes are lived, preparing us for the perfect happiness and joy of Heaven.

Biblical Views on the Family

In biblical times the extended family was the central social institution. Unlike many modern Western families, several generations lived together: a father, mother, and children lived with their grandparents, aunts, uncles, cousins, and all these people's spouses and children. Three or four generations would live in close proximity (adjoining tents or houses) if not in the same household.

Within the hierarchical structure of the extended family, each person had a clearly defined social role. The father earned a living for the family through herding, farming, fishing, or some other trade. He was the head of the family. The mother managed the household. She was subordinate to her husband. Children obeyed their parents. Slaves were also often a part of these households, and slaves obeyed their masters (see Exodus 20:12, Ephesians 5:21—6:9). Fathers and mothers passed on the teachings of the Covenant and the Law. Sons were expected to help with their father's

Other Old Testament Passages on Honoring Parents

Passage	Description
Proverbs 19:26	"He who mistreats his father, or drives away his mother, is a worthless and disgraceful son."
Proverbs 30:17	"The eye that mocks a father, or scorns an aged mother, Will be plucked out by the ravens in the valley; the young eagles will devour it."
Psalm 27:10	"Even if my father and mother forsake me, the LORD will take me in."
Sirach 3:1–16	A long passage with instructions on how to honor parents. Two verses say, "He who honors his father atones for sins; he stores up riches who reveres his mother." (Verses 3–4)

trade, and daughters were expected to help their mothers with household chores from a young age. Sons most often inherited the father's trade. It was based on this custom that Jesus followed Joseph, his earthly father, as a stonemason and woodworker.

Besides faithfulness to God, respect for and loyalty to one's family was the strongest value in biblical cultures. A primary way people practiced this value is by honoring their parents. This is a constant theme in the Old Testament, as seen in the biblical version of the Fourth Commandment: "Honor your father and your mother, that you may have a long life in the land which the LORD, your God, is giving you" (Exodus 20:12). Thus God emphasized the importance of respect for one's family by connecting it to one of the promises of the Covenant, the promise of land. Later on the Israelites are given severe punishments for failures to keep this Commandment: "Whoever strikes his father or mother shall be put to death. . . . Whoever curses his father or mother shall be put to death" (Exodus 21:15,17). See the sidebar "Other Old Testament Passages on Honoring Parents" for more passages that emphasize the importance of loyalty to family and honoring one's parents.

Jesus on the True Meaning of Family

Jesus was a loving and obedient son who honored Mary, his mother, and Joseph, his earthly father. But he shocked his contemporaries with his new and radical understanding of the Fourth Commandment. To start with, he left the family trade and therefore his extended family to preach about the Kingdom of God. Leaving one's family for any reason was considered questionable behavior. At one point, his confused neighbors said: "Is this not Jesus, the son of Joseph? Do we not know his father and mother? Then how can he say, 'I have come down from heaven'?" (John 6:42). In the Gospel of Mark, Jesus' relatives come to find him and forcibly take him home saying, "He is out of his mind" (3:21). Hearing this, Jesus shocks the people listening to him by saying:

> "Who are my mother and (my) brothers?" And looking around at those seated in the circle he said, "Here are my mother and my brothers. (For) whoever does the will of God is my brother and sister and mother." (3:33–35, start at verse 20 for the whole account)

Part of Jesus' mission was to form a new family, a spiritual family who would become his body, the Church. Jesus insisted that loyalty to God and this new family was a higher value than blind loyalty to your blood relatives. If there was conflict between loyalty to God and loyalty to one's birth family, loyalty to God was more important. He taught that his followers formed a spiritual family, based not on blood and Marriage relations, but on a common belief. The New Law taught by Jesus does not take away from the importance

Live It!

Teens' Advice on Honoring Parents

Showing honor to parents is a sensitive topic for teens. For one thing, it is natural for teens and their parents to be in occasional power struggles over curfews, driving, future plans, and so on. During those times it is difficult to feel respectful or respected. Another challenge is that all parents are different; this can cause teens to wish their parents acted more like someone else's parents. Given these and other challenges, here is some good advice from teens that everyone can learn from.

- *Spend time with your parents.* Teens and parents have busy lives with school, work, friends, church commitments, and so on. Because of this teens and parents need to be intentional about spending time together. As one teen says: "How can I have a relationship with my parents if I don't spend time with them? How do they know how important they are to me if it seems like I am avoiding them?"

- *Remember that your parents are people too.* Parents are usually doing their best at parenting even if it isn't perfect. A teen told a story about how she was always complaining about her mother's cooking. Then she spent several months away from home. During that time she realized how much work it takes to cook every day and to please everyone with your cooking. When she returned home, she never complained about her mother's cooking again.

- *Do not misplace your emotions.* When teens are upset with friends or disappointed by something at school, it is easy to let angry or sad feelings spill over into family life. But being angry with their parents when teens are really angry with a friend or even angry with themselves isn't dealing with the real problem—and it is not very respectful to Mom and Dad.

- *Remember, God has given your parents authority over you.* Parents have the responsibility to create family rules that keep their children safe and guide them in living moral lives. One young adult put it this way, "When I show respect for my parents' authority, I feel like I am also respecting God's authority."

© Alain Keler/Sygma/Corbis

Why are the members of the Church sometimes called the family of God? How is the Church like a family?

of the Fourth Commandment but helps us to understand its true meaning. We do not obey the Fourth Commandment because of custom or blind obedience. Rather, the New Law calls us to respect and honor our parents and other family members because we are all part of the family of God. ✝

Article 25 Parent and Child Responsibilities

The most basic meaning of the Fourth Commandment, "Honor your father and your mother," is clear to the casual reader. It commands children to respect and honor their parents. By logical extension, the Commandment also requires us to respect and obey other people God has placed in authority over us for our good—this will be discussed in the next article. Jesus' New Law extends the meaning of the Commandment even further. The Law of Love requires all family members to love one another with the same love God has for us.

The New Law teaches that in addition to children loving and honoring their parents, parents also have a responsibility to love and respect their children. The Letter to the Colossians is an early teaching identifying different roles in the family and how they are rooted in the love of God.

> Children, obey your parents in everything, for this is pleasing to the Lord. Fathers, do not provoke your children, so they may not become discouraged. . . . Whatever you do, do from the heart, as for the Lord and not for others." (3:18–21,23; see also Ephesians 5:21—6:4)

The Colossians passage reveals that parents and children have responsibilities toward each other. Because parents and children have different roles in the family, their specific duties toward each other will also be different. This article explores those responsibilities.

© digitalskillet/istockphoto.com

The Fourth Commandment calls children and parents to love and respect each other. What are some responsibilities that children have toward their parents?

Honoring Parents

What does it mean to honor parents? Instead of a typical list of obligations, the Church defines the duties of this Commandment as *attitudes* that lead to specific actions. The Church teaches that the attitudes children owe parents are respect, gratitude, obedience, and assistance. Showing respect to parents brings harmony to family life.

Respect is the foundation of any healthy relationship. Respect comes naturally for children when they experience the love and respect a parent has for them. When children are young, this usually happens pretty easily because they look up to their parents and believe that their mother or father can do no wrong. However, as children get a little older and develop their own desires and beliefs, they may challenge their parents' values and push against the boundaries that their parents have set. This is a natural and even necessary dynamic, but it means that mutual respect can become more challenging. Even so, the Fourth Commandment requires that we listen to our parents with an open and patient attitude, doing our best to try to understand their point of view.

Another requirement of children is to show gratitude toward parents. Many parents sacrifice a great deal for their children. It is said that it can cost well over one hundred thousand dollars to raise a child from infancy through college. And that doesn't count the hours taking children to and from school and extracurricular activities. Of course, these are parents' responsibilities, but parents occasionally need to know that their children appreciate it! So we shouldn't wait until Mother's Day or Father's Day to say thanks. We should find opportunities to express our appreciation to our parents for providing us with what we need to grow physically, mentally, and spiritually.

Then there is the duty of obedience. That is a word most people really do not like to hear. Most teens generally don't have a problem doing what their parents ask, yet for some

No Family Is Perfect

The teenage years are often a time of disillusionment, as teens see the ways that their family has fallen short in being the community of love God intends families to be. Rather than becoming an occasion to become embittered, the realization that their family isn't perfect can be an opportunity for teens and their families to ask for God's grace to help them grow in love.

No family is perfect, of course. We must acknowledge that some families are so wounded by tragedy or sinful behavior that it may be necessary for the family to separate. Such situations are extremely difficult and painful precisely because they go counter to God's will for family life. Although these situations are not beyond the power of God to heal, such healing often takes many years, or may not be possible at all.

If you find yourself in such a situation, the worst thing you can do is to become isolated. Do not isolate yourself from God; praying and receiving the Sacraments is more important than ever. Do not isolate yourself from other people; find trusted friends and counselors that you can talk to. Your pastor, school counselor, and youth minister are important resources; use them. They can point you to other professionals that can help you keep your life from falling apart.

teens, it is a constant challenge to listen to and do what a parent requests. They may protest, bargain, and delay just to make sure their parents really meant what they said. The Commandment to honor your mother and father should help to provide the motivation teens need to trust their parent's judgment, even when they don't see her or his wisdom. The only exception to the obedience requirement is if your parent, your teacher, or someone else in authority asks you to do something you know is wrong. For example, if an overzealous parent or coach suggests that you cheat to gain an advantage, God's Law requires you to not follow that suggestion.

© Randolph Pamphrey/istockphoto.com

Last in the list of duties for children is the responsibility we have to assist our parents. Assistance may come in the form of regular chores or just helping out when needed to baby-sit, carry in groceries, help cook, or do yard work. As we grow older, we will discover that the Commandment goes deeper than that. It also means that grown children must care for their parents in their old age, giving them the moral and material support they need, especially when they are ill, lonely, or in crisis.

Parents' Responsibility for Children

We don't always like to hear "This is for your own good," a statement parents often make to their children, but parents are supposed to know better than we do what is truly good for us. As infants we received vaccinations that our parents knew were painful, but the discomfort was necessary to prevent dangerous childhood diseases. Our parents winced as we protested those needles, but they knew what was good for us. In a similar way, our parents have the responsibility to teach us about God and the moral life and to make rules for our safety—even if it means telling us things we would rather not hear. Believe it or not, parents do not enjoy telling their children no. In fact, it would be much easier just to let children do whatever they want—but then what kind of parents would such people be?

How do you show your honor for the people God has put in authority over you: parents, teachers, and coaches, for example?

Not only must parents provide for the physical, emotional, and spiritual needs of their children (those things we should be grateful for), but they must also be their children's

catechist

A person called by God to the ministry of the education and formation of Christians by teaching others the essentials of Christian doctrine and forming them as disciples of Jesus Christ.

vocation

A call from God to all members of the Church to embrace a life of holiness. Specifically, it refers to a call to live the holy life as an ordained minister, as a vowed religious (sister or brother), in a Christian Marriage, or in single life.

first educators, especially when it comes to their faith life. They do this first by creating a home in which love, respect, caring, forgiveness, service of others, and faith are the normal values practiced by everyone in the family. Beginning at an early age, parents must also teach their children to have faith in God and to develop a relationship with him through prayer and the Sacraments. Parents are their children's first **catechists**, teaching them the truths revealed by God for our salvation. For this reason, the family home is called the "domestic church." The Christian family is a community of grace and prayer and the primary place where we learn human virtues and Christian charity.

As we grow older, the natural progression that God created requires that parents give us more freedom as we make our own choices. This can be very hard for some parents to do. You are probably familiar with stories of parents who pushed their son or daughter to be a doctor, even though the child's talents and interests were more artistic or mechanical. Even Mary and Joseph had difficulty letting go when Jesus started to become more independent. When they found him in the Temple after being lost for three days, they didn't understand his explanation of being about his Father's business. The Gospel tells us that Mary had to ponder his words in her heart, seriously considering what Jesus was saying about his life's work (see Luke 2:41–51).

Figuring out our **vocation** is something we have to do for ourselves; a parent's responsibility is to encourage and support us in whatever vocation we choose. Of course, the most important thing a parent can do is teach us from an early age that our first calling is to follow Jesus. ✟

Catholic Wisdom

Happiness in the Home

Saint Theophane Venard was a French priest and missionary. He was sent to West Tonkin (Vietnam) in 1854. While he was there, a persecution of Christians began and Father Venard was captured and later killed when he refused to give up his faith. Father Venard was very close to his family and wrote them letters of love and encouragement during his captivity. This is a quotation from one of his letters:

Happiness is to be found in the home where God is loved and honored, where each one loves, and helps, and cares for the others.

Article 26 Respect for Public Life

Discussing the Church's involvement in politics can be a touchy subject. In some families people cannot even talk about religion and politics without it turning into a shouting match. Some people have strong beliefs that faith should not have anything to do with our public life. But they could not be more wrong.

© Jack Hollingsworth/Corbis

Our faith should strongly influence our public life. This book uses the phrase "public life" instead of "political life" to be as expansive as possible. Most people associate politics with local, state, and national governments. Although the Fourth Commandment applies to our relationship with these authorities, it includes other public groups and organizations also. For example, it includes schools, scouting organizations, clubs of all kinds, sports teams, service organizations, and so on. Take a moment to think about how many different groups and organizations you belong to. Have you thought about how the Fourth Commandment applies to your relationship with them? This article and the next one will help you think this through.

Service organizations like Big Brothers Big Sisters clearly contribute to the common good, but all public groups should be committed to the common good.

The True Role and Nature of Public Groups

Recall what was discussed in an earlier part about God's Eternal Law and how every person and every human society can come to know that law through creation and the use of human reason. The understanding of Eternal Law that we come to in this way is called natural law. Thus natural law should be the basis for all public groups, Christian and non-Christian, including all civil authorities. All public groups and organizations are called by God to respect his moral order through their understanding of natural law. He calls public leaders to safeguard the fundamental rights of the human person and to respect and promote human freedom. He calls them to be committed to the common good of society and to work toward this good by morally acceptable means.

The Holy Trinity calls Christians to be part of public life. The Father sent his Son to teach us how to live the Beatitudes and to be models for other people for living a life in communion with God. The Father and the Son send the Holy Spirit to empower us with his supernatural gifts to live that life of faith and holiness. Although it is true that God calls some individuals to remove themselves from public life to live as hermits or in cloistered communities, even these people still participate in society by praying for the common good.

No public group or government perfectly reflects God's will or perfectly follows his moral law. This should not prevent Christians from participating in these groups and witnessing to the moral law. Our participation in public life is obedience to the second Great Commandment: love your neighbor as yourself. By respecting each person's God-given dignity and safeguarding the rights that flow from that dignity, we help the organizations we are part of better reflect the moral law. We also do this through our respect for the leaders of our groups and political communities and through our obedience to their legitimate orders and requests.

To better understand this important concept, let's apply these ideas to being a member of a sports team. A sports team exists to help people be physically active, to develop their physical skills, to build positive relationships with other people, and to provide entertainment for others.

Even groups that are not specifically religious in their purpose must respect God's will. How can a sports team do this?

© Sean_Warren/istockphoto.com

These things are all consistent with God's will, even though the sports team has nothing directly to do with practicing religion. Further, each member of the team has a responsibility to respect the other team members, to help them grow in their skills, and to follow the coach's directions. When everyone on the team fulfills these responsibilities—even when they are challenging—it makes the team members feel happy and fulfilled. What happens if the team loses sight of its real purpose, or if the team members don't respect one another? What happens if they are selfish, or if they don't follow the coach's directions? Being on a team like that is most likely not going to be a happy experience. When any public group or political community is not in line with God's Eternal Law, it cannot fulfill its role in his plan of salvation.

Being in the World but Not of the World

So far the discussion about the role of public groups and civil authorities in God's plan might seem quite optimistic, perhaps too optimistic for those familiar with history. It is easy to point out times and places where governments are guilty of sinful laws and actions directly contrary to the moral law. Fighting unjust wars, allowing slavery, and denying freedom of religion and freedom of the press are just a few examples of the ways societies have failed to follow the moral law. On a lesser scale, some public groups allow and encourage favoritism, prejudice, greed, and misinformation. Some groups discourage or even forbid any mention or outward practice of religious faith.

When faced with these situations, it can be helpful to remember that Christians are called to "be in the world but not of the world." This means that we are called to give witness to our faith and to God's moral law in all that we say and do. This will happen only if we Christians associate with people who do not always share our values, which is why we must be "in the world." And it will happen only if we challenge values that are contrary to God's values, which is why we must not be "of the world." Saint Paul summed this up in a brilliant verse in his Letter to the Romans: "Do not conform yourself to this age but be transformed by the renewal of your mind, that you may discern what is the will of God, what is good and pleasing and perfect" (12:2).

civil authorities

Leaders of public groups that are not religious institutions, particularly government leaders.

Being in the world but not of the world can be a challenging task. It may mean making uncomfortable choices that make you stand out, such as getting up early to go to Church on a school trip. It may mean making the extra effort to speak to a leader privately about something you disagree with. It means that there are some groups or associations that you must choose not to be part of because their core values directly contradict God's Law. However hard these things might be, though, when you do them you will know the peace and joy that the Holy Spirit gives to those who trust in him. ✞

New Testament Teaching on Obedience to Civil Authorities

Saint Paul teaches about the respect and obedience we owe **civil authorities** in his Letter to the Romans, chapter 13. At the beginning of the chapter, he teaches that public institutions should reflect God's will: "Let every person be subordinate to the higher authorities, for there is no authority except from God, and those that exist have been established by God" (verse 1). Later he emphasizes the importance of obedience to legitimate authority: "Pay to all their dues, taxes to whom taxes are due, toll to whom toll is due, respect to whom respect is due, honor to whom honor is due" (verse 7). Finally, he emphasizes that love is the fundamental principle that undergirds all of our public relationships: "Love does no evil to the neighbor; hence, love is the fulfillment of the law" (verse 10).

These passages could seem to suggest that Paul is teaching us to obey civil authorities in every situation. However, in the Acts of the Apostles we find Peter and Paul getting into trouble with civil authorities on several occasions (see 5:17–42; 16:16–23; 21:27–36). Peter and Paul do not directly try to cause these situations, but they do not back away from them. In defense of his actions, Peter simply tells his accusers, "We must obey God rather than men" (5:29). (Tradition says that both Paul and Peter were executed in Rome for crimes against the Roman government, most likely their refusal to worship the emperor.) These and other New Testament passages teach us that all human authority is rooted in God, and because of that we owe civil authority our obedience except when it becomes clear that such obedience is in conflict with God's moral law.

Article 27 Faithful Citizenship

In this article we consider the implications of the Fourth Commandment for governments and for our role as citizens. The bishops of the United States used the phrase "faithful citizenship" in their teaching on this topic. The phrase is clever because it has a dual meaning. On the one hand, it indicates that Catholics are to strive to be faithful citizens of their country, obeying its just laws and being active participants in the political process. On the other hand, it also can be read to mean that Catholics must first be faithful to God in their role as citizens. Our role as citizens must be informed by our faith as we work to make the laws and policies of our country better reflect the moral law of God.

> **solidarity**
> Union of one's heart and mind with all people. Solidarity leads to the just distribution of material goods, creates bonds between opposing groups and nations, and leads to the spread of spiritual goods such as friendship and prayer.

The Role of the State

A basic moral principle is that the state exists for the good of its citizens, not the other way around. The state exists to defend and promote the common good of society. Therefore all states have important responsibilities in regard to their citizens. The most basic of these obligations is to ensure that the basic physical needs of all the state's citizens are met, needs such as food, water, housing, and emergency medical care. But to meet these needs, societies must also promote the exercise of virtue and support the spiritual life of their people. In fact, in order to enable people to reach their God-given potential, societies must give precedence to spiritual values.

Making sure that all people are cared for requires patience, sacrifice, and **solidarity**—in other words, a society that embraces the concept of the common good. If a society does not live out these higher values—the values taught by Christ—then it will inevitably degenerate into a society of the rich and the poor, a totalitarian society in which a minority rule through violence and by restricting the freedoms of its citizens.

As human communities have developed over the centuries and different forms of government have emerged in history, the Church has been active in promoting the values required to create just and peaceful nations. This list summarizes some of the most important values that states must practice to fulfill their duties to their citizens.

- States must protect citizens' basic freedoms, especially the freedom of speech and the freedom to choose and practice their religious beliefs.

- States must provide for the education of their citizens. Civic leaders must not purposely keep citizens ignorant to more easily manipulate them.

- States must allow and promote the formation of associations and groups through which citizens can meet in solidarity to work for social justice and obtain what is their due—groups such as political parties, labor unions, justice education institutes, and so on.

- States must provide the stability and just order that results in a secure and peaceful society. This typically requires laws protecting individuals and their property and some kind of police force enforcing those laws. But these laws and their enforcement must be moral themselves.

- With the growth of worldwide transportation, communication, and commerce, it is more and more necessary to develop international laws and organizations to protect the common good of all people. Nations must not exploit citizens of another country for the benefit of their own citizens.

The Church and the state have unique and complementary roles in protecting and promoting the common good.

© Lori Howard/istockphoto.com

What has become increasingly evident in the last century is how important the Christian virtue of solidarity is in creating a just and peaceful world. People are interconnected through technology, through business and financial practices, and through environmental practices. When one nation pollutes the oceans, many nations are affected. When one nation suffers an economic decline, people all over the world can be affected. Living in solidarity requires us to share food and other material goods and to live in a way that doesn't deprive others, near and far, of what they need to live. It also requires us to show a spiritual solidarity, a commitment to the principle that every person is a child of God—our spiritual brother and sister—no matter where in the world he or she lives. This kind of solidarity will grow only if Christians, empowered by the Holy Spirit, share the spiritual goods of faith that our heavenly Father has so graciously shared with us through his Son, Jesus Christ.

The Role of Citizens

The Fourth Commandment requires that we fulfill the obligations we have as citizens. Governments and other civic institutions are part of God's plan to create human communities that are committed to the common good. Our civic communities require the active cooperation and participation of all citizens to work effectively. By obeying civic laws, by paying taxes, by voting, and by giving our opinion on public policies and issues, we help to build a society based on truth, justice, solidarity, and freedom.

Like some children who find it difficult to obey their parents, some people think that traffic laws, tax laws, or fire safety laws do not apply to them. But think about the consequences if that were actually true. Increased accidents, the

Doesn't Charity Begin at Home?

Some people object to paying taxes and to civic involvement based on the old saying "charity begins at home." They argue that if everyone just takes care of their own family that should be enough. Or they ask why they should have to give time and money for the common good when their family does not yet have everything that they desire.

Although it is certainly important to take care of your family's needs, the New Law of Christ requires us to have a broader vision. When Jesus told his disciples to "love your neighbor as yourself," he was teaching that we have a responsibility to care for people outside our own families. He made this perfectly clear by following up his teaching on the Great Commandments with the Parable of the Good Samaritan (see Luke 10:25–37), a parable that teaches that all people, including our enemies, are our neighbors.

In our modern society, an important way we love our neighbors is by being good citizens. And in the Parable of the Widow's Mite (see Luke 21:1–4), Jesus reminds us that our charity toward others is not measured by how much we give, but by how generous we are when we give. He calls us to be generous both within our families and to those who are outside our families. Our charity begins at home and continues by our reaching out to the entire human family.

civil disobedience

Deliberate refusal to obey an immoral demand from civil authority or an immoral civil law.

loss of money to build roads and fund schools, and increased fatalities and property damage in accidental fires would most likely result. Unless a law is truly unjust, we are obligated to follow it. In democratic countries such as the United States, most laws protect the common good, or at least attempt to do that, and therefore deserve our respect and obedience.

What if a law is truly morally wrong, or what if obeying a law actually works against the common good? If we have properly formed our conscience and believe that a particular law is morally wrong, we are obliged not to follow it. Disobeying the immoral demands of a civil authority or refusing to follow an immoral law is called **civil disobedience**. Examples of civil disobedience throughout history are many. During World War II, courageous people in Nazi-occupied European countries hid Jewish people from the Nazis when the laws required Jews to be turned in. In the struggle for civil rights in the United States, Martin Luther King Jr. and other civil rights activists were arrested for refusing to honor

Pray It!

A Prayer for the Progress of All People

The Church has special liturgies to pray for faithful citizenship. You can pray the prayers from these liturgies on your own. This prayer adapts the opening prayers from the Mass for the Nation and the Mass for the Progress of Peoples.

O God,
who gave one origin to all peoples
and willed to gather from them one family for yourself,
fill all hearts, we pray, with the fire of your love
and kindle in them a desire
for the just advancement of their neighbor.
Graciously receive the prayers
we pour out to you for our country,
that, through the wisdom of its leaders and the integrity of its citizens,
harmony and justice may be assured
and lasting prosperity come with peace.
We ask this through our Lord Jesus Christ, your Son,
who lives and reigns with you in the unity of the Holy Spirit,
one God, for ever and ever. Amen.

(Roman Missal)

In the 1960s, brave individuals protested and even disobeyed unjust laws supporting racism. Are there unjust laws that should be protested today?

© Steve Schapiro/Corbis

laws that were racially prejudiced. Soldiers have refused to fight in wars that do not meet the requirements of a just war.

The privilege of living in a democratic society is that we do not have to wait for unjust laws to pass before doing anything about them. We can work to prevent them before they become law. Doing this requires involvement in the political process. We must encourage and vote for political candidates who respect natural law and the common good. We must educate ourselves about political issues. We must influence our lawmakers to vote for laws that increase the common good and vote against laws that are immoral or that decrease the common good. Christians are called to live as responsible citizens and to ensure that our civil law reflects God's moral law. ✝

Review

1. Besides faithfulness to God, what is the strongest value among biblical peoples? How was this value practiced?

2. How did Jesus' teaching on the meaning of family challenge the people of his time?

3. What attitudes toward their parents does the Fourth Commandment require children to have?

4. What responsibilities do parents have for their children in obedience to the Fourth Commandment?

5. What is the role of public groups and civic communities in God's plan?

6. Explain what it means to be in the world but not of the world.

7. What responsibilities does the state have for its citizens?

8. What obligations do we have as faithful citizens?

Part 2

The Eighth Commandment: Reality versus Illusion

The Eighth Commandment, "You shall not bear false witness against your neighbor," teaches us the virtue of truthfulness, or honesty. Given that God is the source of all truth, it should make perfect sense that if we wish to live in communion with God, we must live in the truth. Yet the Eighth Commandment is probably the most frequently violated Commandment of all the Ten Commandments. Why? Because when we break one of the other nine Commandments, we usually end up lying to ourselves or someone else.

We lie to ourselves to convince ourselves that something wrong is okay. We tell ourselves things like, "There's no harm in making out" or "Everyone else is cheating, so it can't be wrong." We sometimes lie to other people to hide our guilt. We tell them things like, "Mom, I'm not on the phone; I've been doing my homework" or "That wasn't me you saw; it had to have been someone else." Many of the messages we hear through the media today don't help us; they communicate lies too. We see and hear false messages like, "Use this program and you can easily lose twenty pounds in two weeks" or "Sex before marriage is no big deal between two consenting people."

The danger of lies is that the more we use them the less we live in reality and the more we live an illusion—in a false world created by our dishonesty. Illusions, however, almost always break apart, exposing the stark reality we have been trying to avoid, often with disastrous consequences. And there is one more problem with illusions; we cannot find God in them.

The articles in this part address the following topics:

Article 28 Honesty, the Key to Being Real

This is a sad but true story. A woman accused a man of a serious crime. There was a trial, and the man was found guilty and sentenced to a long prison term. The problem was that the woman's accusation was a lie. It turns out that she had been drinking and left the friends she was with to accept a ride from the man. When she returned, her friends were furious at her for leaving them and even started to beat her up. So she made up the story that the man had attacked her to gain their sympathy. Things escalated, and the man was arrested and then put on trial. Out of shame and fear, the woman persisted in the lie through the trial. The man had a long record of violent crimes, and she had no previous record. The jury believed her, and the man ended up spending several years in prison.

This story is an extreme example of a simple but profound truth: lies hurt. The Eighth Commandment instructs, "You shall not bear false witness against your neighbor" for very good reason. Not only do lies destroy trust and may lead to other crimes, they directly affect our relationship with God. Lies are a direct contradiction of the truth and therefore a direct contradiction of God. He is the ultimate truth, the ultimate reality, and when we are dishonest we create false reality, an illusion that denies him.

God Is Truth

Let's use some basic logic to better understand the connection between God and truth. First proposition: what is true is also real. Second proposition: creation is real. Third proposition: God is the Creator of all reality, or to put it another way, all reality has its origin in God. Conclusion: if God is the origin of all reality, then he is also the origin or the basis of all truth. This is why Jesus Christ, the Second Person of the Trinity, says, "I am the way and the truth and the life" (John 14:6). The whole of God's truth has been made evident in him. Other passages in Scripture attest to this too, such as these verses from Psalm 119:

> Through all generations your [God's] truth endures;
>> fixed to stand firm like the earth.
> By your edicts they stand firm to this day,
>> for all things are your servants.
>
> (Verses 90–91)

This may seem a little philosophical, but it helps us to understand that when we tell lies or deny the truth, we are also denying God. Most people don't think of this when they tell a little lie to save themselves some minor embarrassment. Lies not only affect our relationships with other people (which is the focus of the next article), but they also affect our relationship with God, even when we think they are private, hidden, or unimportant.

The **Johannine writings** use the symbolism of darkness and light to symbolize this spiritual truth: "Now this is the message that we have heard from him and proclaim to you: God is light, and in him there is no darkness at all. If we say, 'We have fellowship with him,' while we continue to walk in darkness, we lie and do not act in truth" (1 John 1:5–6). In the Gospel of John, Jesus says, "I am the light of the world" (8:12). The author of the Gospel makes this connection between the light (Jesus) and truth:

> And this is the verdict, that the light came into the world, but people preferred darkness to light, because their works were evil. For everyone who does wicked things hates the light and does not come toward the light, so that his works might not be exposed. But whoever lives the truth comes to the light, so that his works may be clearly seen as done in God. (John 3:19–21)

God calls us to live in the light of truth and not in the darkness of lies, duplicity, and hypocrisy. We exercise the virtue of truth through the honesty of our actions and the truthfulness of our words. By living in the light of reality—that is, God's truth—we grow in our union with God. By living in the darkness of lies, we grow away from him.

Johannine writings

The Gospel of John and the three Letters of John.

"The light shines in the darkness, and the darkness has not over come it."
(John 1:5)

© Chaikovskiy Igor/shutterstock.com

Live in Reality Not in Illusion

It is not a compliment to be told that you are a good liar. Well-practiced liars can create their own version of reality. Their illusion might go like this: "I'm just doing my best, but there are people out to get me, so I'll tell whatever lies are necessary to protect myself." Or, "No one understands the stress I'm under, which is why I have to lie about the things I do to relieve my stress." Some teens are good at keeping an illusion alive with regard to their relationship with their parents: "My parents just don't understand my needs, and I don't want them to be hurt, so I just have to lie to them about some of the things I do with my friends."

Lies are sins, and they endanger both our earthly happiness and our eternal destiny. The danger is that we can begin to believe the lies ourselves. We lose the ability to distinguish between reality and illusion. We cannot find

Live It!

Teens' Insights on Honesty

Teens are aware of the importance of being honest. Many tell stories about the shame they feel when they have been dishonest, and the relief they feel when they finally tell the truth after being dishonest with someone. These experiences give students the following excellent insights on the importance of honesty:

- *Other people often know or find out when you are lying to them.* One student told a story about breaking an uncle's antique vase. When he finally confessed to the uncle, he was surprised to find out that the uncle already knew he had done it. Another student lied to a friend about where she was over the weekend. When she got to school on Monday, her friend—and all her other friends—already knew that she had lied. The conclusion? Just because you think you are getting away with something doesn't mean that you actually are.

- *Lies tend to escalate.* White lies turn into bigger lies when people start getting suspicious. It doesn't matter whether your original motive for telling a "small" lie was to keep from hurting someone's feelings or to avoid a minor punishment; it is better to tell the truth to start with than to have to keep telling more and bigger lies.

- *Lies destroy trust.* When you are caught lying, or even if someone suspects that you are lying, people's trust in you plummets. One student put it like this: "Once you lie it is so much harder to take back the words and explain why you lied in the first place. Building trust starts with the moral decision to tell the truth every moment; this is the foundation of your relationships with others."

God in the darkness of an illusion. Jesus goes so far as to say that the origin of lies and deception is the Devil: "When he [the Devil] tells a lie, he speaks in character, because he is a liar and the father of lies" (John 8:44). When we tell too many lies, we begin to lose our true identity and our eternal reward. We know our true identity only when we are in right relationship with God.

Christians must be committed to the truth and always on guard against lies and the illusions that are created by these lies. We are, of course, responsible for the lies that begin with us, but we are also responsible to some degree for accepting the lies and illusions of others, especially if we do not make efforts to seek the truth.

Witnessing to the Truth of the Gospel

All truth is important, but the truth the Father revealed for our salvation must have the highest priority in our lives. God sent his Son into the world to reveal this truth, so that all humanity might be saved from sin and death. As Christ's disciples, we are called to participate in his mission by testifying to his Father's plan of salvation. Truly there can be no greater honor for us than to help other people to know the saving love of the Father, Son, and Holy Spirit.

Throughout the centuries Christians have made great sacrifices to help all people to know the love of Christ. Missionaries have left their homes to spend their lives preaching the Gospel in foreign lands. Young people volunteer a week, a year, or even several years in programs that serve those in need. People make regular commitments of their time to serve in food programs, immigrant outreach programs, and homeless shelters, witnessing by both their actions and their words to the love of Christ and inviting those they serve to be part of the Body of Christ.

Should you need inspiration for your own Gospel witness, consider the many martyrs who have given their very lives in testimony to the love of God. This is the supreme witness to the truth of faith. The martyrs follow the footsteps of Christ, following him into death with complete confidence that they will share in his resurrected life. There are many stories of martyrs in the lives of the saints; consider making them part of your spiritual reading. ✟

Twentieth-Century Martyrs

Some people think that martyrdom happened long ago and that there are few modern martyrs in the Christian world. But every day, Christians around the world are dying because of their witness to the truth. By some estimates there have been more martyrs in the last century than in any other century since the Resurrection of Christ! Here is just a sampling of some of the thousands of people who have been officially recognized as martyrs in the last century. Many more have died for their faith in recent years and may be declared saints by the Church in the decades to come. Keep in mind that saints are not officially declared until many years after their death.

Martyrs	Reason for Martyrdom
Blessed Martyrs of Nowogródek	Eleven Sisters of the Holy Family of Nazareth were killed by the Nazis in 1943 for protesting the arrest and murder of Polish Jews.
Saints of the Cristero War	A group of twenty-five Mexican martyrs, primarily priests, were executed for carrying out their ministry during the persecution of Catholics from 1926 to 1929.
498 Spanish Martyrs	During the Spanish Civil War (1936–1939), hundreds of Catholics were killed for their faith, especially bishops, priests, and religious sisters and brothers.
Seven Blessed Martyrs of Songkhon (Thailand)	Seven people, including three teenagers, were executed by local police in 1940 because they would not deny the Catholic faith.

This photo was taken during the ceremony in which 498 Spanish martyrs were beatified, a step on the path to full sainthood. Such martyrs inspire us to be courageous in witnessing to the truth of the Gospel.

© CHRIS HELGREN/Reuters/Corbis

Article
29 Becoming a Person of Integrity

The woman who had falsely accused a man of a serious crime (see article 28, "Honesty, the Key to Being Real") was living with enormous guilt. She couldn't sleep at night. She desperately wanted the man to be freed from prison but was too afraid to tell the police the truth. She decided to confess her sin to a priest in the Sacrament of Penance and Reconciliation. She was hoping to relieve her guilty conscience and didn't plan on going to the police. But the grace of the Sacrament caused her to realize that she needed to make **reparation** for her lie. With the encouragement and support of the priest, she met with a lawyer who helped her contact the authorities. Soon the falsely accused man was freed from prison.

Of the many gifts God has given to us, one of the greatest is the gift of **conscience**. Every person has an inner voice attuned to the moral law, a God-given internal sense of what is morally right and wrong. Our conscience continually calls us to integrity—to make our words and actions consistent with the natural law God has placed in every human heart. Just as the woman in the opening scenario discovered, when

reparation
Making amends for something one did wrong that caused harm to another person or led to loss.

conscience
The "interior voice" of a person, a God-given sense of the law of God. Moral conscience leads people to understand themselves as responsible for their actions, and prompts them to do good and avoid evil. To make good judgments, one needs to have a well-formed conscience.

we violate the moral law, our conscience cries out, calling us to recover our integrity, to do what we can to repair the harm we have caused.

Honesty Builds Trust

When teenagers list the important characteristics of good relationships, particularly friendships, the word that surfaces most often is *trust*. We want to be able to trust other people and have them trust us. Without trust, any relationship has a hard time surviving. How long would a friendship last if someone discovered a friend was spreading gossip about him or her? How long would a dating relationship last if a woman found out that her boyfriend was lying about his feelings for her? How hard is it for marriages to survive if one spouse finds out that the other is secretly seeing another person?

All these situations have one thing in common: one of the persons involved is not acting with integrity. Their words or actions are deceitful or dishonest in some way. Honesty builds personal integrity, and integrity builds trust. To be worthy of another person's trust, we must be people who are truthful in all our words and deeds. You cannot be dishonest and hope to be trusted.

Fortunately, God is constantly at work encouraging us to be people worthy of trust. The natural law inclines us toward living truthfully. Our consciences call us to be people of integrity. When we follow these God-given guides, we will know the true happiness he desires for us.

The Effects of Lying

Human beings have a natural orientation to tell the truth, and therefore have to be motivated to tell a lie. Some people lie to cover up something they did wrong, some lie to avoid punishment, and others lie to make themselves appear more important. Well-meaning people sometimes lie to avoid confronting someone with an unpleasant truth. But any of these reasons for saying something false and deceiving someone does not make it morally right. The lie is still a sin against the Eighth Commandment.

We have already discussed that when lies and deception are discovered, trust and relationships are damaged or even

© Lou Oates/shutterstock.com

Because someone lied about a crime, an innocent man was sent to prison. What are some of the other effects of lies that you have experienced or heard about?

destroyed. What if they are not discovered? A lie can still hurt and wound others, even if they never discover the lie. Consider the following scenario: Javier and Sofia are dating. They have a mutual understanding that their relationship is exclusive—that is, they don't date anyone else. But when Sofia goes out of town one weekend, Javier goes out with her best friend. The two believe that what Sofia doesn't know won't hurt her. Are they correct in that assumption? Has the relationship between Sofia and Javier been hurt in some way, even if Sofia never finds out that her boyfriend broke the trust? Yes, their relationship has been hurt because Javier's guilty conscience will change the way he relates to Sofia in small and subtle ways. Their relationship should be built on

Making Reparation

We are morally obligated to make reparation, or amends, for sins against the truth. Owning up to our lies is often more difficult than telling the truth in the first place. Even if the damage is great, we must try to undo the harm we have caused by deceit and dishonesty.

Take as an example this true story. A high school cheating scandal began with two students finding copies of a final exam. They made multiple copies for their friends, who in turn made copies for their friends, so that more than a hundred students saw at least some part of the exam. Some students, who felt strongly about integrity, came forward to tell authorities. A few of the students who had cheated turned themselves in; others turned their friends in. The consequences were many: lower grades; expulsions from school, sports teams, and honor societies; and broken friendships. The scandal made the local paper, embarrassing the school, its administration, and its alumni. Despite the damage, the students who made reparation by coming forward, confessing, and accepting the consequences helped the school and their classmates to regain needed trust and integrity.

The duty to make reparation is binding on our conscience, which means we will not be free from responsibility and the pangs of guilt until we have made the best efforts possible to repair any damage caused by our dishonesty. If it would cause additional harm to make public reparation—for example, opening a victim to additional embarrassment—than we must do it privately. If we cannot directly pay back the person we have harmed, then we must do some other act of charity, and the effort we make should in some way be equal to the harm we have caused.

trust and honesty. But now Javier has been dishonest with Sofia. If that dishonesty continues, it will weaken the relationship and most probably destroy it over time.

Or consider another form of deception—cheating on homework, quizzes, tests, or projects. How is the teacher hurt if she or he never finds out? What about your classmates? How will they be negatively affected by your dishonesty?

Dishonesty in relationships destroys trust and damages our personal integrity.

© ESLINE/shutterstock.com

Pray It!

A Prayer for Integrity

Dear Heavenly Father,
Give me the desire to be a person of integrity.
Help me to be honest in all my words and deeds,
so that I am worthy of people's trust.
Give me a well-formed conscience to guide me
and help me to follow my conscience in every decision.
And if I fail to be truthful in any word or action,
help me to acknowledge and confess my sin
and make quick reparation to those who have been harmed by it.
I am confident that empowered by the sacrifice of your Son
and the Gifts of the Holy Spirit,
I can live in truth and grow ever closer to you.
Amen.

When we fail to be honest, at the very minimum we damage our own personal integrity. We think less of ourselves and find it harder to love ourselves. But because every sin has social implications, the web of deceit often gets larger without our even realizing it. Sir Walter Scott's statement, "Oh, what a tangled web we weave when first we practice to deceive," is as true today as it was when God asked Cain where his brother was. Cain had murdered Abel but tried to deceive God by answering: "I do not know. Am I my brother's keeper?" (Genesis 4:9). We must remember that just as God saw through Cain's deception, he will see through our lies and deceptions. ✝

^{Article}

30 Other Sins against Honesty

The story of the woman who falsely accused a man of a serious crime (see articles 28 and 29) concludes with her being found guilty of perjury and sentenced to one to three years in prison. Perjury is a sin against the Second and the Fourth Commandments, but it is also a federal crime. As part of her reparation, the woman was ultimately willing to accept the criminal consequences for her crime. People will disagree about whether her punishment was too lenient or too harsh, but everyone should agree that she took the steps necessary to begin the process of forgiveness and reconciliation with God, with the person she harmed, and with society.

Telling a lie is the most direct offense against the Eighth Commandment, but we can sin against it in other ways, perjury being just one of those ways. Even telling the truth can be a sin against the Eighth Commandment in certain circumstances. In this article we discuss some of these other sins against honesty.

Public Lies

In public communication, lies and misinformation take on even greater seriousness because they potentially affect a greater number of people. Unfortunately, examples of public lies and misinformation abound, from pharmaceutical companies not revealing all the effects of their drugs, to public officials giving inaccurate information about the cost

Confidentiality

Sometimes it is inappropriate to reveal the truth to someone who asks for it. The welfare and safety of others, respect for privacy, and the common good are sufficient reasons for being silent or discreet about the truth. You are not morally bound to tell the truth to someone who will use it to harm another person. For example, if you have a friend who is staying at your house because she is being harassed or abused by an ex-boyfriend, you have a duty to protect her. If the boyfriend calls and wants to know if she is with you, it is morally permissible to deny that she is there to protect her from further harm.

Sometimes professional confidentiality requires secrecy. Religious leaders, counselors, public officials, lawyers, therapists, and doctors must not reveal confidential information given under the seal of secrecy, except in extreme situations when keeping the secret might cause serious harm to someone. Even if it is not a matter of professional confidentiality, private information that could lead to prejudice against a person must be kept confidential unless a serious reason exists to tell it.

The one place where everyone's secrets are completely safe is in the Sacrament of Penance and Reconciliation. The seal of confession is so sacred that a priest can never tell anyone what he has heard in someone's confession, even in the most serious circumstances. A priest is expected to go to jail, and some have even chosen death, rather than reveal what is said under the seal of confession.

of school renovations. Keep in mind that failing to give relevant information is just as morally wrong as giving false information. Public speakers and writers have a responsibility to present information completely and accurately.

Telling the truth in a public hearing or court of law, where often the common good or another person's reputation and freedom are at stake, is an especially serious obligation. A lie told in these circumstances is called false witness. A lie told while under oath is called perjury.

© Reuben Schulz/istockphoto.com

Perjury was also discussed in article 20, "Other Sins against the Second Commandment," because most oaths are taken using the name of God.

Sins against Reputation

Another category of sins against the Eighth Commandment is when words are used intentionally to hurt or do violence to another person. A good example of this is telling people about someone's faults and failures without any valid or necessary reason. Even if the information is true, when we pass it on unnecessarily, we injure someone's reputation. This sin is called gossip, or **detraction**, because it detracts from another person's good name.

Even worse is telling a false story about someone to hurt their reputation. This kind of sin is called **calumny**, or slander.

A final sin to be careful of in this category is called rash judgment. Rash judgment is assuming the worst about something a person says or does without knowing all the facts. For example, let's say you see an aide in a nursing home refuse to give an elderly resident a piece of candy. Rash judgment would be thinking, "That aide is a lazy person who just doesn't want to be bothered with a little extra effort." However, by asking, you might find out that the elderly person is diabetic, and the extra sugar would be unhealthy for her.

Putting ourselves in the place of the other person is a good way to avoid the moral pitfalls of gossip, slander, and rash judgment. Think about how it would feel if people

detraction
Unnecessarily revealing something about another person that is true but is harmful to his or her reputation. It is a sin against the Eighth Commandment.

calumny
Ruining the reputation of another person by lying or spreading rumors. It is also called slander and is a sin against the Eighth Commandment.

Catholic Wisdom

The Saints on Gossip

"Don't let the tongue that has confessed Christ speak evil or cause disturbances; don't let it be heard clamoring with reproaches and quarrels." (Cyprian of Carthage)

"Would we want our own hidden sins to be divulged? Then we should be silent about the hidden sins of others." (John Baptist de La Salle)

"If something uncharitable is said in your presence, either speak in favor of the absent person, or withdraw, or if possible stop the conversation." (John Vianney)

gossiped about you. Then you can empathize with how that person might feel about your gossip. True empathy with other people can break the vicious cycle of gossip and rumors.

To injure someone's reputation through detraction or calumny is a sin against the Eighth Commandment. When have you seen these sins committed in your school or local community?

© coka/shutterstock.com

adulation

Excessive flattery, praise, or admiration for another person.

Flattery and Boasting

Some sins, like detraction, may not be so much about lying as they are about misusing the truth. One example of this is the misuse of flattery, or **adulation**. It is a good thing to give people honest compliments and affirmations about a job well done or about the progress they've made on a difficult project or challenge. But praising someone for something that you know isn't true is wrong. And praising someone for doing or saying something wrong can even make you an accomplice in that person's sin. For example, let's say your underage friend got drunk at a party and acted outrageously. It would be wrong for you to say to your friend the next day, "The way you acted last night was awesome!" Sometimes people offer false flattery to be nice, to fit in, or to seek some advantage in a situation, but none of these make it moral.

Boasting or bragging is another sin that often involves a misuse of the truth. It is certainly moral to share our accomplishments and successes with other people. But if we exaggerate those things to make them seem more praiseworthy, or if we share our accomplishments in a way that draws attention to ourselves at the expense of others, it is morally wrong. For example, someone shouldn't say, "If it wasn't for me, we would have lost the game," when the person knows that other team members also played critical roles. We must remember that we are called to follow the example of Christ's

humility. If any person had reason to boast, it would certainly be Jesus Christ. Yet

> he humbled himself,
> becoming obedient to death,
>   even death on a cross.
>   (Philippians 2:8)

Finally, another sin that is a misuse of the truth is making fun of another person to humiliate the person and to
hurt his or her feelings. This sin is prevalent among teenagers, as some teens attempt to raise their own social status by
putting other people down. Unfortunately, such behavior can
also be especially damaging during adolescence, when many
teens are forming their values and identity and, as a result,
have a fragile self-image. Some people may think they are
just being funny by pointing out a flaw in someone's physical
appearance or by exaggerating someone's behavior, but their
actions can deeply wound that person's ego. ✝

When to Break a Confidence

Sometimes it is morally permissible—even morally necessary—to reveal a
secret. This situation occurs when keeping a secret means that someone
might experience serious harm. For example, if your friend tells you he is
thinking about suicide, it is important for you to go to an adult trained to
help in these situations—a teacher, counselor, coach, or youth minister—
and tell that person about your friend's plan, even if you promised your friend
you wouldn't tell a soul! A person contemplating suicide needs more help and
support than you alone can give, and the best way for you to be a friend is
to tell the secret to someone trained to help. Your friend may be angry with
you at first, but it's better to lose the friendship for a while than to lose
the friend forever! Some other situations when you might need to break a
confidence are these:

- if someone reveals that she or he has committed a serious crime and
  refuses your advice to confess it to the authorities
- if someone reveals that he or she intends to cause serious physical or
  emotional harm to another person
- if someone reveals that she or he is in an emotionally, physically, or sexually
  abusive situation
- if for some reason keeping the confidence puts you in danger or could make
  you a criminal accomplice

Article 31 Calling Society to Integrity

A feature of many Internet social networking sites is a comment section where readers of posts and blogs can make comments on the topic being discussed. Reading the comments left by some people in these public forums can be troubling, especially on sites dealing with controversial topics. It is not uncommon to find comments that are mean-spirited, that are laced with profanity, that presume the worst motives of others, and that attack other people rather than calmly discuss the issues. And you can find these kinds of comments even on religious-based Web sites.

We live in changing times. Not too many years ago, the media were controlled by relatively few people without any access by ordinary people. But the development of the World Wide Web and the technology to access it has given public voice to many more people. Even the comment sections in social networking sites could be considered a form of public media. The Eighth Commandment has an important social dimension that should guide the creation and use of public media.

© Vlue/shutterstock.com

Truth in the Media

In modern societies media sources (which include but are not limited to radio, television, movies, newspapers, magazines, and the Internet) are the primary sources of information about our local communities, our nation, and the world. In many ways media sources have the same responsibilities for the common good as nations do. God's will is that media outlets be sources of truth and moral entertainment. Society has the right to information based in truth that promotes human freedom and that calls society to act justly. Society also has the responsibility to see that the media provide such information. The media, especially the news media, must be held accountable for providing information that is balanced, fair, and disciplined in presenting the truth.

Using Media Critically

The average person is exposed to hours of media every day. This exposure has the potential to affect our attitudes and values, even unconsciously, which is why we must be discerning in our use of media. Here are some suggestions for critically using the media:

- Evaluate the moral message of the songs, TV shows, movies, books, and games you listen to, watch, read, and play. Does the message support the values of God's moral law, or does it undermine the values of the moral law?

- Seek reliable sources to evaluate the moral messages in media and to help you choose which media you will use. For example, you might visit the United States Conference of Catholic Bishops' Web site for movie reviews.

- If, for example, a particular artist, TV series, or radio station consistently promotes values and actions that are contrary to God's moral law, stop watching or listening. Don't make yourself an accomplice to an immoral media source.

- Consider going one step further if you find a particular media source consistently promoting sinful actions and values. Write to the organization or person in charge of the media source and let them know of your disapproval.

What about Art?

Art is a form of social media too. Art can inspire, entertain, educate, and cause us to question and wonder. It is a uniquely human form of expression; many consider the creation of art as a kind of spiritual task. The ability to create art is a gift from God, and in some way the creation of a unique piece of art is a sharing in God's creative power.

© Hazlan Abdul Hakim/istockphoto.com

The creation of sacred art has a long history. Sacred art can teach us about Revelation, can inspire us to live holy lives, and can evoke awe and wonder, which leads to praise of God.

sacred art

Art that evokes faith by turning our minds to the mystery of God, primarily through the artistic depiction of Scripture, Tradition, and the lives of Jesus, Mary, and the saints.

A society must protect an artist's basic freedom of expression. But even in countries that accept this moral principle, artists should use their skills to create art in keeping with God's will. The fine arts should portray life, beauty, and truth. Art that is dark and disturbing may also be moral if it is clearly a warning to society about the things that threaten beauty, truth, and life.

The Church encourages the creation of **sacred art**, art that evokes and glorifies the mystery of God. Sacred art reflects the beauty of truth and love visible in Christ. It frequently illustrates themes from Scripture, Tradition, and the lives of the saints. It draws us to adoration, to prayer, and to the love of the Holy Trinity. ✝

Review

1. How are the Johannine symbols of light and darkness connected to the Eighth Commandment?

2. What kind of truth should have the highest priority in a Christian's life? How can you witness to this truth?

3. Explain how honesty is related to trust and integrity.

4. What is reparation?

5. Name and explain three sins against a person's reputation.

6. Is it ever inappropriate to reveal the truth, and if so, when?

7. What responsibility do social media have for safeguarding the truth?

Part 3

The Seventh and Tenth Commandments: Justice versus Injustice

The Seventh Commandment, "You shall not steal," seemed so simple when we were children; it just meant that you didn't take other children's toys. As we grow older though, this simple Commandment becomes far more complex. We come to understand that there are many ways of stealing—laziness at work, tax fraud, corporate espionage, and misleading product advertising—that do not involve taking someone else's physical property.

The Tenth Commandment, "You shall not covet your neighbor's goods," addresses the sinful attitudes of envy and greed that are often at the root of stealing from others. We open ourselves up to committing many other sins when envy and greed control our heart's desires. God's grace helps us to embrace the poverty of spirit that is necessary, especially in our materialistic culture, to avoid the unholy influence of envy and greed.

Both the Seventh and Tenth Commandments give witness to a basic moral truth that is related to the common good: God has given the earth and all its resources to the whole human race to take care of and enjoy. When we take care of the earth and distribute its resources equitably, no person needs to live in poverty or hunger. Unfortunately, the world's history is marked by the unjust distribution of wealth and a division between rich and poor. The prophets and Jesus repeatedly warn us against the dangers of failing to take care of the needs of the poor, and the Church continues to give society moral guidance through its social teaching on issues of justice and peace.

The articles in this part address the following topics:

Article 32 The Moral Law and Material Possessions

Back when your parents were teenagers, there was a popular bumper sticker that said, "He who dies with the most toys wins." It expresses a still-common attitude for acquiring material possessions. The human race has struggled with the moral issues of private property, material wealth, and the just use of the earth's resources since the beginning of human history. Have you ever thoughtfully considered what the moral law has to teach us about possessions and wealth?

Two Commandments directly instruct us about the role material possessions are to have in life. The Seventh Commandment says simply, "You shall not steal." The Tenth Commandment, "You shall not covet your neighbor's goods," has a slightly different emphasis. Christ's interpretation of these two Commandments in the New Law helps to put material possessions in their proper perspective. A hint: the one who dies with the most toys doesn't necessarily win in God's plan for our salvation.

The Old Law on Possessions

The Old Testament account of Creation reveals this foundational principle about material possessions: God has given the earth and all its resources to the whole human race to care for and enjoy. He tells the first man and woman: "Fill the earth and subdue it. Have dominion over the fish of the sea, the birds of the air, and all the living things that move on the earth. . . . See, I give you every seed-bearing plant . . . to be your food" (Genesis 1:28–29). Adam and Eve stand for all humankind, and God's command to them to care for the earth and his promise to provide them food extends to every human being. Passages such as Psalm 8 affirm this:

> What are humans that you are mindful of them,
>> mere mortals that you care for them?
> Yet you have made them little less than a god,
>> crowned them with glory and honor.
> You have given them rule over the works of your hands,
>> put all things at their feet;
> All sheep and oxen
>> even the beasts of the field,

> The birds of the air, the fish of the sea,
>> and whatever swims the paths of the seas.
>
> (Verses 5–9)

The fact that the earth's resources are meant to be shared by all people does not negate the principle of private property though. Revelation and reason teach us that in just societies families and individuals need certain material possessions to survive: clothing, shelter, tools, food, and so on. In the Books of Exodus and Leviticus, the moral laws that accompany the Sinai Covenant recognize the right to personal possessions through specific laws dealing with property damage, theft, and lending (see Exodus 21:33—22:14 and Leviticus 25:23–55).

The most fundamental law regarding personal possessions is given in the Ten Commandments: "You shall not steal" (Exodus 20:15). Outside of some exceptional circumstances, we cannot take someone else's property without their permission, ever. This includes borrowing someone's property and not giving it back, finding a lost object and not returning it to its owner, willfully destroying someone's property, following dishonest business practices, breaking a personal or business contract, or paying unjust wages to your employees if you own a business. Theft brings chaos and injustice, upsetting the order and fairness that societies need to thrive.

God intends that the earth's resources be used for the good of all human beings. How well do you think this is being done in the world today?

However, the right to private property is not absolute, even in the Old Testament. The right to private property is subordinate to the just distribution of the earth's resources and the common good. The Jubilee Laws described in Leviticus, chapter 25, attest to this truth. These laws describe how every fifty years the Israelites are to return any land that was bought and sold during that time to the families that originally owned it, selling it back to

© Andrew Parfenov/istockphoto.com

parables
Stories rooted in daily life that use symbolism or allegory as a teaching tool and that usually have a surprise ending.

mammon
An Aramaic word meaning wealth or property.

them at a fair price. Because farming and herding were the ways that people survived, land was their most basic possession. Redistributing the land on a regular basis kept families from experiencing long-term poverty. We are not sure how well this law worked in practice, but the fact that it is part of the Old Law testifies that God expects the earth's goods to be fairly distributed among his people.

The New Law on Possessions

Christ had a lot to say on material possessions and wealth; it was one of the topics he taught about most frequently. Let's begin by looking at the Sermon on the Mount, the summary of the New Law. In the first beatitude, Christ says, "Blessed are the poor in spirit, for theirs is the kingdom of heaven" (Matthew 5:3). The Lukan version is more direct:

> Blessed are you who are poor,
>   for the kingdom of God is yours.
> Blessed are you who are now hungry,
>   for you will be satisfied.
>   (6:20–21)

In Luke, Jesus also pairs this beatitude with a warning:

> But woe to you who are rich,
>   for you have received your consolation.
> But woe to you who are filled now,
>   for you will be hungry.
>   (6:24–25)

Most of Jesus' hearers would have been shocked at this teaching. The common belief at the time was that wealth was a sign of God's favor and blessings. Jesus seemed to be saying the exact opposite. Or more precisely, he was saying that detachment from wealth is necessary for entering the Kingdom of God. He makes this point even more clearly in later sections of the Sermon on the Mount and the Sermon on the Plain:

> Do not store up for yourselves treasures on earth, where moth and decay destroy, and thieves break in and steal. But store up treasures in heaven, where neither moth nor decay destroys, nor thieves break in and steal. For where your treasure is, there also will your heart be. (Matthew 6:19–21)

Parables on Material Possessions and Wealth

Jesus taught about the just use of material possessions in many other places besides the Sermon on the Mount (or Sermon on the Plain). Much of this teaching was in the form of **parables**. Some of these parables were directly about the dangers of wealth; others used the just distribution of goods as a metaphor for what the Kingdom of God is like; and others held up people who forgave debts as positive role models. Here is a list of those parables. Notice how many come from the Gospel of Luke, which is why Luke is sometimes called the Gospel of social justice.

Parable	Location
Canceled Debts	Luke 7:41–43
The Dishonest Manager	Luke 16:1–8
The Great Dinner	Luke 14:12–24
Laborers in the Vineyard	Matthew 20:1–16
Lazarus and the Rich Man	Luke 16:19–31
The Rich Fool	Luke 12:16–21
The Unforgiving Servant	Matthew 18:23–35

No one can serve two masters. He will either hate one and love the other, or be devoted to one and despise the other. You cannot serve God and **mammon**. (Matthew 6:24)

If you lend money to those from whom you expect repayment, what credit (is) that to you? Even sinners lend to sinners, and get back the same amount. But rather, love your enemies and do good to them, and lend expecting nothing back; then your reward will be great and you will be children of the Most High. (Luke 6:34–35)

In these teachings Jesus makes clear at least four things. First, poverty is not a sign that God is displeased with someone. Second, God has a preferential concern for those who experience poverty. Third, lust for wealth is a danger to our spiritual welfare. It causes us to trust in money and material possessions for our happiness rather than trusting in God. Fourth, wealth is to be shared with others, especially those in need. God wants the bounty of creation to be shared fairly and justly among all people, not hoarded by a few.

© Richard Baker/In Pictures/Corbis

Scripture teaches that God wants our wealth shared with others, especially those in greatest need. How does Jesus make this point in his teaching and parables?

Jesus continues to make these points in his encounters with people and in the parables he uses to teach about the Kingdom of God (see the sidebar "Parables on Material Possessions and Wealth," on page 159). Let us look at two encounters that Jesus had with wealthy people, the rich young man and Zacchaeus. The account of the rich young man is told in all three synoptic Gospels (Matthew 19:16–30, Mark 10:17–31, Luke 18:18–30). In this encounter a rich young man approaches Jesus and asks what he must do to have eternal life. The young man had kept the Ten Commandments all his life. Jesus tells him he must do one thing more: sell what he has and give the money to the poor so that he will have treasure in Heaven. This is a significant challenge for him to make, and we are told that the young man "went away sad, for he had many possessions" (Mat-

thew 19:22). Mark adds the detail that Jesus looked at the young man with love (see 10:21), a reminder that God loves both the rich and the poor.

Although we do not know what the rich young man ultimately did with his wealth, we do know Zacchaeus's decision (see Luke 19:1–10). Zacchaeus, a wealthy tax collector, announces without any prompting from Jesus, "Behold, half of my possessions, Lord, I shall give to the poor, and if I have extorted anything from anyone I shall repay it four times over." Jesus replies, "Today salvation has come to this house" (19: 8–9). Zacchaeus's generous redistribution of his wealth and his willingness to correct any dishonesty is seen by Jesus as a sign of his faith and moral conversion. Zacchaeus also practices reparation, a requirement for repairing the harm caused by unjustly taking someone's property or money. This is an example of **commutative justice**, which requires that we return what we have stolen in the same condition it was when we stole it, or its equivalent.

In summary, the New Law of Christ helps us to see the deeper meanings of the Seventh and Tenth Commandments. Besides teaching that stealing is wrong, the Seventh Commandment teaches us that the goods of the earth and the wealth that comes from human labor are to be distributed fairly and lovingly to all people. No person should have more

commutative justice

This type of justice calls for fairness in agreements and contracts between individuals. It is an equal exchange of goods, money, or services.

plagiarism

Copying someone else's words or ideas without permission or giving proper credit to the person.

Modern Sins of Stealing

The digital world that we live in has given an old sin of stealing new life and made a new sin of stealing possible. The sin of **plagiarism**—copying someone else's words or ideas without permission or giving proper credit—has been around for centuries. But it has become far easier to do because of the vast amount of information on the Internet. All you have to do is search, copy, and paste. This form of stealing is also cheating, and schools and businesses have severe penalties when people are caught doing it.

Pirating music, video, and software is a relatively new form of stealing. Pirating music was much harder when music was distributed on vinyl records, and you could only see movies at the theater or as a TV broadcast. Now digital recordings make it much easier to do. If people download an illegal copy of a song or movie, they are stealing from hundreds of people—not only the artists who created it but also the technical crew, the support staff, and the local store owners who depend on your purchase to make their living.

social doctrine

The body of teaching by the Church on economic and social matters that includes moral judgments and demands for action in favor of those being harmed.

corporal works of mercy

Charitable actions that respond to people's physical needs and show respect for human dignity. The traditional list of seven works includes feeding the hungry, giving drink to the thirsty, clothing the naked, sheltering the homeless, visiting the sick, visiting prisoners, and burying the dead.

than she or he needs while other people go without basic necessities. The Tenth Commandment teaches us that envy for our neighbor's material goods results in greed, one of the capital sins. Greed is the passion for wealth and the power that comes from it, a passion that takes over the place that God should have in our life. ✞

Article 33 Called to Be Just

Sometimes people think about what it means to be Christian in an either-or sort of way. They think that to be a true disciple of Jesus you must be either focused on your personal morality and relationship with God, or on social justice and following Jesus' call to care for the poor, but that you cannot focus on both. But the New Law of Christ reveals that we are indeed called to do both. We must grow in our loving communion with God, which begins in this life and will be fulfilled in Heaven, and we must grow in the love of our neighbor, which means working for a just society in this life that will also only be ultimately fulfilled in Heaven.

The human person is composed of both body and soul, so the Church's concern for people's material needs is as essential as her concern for their souls. The Church has a responsibility to make judgments about social issues that affect both our material and our spiritual welfare and, when necessary, to be prophetic in calling society to greater justice. The New Law of Christ demands that the Church use its moral authority to address social issues that affect the common good.

Especially in the last century, the Church has provided clear and consistent teaching on issues of economic justice, war and violence, respect for life, and environmental justice.

© Arte & Immagini srl/CORBIS

The teaching of the Church on these and other social issues is sometimes called the **social doctrine** of the Church. In this article we consider the basic social doctrine themes, and in future articles we consider specific social issues in light of this doctrine.

The Two Feet of Social Action

Our response to social injustice can be thought of as having two components. On the one hand, we must try to alleviate immediate needs by giving food to the hungry, clothing to the naked, comfort to the sick and imprisoned, and so on. This is sometimes called the work of service, or charity, and is often summarized in the **corporal works of mercy**. *On the other hand, we must also work to change the structures of society that keep people hungry or poor or motivate them to commit crimes. This is called the work of justice. Charity and justice are like two feet that walk together in our faith.*

Both service and justice are needed as part of our response to social injustice. Works of service are more immediate, and often the results are easier to see. Works of justice are more long term, more complex to deal with, and the results may never come. But Christ calls us to be faithful—though not necessarily successful—and he will strengthen and guide us in this work.

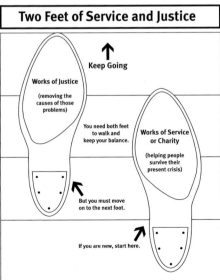

Two Feet of Service and Justice

Keep Going

Works of Justice

(removing the causes of those problems)

You need both feet to walk and keep your balance.

Works of Service or Charity

(helping people survive their present crisis)

But you must move on to the next foot.

If you are new, start here.

conciliar

Something connected with an official council of the Church, normally an Ecumenical Council such as the Second Vatican Council.

Catholic social doctrine emphasizes the theme of solidarity, which is the principle that all people are connected by an intricate web of life. We are all beloved children of God and must treat one another with love and respect.

Basic Social Doctrine Themes

The Church's social doctrine has been taught in the last century by a rich treasure of **conciliar**, papal, and bishops' documents. These documents are readily available online on the official Vatican Web site and the Web sites of national and regional conferences of Catholic bishops. Only by reading these documents directly can you learn the full scope of this tradition and the nuanced and reasoned judgments on particular social issues. However, the bishops of the United States have highlighted these seven key themes that are at the heart of all Catholic social doctrine.

© Alberto Ruggieri/Illustration Works/Corbis

The Life and Dignity of the Human Person

A just society is based on the principle that human life is sacred, and every individual has an innate, God-given dignity. This means that people are always more important than things. Society must protect human life and dignity from the beginning of life at conception until its natural end. Attacks on the life and dignity of the human person come from evils such as abortion, euthanasia, cloning, poverty, hunger, war, torture, and terrorist attacks. The equal dignity of human persons calls society to ensure that the goods of the earth are distributed in just and charitable ways to every person in the world and to eliminate sinful inequalities.

The Call to Family, Community, and Participation

Human beings are social creatures, created by God to live in loving and caring communities. Marriage and family is the fundamental human community that forms the foundation of all other social institutions. Thus Marriage and the family must be supported and strengthened by society, not undermined by it. As members of communities, all people have both a right and a responsibility to work together for the common good and well-being of all, especially those who are poor and vulnerable.

Rights and Responsibilities

Human life and human dignity can be protected only if society safeguards basic rights such as food, clothing, shelter, education, dignified work, health care, religious freedom, and freedom of speech. The most fundamental right is the right to life, which must be protected from conception to natural death. Every person shares in the responsibility to support and protect these rights.

The Option for the Poor and Vulnerable

A basic test of any just society or state is how its most vulnerable members are treated. Christ's teaching and example are clear that we are to love both rich and poor, but that we have a special obligation to put the needs of the poor and vulnerable first, even above our own comforts and wants. Societies that are marked by sharp division between rich and poor must work to reduce those inequalities and provide for a more just distribution of the goods of the earth.

The Dignity of Work and the Rights of Workers

A fundamental theme in the Church's social doctrine is that economies exist to serve people; people do not exist to serve economies. All people have a right to dignified work by which they can contribute to society and support themselves and their families. For this to happen, the basic rights of workers must be respected, such as the right to fair wages, the right to organize and join labor unions, and the right to take economic initiatives to start new businesses and industries.

Solidarity

As members of a global family, we are all connected by an intricate web of life, whatever our national, racial, ethnic, economic, and ideological differences. This interconnectedness requires us to live together, united as brothers and sisters, in relationships that are marked by peace, love, and reconciliation instead of war, hatred, and mistrust.

Care for God's Creation

At the beginning of Genesis, God calls Adam and his descendants to be stewards and caretakers of the earth. Human beings are called to live in right relationship with all of God's creation, protecting both people and the planet. Modern life and technology have created serious environmental challenges that must be addressed in solidarity. Failure to do so imperils future generations. ☦

Pray It!

Prayer for Justice

Just and loving God,
You are the Father of all people, making us all brothers and sisters.
Give me a vision of the world as you would have it,
a world in which the weak are protected, and no one is poor or hungry,
a world in which the riches of your creation are shared by all,
a world in which all races and cultures live in harmony and mutual respect,
a world in which the earth and all its creatures are protected and cared for,
a world in which peace is built on justice, and justice is guided by love.
Help me to follow your Son by speaking out for those in need and calling society
    to justice.
And empower me with the gifts of the Holy Spirit
to be faithful in following your call even when I do not see success. Amen.

Article 34 Calling Society to Justice

A principle at the heart of the social doctrine of the Church is this: "Man is himself the author, center, and goal of all economic and social life. The decisive point of the social question is that goods created by God for everyone should in fact reach everyone in accordance with justice and with the help of charity" (*Catechism of the Catholic Church [CCC]*, 2459). The previous article, "Called to Be Just," explored how this principle applies to society today by outlining seven key themes in Catholic social doctrine. This article applies this principle to three contemporary social issues: labor issues, environmental issues, and international issues.

Labor Issues

As a young person, your primary work is to be a student and to study and learn. You are probably still discerning what your future vocation will be. Whatever your future vocation ends up being, you will probably work in several different full-time jobs or positions throughout your life. Remember that the primary value of all work is to benefit ourselves and society; we should work to live, not live to work. By contributing our talents to society, we participate in the divine work of creation. Even more, when we work in such a way that our labor reflects Christ's teachings and values, we share in Christ's saving mission, our ultimate vocation in life.

What are some of the rights that all workers have in light of the Seventh Commandment? What responsibilities do workers have toward their employers?

In light of the Seventh Commandment, "You shall not steal," workers have important responsibilities to their employers and to society.

© mangostock/shutterstock.com

People need to give their best to the work they do. Coming in late, slacking off at work, or not getting enough sleep to do your best work is, in a sense, stealing from the company. More important, workers need to keep a humble and positive attitude toward their work and their fellow workers. Following instructions carefully and cheerfully, being willing to learn from other employees, being willing to assist other employees, and taking initiatives to improve personal work performance are all ways workers reflect the values of Christ in their workplace.

Companies and employers also have responsibilities in light of the Seventh Commandment. First and foremost, they have the responsibility to make sure the goods and services they provide contribute to the good of society and not to its harm. They must be sure that their manufacturing processes do not harm their workers or the environment. They have a responsibility to provide their employees with fair and just wages and benefits. They must not practice discrimination in their hiring practices. They must not ask their employees to do anything immoral or illegal.

The Church recognizes that there may be times when the interests of the worker and the interests of the employer come into conflict. In these cases efforts at negotiation that respect the rights and duties of both employees and employer must be made. The Church affirms the rights of workers to form trade and labor unions that speak and negotiate for the rights of workers. Recourse to labor strikes should be a last resort after all other attempts at negotiation fail. Workers and employers should never resort to violence in labor disputes.

When it comes to work and workers, we should be aware of one more social justice issue—slavery. Slavery still exists, and it exists because it provides some people with an economic advantage. Estimates are that every year, millions of people are forced into slavery across the globe. This slavery takes many forms. For example, people are forced into prostitution, or lured into another country and forced to work in prisonlike conditions, or even under the control of totalitarian governments that severely limit personal freedoms. The moral law condemns any act that leads to the enslavement of human beings—people bought, sold, or exchanged like merchandise.

Environmental Issues

Today almost all people recognize that caring for the environment is an important moral issue. Environmental pollution, overgrazing, overplanting, overfishing, the destruction of the rainforests, the destruction of plant and animal species, and global warming are all issues we hear about regularly. It took decades for human beings to recognize the damage that modern manufacturing, modern agriculture, and rampant consumerism were causing to the environment, and the Church was one of the early voices in recognizing care for the environment as a moral issue.

Renewing the Earth: An Invitation to Reflection and Action on Environment in Light of Catholic Social Teaching is a key document

The consequences of not caring for the earth have been made clear in recent environmental crises and catastrophes. In order to prevent future catastrophes, every person will need to do his or her part to protect the environment.

© Austin Adams/shutterstock.com

Safeguarding the Integrity of Creation

In his World Day of Peace message in 1990, Pope John Paul II had this to say about safeguarding creation:

> Theology, philosophy and science all speak of a harmonious universe, of a "cosmos" endowed with its own integrity, its own internal, dynamic balance. *This order must be respected.* The human race is called to explore this order, to examine it with due care and to make use of it while safeguarding its integrity.
>
> On the other hand, the earth is ultimately *a common heritage, the fruits of which are for the benefit of all.* In the words of the Second Vatican Council, "God destined the earth and all it contains for the use of every individual and all peoples" (*Gaudium et Spes,* 69). This has direct consequences for the problem at hand. It is manifestly unjust that a privileged few should continue to accumulate excess goods, squandering available resources, while masses of people are living in conditions of misery at the very lowest level of subsistence. Today, the dramatic threat of ecological breakdown is teaching us the extent to which greed and selfishness—both individual and collective—are contrary to the order of creation, an order which is characterized by mutual interdependence. (8)

published by the United States Catholic Conference in 1991. In the document the bishops call on different groups to take action on behalf of the environment. Their call still needs to be listened to today. Here are some of the people they addressed:

- We ask *scientists, environmentalists, economists, and other experts* to continue to help us understand the challenges we face and the steps we need to take. Faith is not a substitute for facts; the more we know about the problems we face, the better we can respond.

- We invite *teachers and educators* to emphasize, in their classrooms and curricula, a love for God's creation, a respect for nature, and a commitment to practices and behavior that bring these attitudes into the daily lives of their students and themselves.

- We remind *parents* that they are the first and principal teachers of children. It is from parents that children will learn love of the earth and delight in nature. It is at home that they develop the habits of self-control, concern, and care that lie at the heart of environmental morality.

- We ask the *members of our Church* to examine our lifestyles, behaviors, and policies—individually and institutionally—to see how we contribute to the destruction or neglect of the environment and how we might assist in its protection and restoration.

- As *citizens,* each of us needs to participate in this debate over how our nation best protects our ecological heritage, limits pollution, allocates environmental costs, and plans for the future. We need to use our voices and votes to shape a nation more committed to the universal common good and an ethic of environmental solidarity.

International Issues

It is an interesting exercise to look at the labels on the things you own and the things you eat and see which country they came from. Chances are that the majority of these things came from outside the United States. The reality that ordinary people routinely buy goods manufactured in other countries and create goods that will be sold in other countries is a sign that we live in a truly global economy. The moral law requires that our global economy must be just; nations must treat one another—and the people that live in those nations—with respect and fairness.

Working for international justice is most needed to overcome the gap between the world's richest nations and poorest nations. It is estimated that half the world's population lives on less than $2.50 a day. The richest 20 percent of the world's population earns three-quarters of the world's income (2005 statistics). The causes for this gap are many: poor national leadership and planning, the lack of natural resources, natural disasters, corrupt government officials, and warfare are some examples. Whatever the causes, rich nations must not exploit poor nations through practices like

Justice must also be practiced in relations between nations. People in wealthy nations must not take advantage of the workers in other nations by paying low wages for inexpensive goods.

© Jessica Liu/istockphoto.com

Catholic Wisdom

The Gospel of Work

The following is part of an encouraging message about the dignity of work sent by Pope Benedict XVI to young people gathered for the Ninth International Youth Forum in 2007.

> Today, more than ever, it is necessary and urgent to proclaim "the Gospel of Work," to live as Christians in the world of work and become apostles among workers. In order to fulfill this mission it is necessary to remain united to Christ through prayer and a deep sacramental life, and for this purpose, to hold Sunday in special high regard, for it is the day dedicated to the Lord. . . . It is only in this way that young people— with the support of their respective parishes, movements and communities . . . — will be able to experience work as a vocation and true mission.

envy

Resentment or sadness because of another person's good fortune. It is one of the capital sins and contrary to the Tenth Commandment.

greed

The desire to accumulate earthly goods beyond what we need. It is one of the capital sins and contrary to the Tenth Commandment.

forcing poor nations into high interest international loans, supporting corrupt government officials, selling weapons to governments that oppress their people, or buying goods from companies that abuse their workers or do not pay their workers just wages.

Nations have a responsibility to help one another's economic and social development. By helping individual nations to develop just and fair economic systems and to develop government systems that support human rights, the entire international community grows stronger. True development does more than just increase a nation's wealth or economic productivity; it is concerned with the whole person and helps to increase each person's ability to respond to God's call and live out his or her vocation.

The Church is a strong advocate for international justice and cooperation. Although it is not the role of the clergy of the Church to get directly involved with national or international politics, the Church's leaders do speak out in support of just economic development and against unjust economic and political systems. They call the laity to take initiative in addressing the causes of poverty and to bring greater justice to economic and political systems. The members of the Church, the living Body of Christ, take seriously their responsibility to be agents of justice and peace in the world. ✟

Article 35 Envy and Greed

So far in this part we have focused on sins that are primarily against the Seventh Commandment. But **envy** and **greed**, the two primary sins against the Tenth Commandment, usually precede sins against the Seventh Commandment. The desire to have more than we need and the desire to have something that someone else has can lead us to sins of fraud, theft, and injustice. In this article we look more closely at envy and greed and how to combat their influence in our lives.

Controlled by Envy or Greed

Have you ever been controlled by envy—that feeling that grows in you when you see other people with something that you want too? Before envy takes control, we are usually content with things we have. Then we notice a friend, acquaintance, or maybe just someone in an advertisement with something we don't have. The other person seems so happy, and we start to think that we'd be happier if we just had this thing too. We start to feel sad for ourselves because we can't afford it or maybe we would be embarrassed to be seen with it. We start to imagine ways we could get it, and it occupies more and more of our thoughts. We even start thinking of ways to steal it or secretly buy it. Before we know it, we are no longer controlled by our own conscience and reason; our envy is fully in charge now.

© Jake Holmes/istockphoto.com

Greed is the cousin of envy. When we are under the control of greed, there is no limit to our desire for something: money, stocks, gold, power, fame—just about anything can be the object of greed. Like envy, greed also leaves us feeling dissatisfied and sad, for no matter how much we have of the thing we desire, there is always an empty place in us that wants more. The greedy heart has a thirst that is never quenched.

Our culture's focus on having lots of things makes it easy to be envious of the things other people have. When are you most tempted to feel envious of other people?

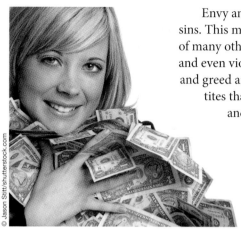

Envy and greed are two of the seven capital sins. This means that they are often at the root of many other sins such as cheating, theft, lying, and even violence against other people. Envy and greed are also disorders of the natural appetites that we have for food, drink, comfort, and protection from the elements. These desires are good in themselves, but when they become exaggerated and control our thoughts and behavior they are no longer good, but are sinful instead.

Why are greed and envy capital sins? How do you combat envy and greed?

Combating Envy and Greed

Feelings of envy and greed are not sins in themselves. These negative feelings creep into our hearts unbidden; they are the result of concupiscence, the vestiges of Original Sin in our lives. However, once we recognize those feelings, we then have a choice to make. If we choose to hold on to them, dwell on them, and let them grow in our heart and mind, sin begins. Or we can choose to banish them and replace them by exercising the virtues of goodwill toward others, personal humility, and trust in the **providence** of God. Our practice of these virtues will combat our feelings of envy and greed, making them less and less an influence in our lives. Here are some suggestions for cultivating these three virtues in your life:

- To have goodwill toward others is to desire what is best for other people and to take joy in their happiness. Goodwill requires that you take your mind's focus off your needs and wants and focus it on the needs of the other person. In this way, goodwill is the opposite of envy. A good way to cultivate goodwill when you start feeling envious of someone else is to say a simple prayer like this: "Father, I pray for (person's name) happiness. Help me to rejoice that you have blessed her (or him)."

- Envy often comes from pride, the belief that we deserve special treatment or are more important than others in some way. It happens when we think something like this: "Why does he have that and I don't? I'm just as good as he is." The antidote to pride is personal humility, which is the recognition that God already loves us completely and blesses us, and that there is nothing we can do to earn more of his love. We recognize that material possessions are not a sign of God's love for us. This helps to free us from envying other people's situations and material things.

- Greed is a sign that we really don't trust in God. It is based in the fear that we will not have enough of something to meet our needs. But Jesus tells us that this fear is without basis: "Look at the birds in the sky; they do not sow or reap, they gather nothing into barns, yet your heavenly Father feeds them. Are not you more important than they?" (Matthew 6:26). Develop your trust in the providence of God by praying something like this every day: "Father, help me to trust that you will provide everything I need today. Help me to understand that you are the source of true happiness. Do not let me succumb to the belief that I need more of anything than you give me." ☦

providence

The guidance, material goods, and care provided by God that is sufficient to meet our needs.

The Saints on Envy

"Whenever you envy your neighbor, you give demons a place to rest." (Saint Ephraem the Syrian)

"When a man envies his brother the good that God says or does through him, it is like committing a sin of blasphemy, because he is really envying God, who is the only source of every good." (Saint Francis of Assisi)

"If we were to . . . esteem everything according to its true nature, rather than according to people's false opinion, then we would never see any reason to envy any person, but rather we would pity every person—and pity those most who have the most to be envied for, since they are the ones who will shortly lose the most." (Saint Thomas More)

Article 36 Living Simply So Others May Simply Live

Money can be a touchy subject. Our culture places a great deal of importance on having it. We often measure our worth by how much we have. We get stressed when we think we don't have enough—which for some people is most of the time. We sometimes compromise our values and even our physical and emotional well-being to get more money. But there is a simple, Gospel solution to this trap. It's called living simply so that others can simply live.

Besides avoiding the sins of greed and envy, there is also a justice reason for simple living. Reason and science are making it clear that the earth has limited resources. Our God-given stewardship over the earth's resources cannot be separated from our moral obligation to use these resources wisely and justly. God has provided us with enough resources so that when they are shared fairly among all the people of the earth, everyone can live without hunger and poverty. But when some people accumulate too much money and material goods, it often means that other people have less and sometimes so much less that people are kept poor and hungry.

Christ provides the example of simple living for us to follow. He embraced a lifestyle of voluntary poverty even though he could have been born to wealthy parents and lived in wealth and luxury. Let's look first at Christ's example and then at the challenge of living a simple lifestyle.

This painting by Rembrandt depicts the parable of the rich fool counting his money. If Rembrandt were painting this today, in what setting might he depict the rich fool?

Christ's Example

Jesus' life and teaching revealed that **poverty of heart** (sometimes called spiritual poverty) is necessary for us to be in communion with God. People who have poverty of heart recognize their need for God. This is why Jesus says, "Blessed are the poor in spirit" (Matthew 5:3). Without God we are truly empty and alone; no amount of material wealth can fill that void. In fact, material wealth often gets in the way of our recognizing our need for God. For this reason, Jesus warns us that material wealth can be dangerous to our salvation: "How hard it is for those who have wealth to enter the kingdom of God!" (Mark 10:23).

poverty of heart
The recognition of our deep need for God and the commitment to put God above everything else in life, particularly above the accumulation of material wealth.

Christ's actions reflected his words. During the three years of his active ministry, he did not own a home or any material possessions beyond the clothes on his back. When a scribe approached Jesus to become one of his followers, Jesus responded, "Foxes have dens and birds of the sky have nests, but the Son of Man has nowhere to rest his head" (Matthew 8:20), indicating his lack of possessions. He depended entirely on the generosity of others to finance his mission (see Luke 8:3). He traveled everywhere by foot, the transportation method of poor people (except for his triumphal entry into Jerusalem before his Passion).

Gospel Teaching on Poverty of Heart

In many places in the four Gospels, Jesus teaches about the importance of poverty of heart, which is the basis for living simply.

Gospel Passage	Summary
Mark 12:41–44	the widow's mite
Matthew 13:44–46	Parable of the Treasure Buried in the Field, The Pearl of Great Price
Luke 12:15–21	Parable of the Rich Fool
Luke 12:22–32	"Do not worry about what to eat or what to wear."
Luke 12:33–34	"Where your treasure is, there also will your heart be."
Matthew 6:19–21, 24	"Store up treasures in heaven," and "no one can serve two masters."

almsgiving
Freely giving money or material goods to a person who is needy, often by giving to a group or organization that serves poor people. It may be an act of penance or of Christian charity.

Jesus calls his disciples to follow his example in being unattached to material wealth. After the rich young man leaves in sadness because of his attachment to his wealth, Jesus tells his disciples, "Amen, I say to you, it will be hard for one who is rich to enter the kingdom of heaven." His disciples are astonished and ask, "Who then can be saved?" Jesus replies, "For human beings this is impossible, but for God all things are possible." Jesus also promises that there is a reward for those who embrace his voluntary poverty. When Peter asks him: "We have given up everything and followed you. What will there be for us?" Jesus replies, "Everyone who has given up houses or brothers or sisters or father or mother or children or lands for the sake of my name will receive a hundred times more, and will inherit eternal life." (See Matthew 19:23–29.)

The Challenge of a Simple Lifestyle

Living a simple lifestyle or choosing voluntary poverty is a challenging and complex topic. First of all, God does not call every Christian to a vow of poverty, especially the radical poverty of Jesus. Second, people will have different definitions of what a simple lifestyle is depending on their country, their culture, and their current economic status. Third, people's situations may limit their economic choices; this is especially true for teenagers who are usually not in control of their own economic situation.

These challenges should not deter us from taking Jesus' call to live a simple lifestyle seriously. We can make many choices to live more simply (see the sidebar "Teens' Advice for a Simpler Lifestyle" on page 179). If you are already making choices to live simply, congratulations, and keep working at it. If you have never seriously considered this call, spend some time praying about it and ask God to point out one way that you can make your life simpler. This is an important topic for families to discuss too. If your family hasn't talked about it recently, maybe you can bring it up for a family discussion.

Living simply often leads to less consumption of the earth's resources. For example, you and your family might decide that rather than having multiple TV sets in your home, one will be enough. This decision leads to lower energy use, a reduction in the use of materials used in the manufacturing of televisions, and even reduced use of landfill space when the televisions become old or malfunction and need to be disposed of. When you use less of the world's resources, you allow a more equitable share for people in greater need. Further, in choosing to live simply, money saved might be used for **almsgiving**, which is making monetary contributions to help people who are poor and needy. This is a work of justice that is pleasing to God. As a teenager you might not feel wealthy, but do not neglect this important practice of giving to those in need, even if what you can give is very little (remember the story of the widow's mite?). Almsgiving should be a lifelong habit, one that will be easier if you begin now. ✝

Living a simpler lifestyle can be as simple as riding a bike instead of driving a car for short trips.

© Tetra Images/Corbis

Live It!

Teens' Advice for a Simpler Lifestyle

Teens have lots of suggestions for living a simpler lifestyle, especially in the areas of clothing, transportation, and leisure activities. When it comes to buying clothes, many students recommended going to thrift shops and secondhand clothing stores. "I bought a whole season's wardrobe for ten dollars," said one student, "and I kept those clothes from going into the dump." Someone else said that they traded clothes with friends. Another student said that his school had a clothing exchange for clothes that fit the school dress code, so that many students did not have to buy new clothes each new school year.

One student said that he almost never goes anywhere in a car, that he and his friends ride their bikes everywhere they go. Public transportation and ride sharing were other ways mentioned for keeping it simple and being environmentally responsible.

For leisure activities, young people said there is no need to spend lots of money. "Watch movies at home with friends and save on the expensive movie tickets" was a common suggestion. Others suggested going without electricity altogether, playing board games and spending time outside. One student even said, "Skip the prom; it's just become one big excuse to spend money needlessly." These practices help students to consume fewer resources and to have more to share with others in need.

Review

1. Summarize the Old Law's teaching on material possessions.

2. Why did Jesus Christ's teachings on poverty and wealth shock the people of his time?

3. Define the concept of social doctrine.

4. Choose two key principles of the social doctrine of the Church and explain their significance.

5. What responsibilities do employers have in regard to their workers?

6. What responsibilities do rich nations have toward poor nations according to the social doctrine of the Church?

7. Why does envy or greed leave us feeling sad and dissatisfied?

8. What are some ways that you can combat envy and greed?

9. How did Christ provide us with an example of living simply, and how does he call us to do likewise?

Respecting Life and Sexuality

Part 1

The Fifth Commandment: Respecting Life

The gift of life is God's greatest gift to us. All human life is sacred because God creates human beings in his image, sharing his divine life with us. Thus to murder or to intentionally harm yourself or another person is a sin against human dignity and against God's gift of life. These are the minimum requirements of the Fifth Commandment. In the New Law, Christ teaches us to put away all thoughts of anger and vengeance and even to love our enemies.

The moral law calls us to respect human life from its beginning at the moment of conception until natural death. Forces in society are attacking human life when it is most fragile, at the very beginning and at the end of life. Both abortion and euthanasia are grave sins, and we must resist the efforts of those who would make them morally acceptable choices.

The Beatitudes also call us to be peacemakers and to work for an end to war, terrorism, and genocide. However, human beings have the right to legitimately defend their lives against unjust aggressors. War can be morally permissible under certain strict criteria. However, we must not seek war, and we must work to end the race to build and stockpile more and more weapons, especially weapons of mass destruction. Even unused, their cost to society leads to other social injustices.

The articles in this part address the following topics:

Article 37 Life, God's Greatest Gift

What is the one thing every human being must have in order to think, speak, and act? Did "the gift of life" immediately occur to you as the answer to this question? The gift of life is so basic that it is easy to take for granted. Sometimes it is only after witnessing a birth, spending time with someone who is dying, or having a near-death experience that we are reminded that life is a precious gift. Human beings naturally struggle against death. Take a minute to think about that last statement: human beings naturally struggle against death. Popular culture tends to present death as an unfortunate but natural part of life. But if death is so natural, why do we struggle so hard to prevent it? Our faith gives the answer: God did not create human beings for death but for eternal life. The Fifth Commandment, "You shall not kill," teaches us this important truth.

The Sacredness of Human Life

In the biblical account of creation, God blew the breath of life into Adam, the first man (see Genesis 2:7). This action conveys the truth that at the beginning of life God creates our soul, our spiritual principle, and unites it with our physical body, thereby sharing his divine image with us. For this reason human life is qualitatively different from the life of every other creature. Every human life is sacred from its beginning at the moment of conception because every person has been created in the image and likeness of God (see

Michelangelo's famous painting in the Sistine Chapel shows God sharing the spark of life with Adam and depicts the sacredness of human life.

© estelle75/istockphoto.com

Genesis 1:26) and shares in his divine life. Because of this, human life is uniquely sacred; killing a human being is not the same thing as killing a plant or animal. The murder of a human being is a sin against the sacred dignity of the human person and against the holiness of God.

Murder is also wrong because God alone is the author of life and death. Two Old Testament songs witness to this truth. Moses' song in the Book of Deuteronomy proclaims:

> Learn then that I, I alone, am God,
>   and there is no god besides me.
> It is I who bring both death and life.
>   (32:39)

In her song, Hannah, the mother of Samuel, proclaims, "The LORD puts to death and gives life; / he casts down to the nether world; he raises up again" (1 Samuel 2:6). The power of life and death is God's alone, so the murder of another person assumes a power that is not for human beings to claim.

But the Fifth Commandment is about more than murder. In the Sermon on the Mount, Jesus commands us to have a deep and radical respect for the sacredness of the human person.

> You have heard that it was said to your ancestors, "You shall not kill; and whoever kills will be liable to judgment." But I say to you, whoever is angry with his brother will be liable to judgment, and whoever says to his brother, "Raqa," [an abusive word probably meaning "imbecile"] will be answerable to the

Catholic Wisdom

Human versus Animal

Saint Augustine (AD 354–430) is known for his wit and intelligence. In this amusing reflection he answers the question, how are human beings better than animals?

> You do not differ from the cattle except in your intellect; do not glory in anything else. Do you believe that you are strong? By the wild beasts you are surpassed. Do you believe that you are swift? By the flies you are surpassed. Do you believe that you are beautiful? There is greater beauty in the feathers of a peacock. How then are you better? In the image of God. Where is the image of God? In the mind, in your intellect! (*Homilies on the Gospels*, 3,4)

Sanhedrin, and whoever says, "You fool," will be liable to fiery Gehenna. (Matthew 5:21–22)

You have heard that it was said, "An eye for an eye and a tooth for a tooth." But I say to you, offer no resistance to one who is evil. When someone strikes you on (your) right cheek, turn the other one to him as well. (5:38–39)

You have heard that it was said, "You shall love your neighbor and hate your enemy." But I say to you, love your enemies, and pray for those who persecute you, that you may be children of your heavenly Father, for he makes his sun rise on the bad and the good, and causes rain to fall on the just and the unjust. (5:43–45)

In these passages Jesus is teaching that respect for human life goes beyond not killing other people. It prohibits harm of any kind to another person, physical or otherwise. In fact, it prohibits harboring thoughts of anger and revenge that lead to violent and abusive actions. Jesus even commands us to love our enemies and pray for them!

Thus any word or action that causes harm to another person is a sin against the Fifth Commandment. This includes violent assaults, rapes, torture, and acts of terrorism. It includes hazing rituals and name calling. In fact, your

Why would texting while driving be a sin against the Fifth Commandment?

actions only have to have the potential to harm someone to be wrong. Reckless or unsafe driving, for example, is a sin against the Fifth Commandment, even if no one gets hurt. So are practical jokes that could accidently cause embarrassment or physical harm to someone.

The Fifth Commandment covers business practices and governmental policies as well. It forbids endangering people by selling unsafe products or services. It forbids medical or psychological experimentation on human beings that might seriously endanger their lives or health, even with their consent. It forbids business practices or legal policies that take advantage of poor people or poor nations, possibly leading to starvation and disease. It is a sin to put profit above peoples' safety.

The Fifth Commandment reminds us that every person on earth is made in the image of God and is precious to him. There are no exceptions. This truth is at the heart of Christian morality. It is the foundation for loving other people and loving ourselves. ✝

The Fifth Commandment and the Sin of Scandal

The Fifth Commandment also requires that we care for the spiritual lives of other people. One way we harm other people's spiritual lives is through the sin of **scandal**, which is leading another person into sin through our words or actions. For example, offering alcohol to someone who is underage is scandalous behavior. Scandal can also be a sin of omission, such as skipping Mass on Sunday, which sets a bad example for others about their spiritual well-being. Scandal is a grave or mortal sin when we deliberately lead another person to commit a serious sin.

Scandal is particularly wrong when committed by those who are supposed to teach and educate. Remember Jesus' words, "Whoever causes one of these little ones who believe in me to sin, it would be better for him to have a great millstone hung around his neck and to be drowned in the depths of the sea" (Matthew 18:6).

^{Article}
38 Beginning-of-Life Issues

The Fifth Commandment calls individuals and society to respect and protect human life at all stages of development. Most people would agree that it is a serious evil to kill a child, a teenager, or an adult in the prime of life. But opinion changes when talking about the beginning of life or the end of life. In the last forty to fifty years, many people have come to accept abortion and euthanasia as acceptable moral choices. This change in public opinion goes directly against God's moral law.

Revelation is clear that life begins at conception and must be protected to its natural end. The Catholic Church has been a strong moral voice calling society to protect human life from "womb to tomb." This concept is sometimes called "the seamless garment of life," a reference to Christ's seamless garment that the soldiers cast lots for at his Crucifixion (see John 19:23). The seamless garment of life concept emphasizes that all Fifth Commandment issues are interconnected and are rooted in the same principle: that all human life is sacred and precious to God. This article looks at Fifth Commandment issues that come up at the beginning of life, and the next article looks at issues that come up at the end of life.

scandal

An action or attitude—or the failure to act—that leads another person into sin.

abortion

The deliberate termination of a pregnancy by killing the unborn child. It is a grave sin and a crime against human life.

Abortion

Abortion is the deliberate termination of pregnancy by killing the unborn child in the womb. The ability to abort children has existed for a long time, but until recently most societies and religions considered this act a moral evil. In the 1970s the United States made abortion legal, and many other countries have done the same. But remember: acts that are legal are not necessarily moral. What is legal often becomes commonplace and acceptable, and today abortion has tragically become commonplace.

The Church, however, has never wavered in her complete support for the right to life of unborn children from the moment of their conception (when the egg and sperm unite). Direct abortion, that is, abortion performed to end a pregnancy and the life of the unborn child, is a serious sin and strongly forbidden by the Law of God. The woman who is having the abortion and the people who perform the abortion are all guilty of mortal sin. (An example of an indirect abortion is the rare case of a critically ill mother or a mother with an ectopic pregnancy who requires a medical procedure that is not an abortion but that indirectly results in the death of her unborn child. The medical procedure has double effect: saving the life of the mother and ending the life of the child. The first is intended. The second is not. This tragic situation would be morally tolerated because the death of the child is not directly intended.)

When Does Life Begin?

The controversy surrounding abortion and other beginning-of-life issues is partly over the question of when a human life begins. Those who promote legalized abortion argue that a human embryo, or fetus, at least in the first days, weeks, and months after conception, is not a unique human being with his or her own rights and dignity. To make this argument they must ignore or overlook the following facts:

- From the moment the sperm and ovum meet, the cell formed has its own unique human DNA, which no other human being has. Left to its natural development, this cell will always develop into an adult human being, not a frog, a dog, or a tree.

- As early as twenty-one days after conception, the embryo's heart begins to beat. At nine weeks the fetus has fingerprints. At twelve weeks the fetus sleeps, exercises, curls its toes, and opens and closes its mouth. At eighteen to twenty weeks, the fetus is fully capable of feeling pain.

- The fetus's body is clearly differentiated from its mother's body. Although the mother's body provides oxygen and nourishment, the baby has its own intact and separate body. Its blood is not shared with the mother, and it often even has a different blood type.

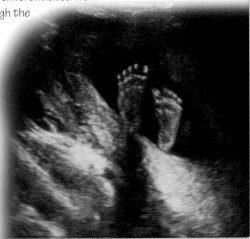

© istockphoto.com

These facts and others lead to one inevitable conclusion: a unique human life begins at the moment of conception.

Many of the arguments for abortion may seem reasonable at first glance but do not hold up under scrutiny. Some people argue that in the first weeks or months after conception the embryo is not a human being. But modern biology, particularly the study of genetics, has conclusively shown this not to be true (see the sidebar "When Does Life Begin?" on page 188). People also argue that a pregnant woman has the right to make choices about her own body, including the baby growing inside her womb. It is true that a woman does have the right to make choices about her body, but science provides clear proof that the baby's body is separate and unique from the mother's body. The baby's right to life is an infinitely greater value than the mother's right to terminate the pregnancy. Some people also argue that if a baby's father abandons the unborn child and its mother, the woman should not have to carry the burden of having the child by herself. But as the saying goes, two wrongs do not make a right. Society must make fathers accountable for the children they conceive and provide pregnant women with options such as pregnancy support and adoption.

Because abortion is a serious sin against the moral law, society has a responsibility to prevent this tragedy. We must work to change societal acceptance of abortion and overturn the laws that make it legal. Providing material, emotional, and spiritual help for women facing a crisis pregnancy can help to stop abortions. Encouraging people to see adoption as a loving alternative to abortion can help to save lives too. And greater respect for the gift of sexuality will prevent the situation in the first place.

The Catholic Church stands as a strong voice for those who cannot speak for themselves. Parishes, dioceses, and conferences of bishops, for example, foster respect for life by communicating the evil of abortion and finding ways to help women avoid this tragedy. And even though the canonical penalty for having an abortion is **excommunication**, the Church actively reaches out to women who have had abortions to assist in their healing and reconciliation. If someone you know has had an abortion only to realize later what a great wrong it was, programs like Project

excommunication
A severe penalty the Church imposes on a Catholic who has committed a grave sin or offense against canon law in which the person is banned from celebrating or receiving the Sacraments. The Church imposes excommunication in the hope that the sinner will repent and be reconciled with God and the Church.

What are some ways that we can provide support for women facing difficult or unplanned pregnancies?

© David Sucsy /istockphoto.com

Rachel can help them to find healing and can lead to reconciliation with God and the Church, especially through the Sacrament of Penance and Reconciliation.

Prenatal Testing, Genetic Engineering, and Stem Cell Research

Modern advances in genetics research raise new beginning-of-life moral issues. With the guidance of the Holy Spirit, the Magisterium teaches how to apply the moral law to these issues. One issue is prenatal testing, also called prenatal diagnosis, which is testing the embryo or fetus for diseases or birth defects while it is still in the womb. The Church teaches that prenatal testing is morally permissible as long as it does not harm the fetus and is done for the purposes of safeguarding and healing the developing baby in the womb or after birth. But prenatal testing for the purpose of deciding whether to abort the baby is morally wrong. The Church's 1987 instruction *Donum Vitae* explains: "It is gravely opposed to the moral law when this is done with the thought of possibly inducing an abortion, depending upon the results: a diagnosis must not be the equivalent of a death sentence"[1] (*CCC*, 2274).

Genetic engineering is the manipulation of an ovum or fetus' genetic coding. This could be used to produce a "designer baby," that is, to create a person with predetermined qualities such as a specific gender, hair color, and so on. Genetic engineering for this purpose is morally wrong because it falsely puts human beings in God's role of determining the uniqueness of every human person. However, certain forms of genetic engineering, called gene treatment or gene therapy, are used to prevent diseases or physical handicaps. These uses are morally permissible and encouraged as long as there is no significant possibility of harm to the fetus.

Stem cell research has been a controversial political issue. Stem cells are unique cells that have the potential to reproduce themselves as different human tissues and organs. Stem cell therapy is already used for bone marrow transplants and to treat leukemia. Scientists hope that it can be used to treat many other diseases and maybe even to grow new organs. However, one of the main sources for stem cells is fetal tissue, and some stem cell researchers want to use aborted embryos and fetuses for their research. Though stem

cell research is not itself immoral, for obvious reasons the Church has condemned stem cell research that uses aborted embryos and fetuses and embryos created through in vitro fertilization. A good intention cannot justify an evil act.

These beginning-of-life issues are clear examples of an important moral principle: just because human beings have the technology and knowledge to do certain actions doesn't mean those actions are morally right. Remember that we must defend the rights of human beings from conception through all the stages of life. For that reason we must defend, care for, and heal embryos as we would any other human being. ✝

euthanasia

A direct action, or a deliberate lack of action, that causes the death of a person who is handicapped, sick, or dying. Euthanasia is a violation of the Fifth Commandment against killing.

Article 39 End-of-Life Issues

We now turn our attention to moral issues connected with the end of our life on earth. As we do this, remember that death is only the end of life for our physical body. Because our compassionate and loving Father sent his only Son for our eternal salvation, our soul lives on and we will know eternal life in resurrected bodies. In that life "he will wipe every tear from their eyes, and there shall be no more death or mourning, wailing or pain" (Revelation 21:4). If we focus on the promise of this ultimate destiny, we will more easily make the right moral choices—those rooted in respect for the human person and using scientific research that is carried out according to moral criteria—at the end of life.

By loving and caring for people who are approaching death, we can help them reach the natural end of their life with dignity.

Euthanasia

The end-of-life issue that we probably hear about most frequently in the news is **euthanasia**, also called mercy killing. Euthanasia is a serious offense against the Fifth Commandment. God's Law is clear that intentionally causing the death of a human being is murder, regardless of the motive or the circumstances. The person choosing to die by euthanasia and the people helping her or him do it are all guilty of this mortal sin.

© Andrew Gentry/shutterstock.com

Proponents of euthanasia make it an issue of human freedom, saying that people who have a serious physical handicap or people who are terminally ill and in severe pain—or their families if the people are incapable of making their own decisions—have a right to choose to end their suffering. This sounds like a good and noble intention, but does it ever make euthanasia right? Remember the three elements that determine the morality of any human action: the object, the intention, and the circumstances. If either the object or the intention is bad, the action is a sin. In the case of euthanasia, the object—that is, the act itself—is a violation of God's Law. It violates human dignity and the respect we owe to our Creator, the author of human life. Even the best of intentions—for example, sparing family members the anxiety of watching a loved one go through a long and painful disease or easing a sick person's suffering—does not justify euthanasia. The *Catechism* acknowledges that thinking of euthanasia as moral is an "error of judgment into which one can fall in good faith," but it stresses that this "does not change the nature of this murderous act, which must always be forbidden and excluded" (*CCC*, 2277).

Autopsies, Organ Donation, and Cremation

Although it may seem a little morbid, there are moral questions concerning the treatment of dead bodies. Even though the soul has departed the physical body, corpses should be treated with all due reverence out of respect for the person who has died. Burying the dead is one of the corporal works of mercy.

The donation of a dead person's organs for either organ transplants or medical research is morally permissible and even encouraged. These donations must be free gifts, however, and the organs must not be taken without the permission of the person or his or her legal representatives. The donation of organs after death can be a lifesaving gift. Carefully consider this option and make whatever legal preparations are necessary to see that your wishes are carried out.

Similarly, autopsies are morally permissible if necessary to determine the cause of death or for medical research. Again the corpse should be treated with care and reverence. Finally, bodies can be either buried or cremated, as long as cremation doesn't signify a denial of faith in the resurrection of the body and the ashes are reverently laid to rest through interment or inurnment. Also, it is important that the Rite of Christian Burial be celebrated.

When discussing euthanasia, it is important to understand the Church's teaching on natural death. Rejecting euthanasia as a moral choice does not mean that we must prolong the life of a person who is near death through extraordinary measures. When a person has come to the end of his or her life, it is legitimate to reject treatments such as heart pacemakers, special breathing apparatus, and medications that are used only to prolong life. Likewise, the use of painkillers is allowed even if their use risks bringing death more quickly because the direct intention is to relieve the dying person's suffering, not to cause his or her death. The painkillers have a double effect, one that is intended and one that is not.

Rejecting euthanasia is not a lack of compassion for people who are suffering and dying. To the contrary, it rejects the false solution offered by euthanasia in favor of the sometimes harder but morally right response: placing our trust in God until the natural end of our days on earth. We do this with the help of God's grace and the compassionate support of others. Christians have an outstanding history of caring for people who are sick, disabled, and dying. Through hospice programs, medical advances in relieving pain, and spiritual support, we help one another make that transition from death into new and eternal life with God.

suicide
Deliberately taking one's own life. It is a serious violation of the Fifth Commandment for it is God's will that we preserve our own lives.

Suicide

Suicide is also a grave offense against the Fifth Commandment. Sacred though life is, for some people it can at times seem overwhelming, and they seek desperate solutions. But the answer is not **suicide**; by committing suicide a person takes over a decision that is God's alone to make: when and how we die. It is always God's will that we preserve our own lives as well as the lives of others. Suicide is the ultimate rejection of God's gifts of hope and love. It causes devastation

In the darkest times, remember to trust in God's love for you and persevere in seeking help. There are many people you can turn to for help and comfort, including family, friends, pastors, teachers, and counselors.

© @erics/shutterstock.com

to the surviving family and friends, and it also wounds the greater human family, which is prematurely deprived of the gift of the life of the person who commits suicide.

Although suicide is always wrong, the Church recognizes that serious mental illness or suffering can contribute to the decision a person makes to take her or his own life. If you know someone who is thinking about suicide, it is essential that you do what you can to get the person the medical or psychological help she or he needs, even if it breaks a promise of confidentiality. If you know someone who has committed suicide, you should not consider her or him forever lost to the love of God or condemned to Hell. As the Church, we pray for those who have committed suicide, placing them in God's love and mercy. ✟

Article 40 Called to Be Peacemakers

War is a failure on someone's part to obey God's Law. We are only permitted to engage in war as an act of legitimate self-defense and when very specific criteria are followed to ensure a minimum of violence and harm.

War has been one of the greatest threats to the sacredness of life throughout the millennia of human existence. Whether fought with spears and clubs or with nuclear weapons, the loss and devastation to human life has been horrific. It is estimated that between forty and seventy million people died as a direct result of World War II. And it is not just soldiers who die; sometimes more civilians die owing to the famines, diseases, and genocides that accompany the evil of war. One shudders to think of the devastation and death that would be caused by a worldwide war today using nuclear, chemical, and biological weapons.

This is why the beatitude "Blessed are the peacemakers, for they will be called children of God" is more important than ever. God calls people of faith to be ambassadors of peace and reconciliation and to tirelessly work for the creation of just

© Ivan Cholakov/istockphoto.com

societies. Injustice is the breeding ground for armed conflict; societies built on justice have little need to resort to war.

In Scripture we see a growing awareness that love is incompatible with violence. The early history of the Old Testament has many of stories of war; often these battles are waged in God's name or at his command. Yet even in the Old Testament, glimpses of insight show that God is not a God of violence but of nonviolent love. See Isaiah's prophecies of the Messiah (2:4) and of the suffering servant (52:13—53:12). When Jesus, the prince of peace, breaks into history, he tells us, "Love your enemies, and pray for those who persecute you" (Matthew 5:44). By his own example of accepting humiliation and suffering rather than resorting to violence to protect himself and destroy his enemies, Jesus sets a new standard. We, his disciples, are called to do everything possible to promote peace and convert hardened hearts through nonviolence and love, even sacrificing our own lives if necessary.

And this is what Christians have done throughout the last two thousand years. Starting with Saint Stephen, whose story is told in Acts of the Apostles 6:8—7:60, hundreds of thousands, maybe even millions, of Christians have given their lives as martyrs. The exact number is hard to determine. These Christians chose to die for their faith, loving their enemies instead of turning to violence.

legitimate defense
The teaching that limited violence is morally acceptable in defending yourself or your nation from an attack.

Legitimate Self-Defense

Does the New Law of Christ demand that we never resort to violence to defend ourselves? No, it does not. Our love for others, including our enemies, is balanced by our love for ourselves. It is perfectly correct to insist on our own right to life. Thus when threatened with bodily harm by an unjust aggressor, we have a legitimate right to defend ourselves and others. But harming the aggressor must be a last resort. For example, if a burglar wants to steal from you, it is far better to allow the theft than to kill the thief. If we must fight to protect ourself, our direct intention must always be to protect our own life, not to hurt or kill the aggressor. However, if a threat to our own life exists and we have no alternative except to kill or be killed, it would be permissible to kill in self-defense. This principle of **legitimate defense** of life is the basis for civil law and the right to self-defense.

The Death Penalty

The moral law, when applied to the death penalty, is complex and nuanced. The Old Law dictated the death penalty for a strikingly large number of offenses (see Exodus, chapter 21, or Leviticus, chapter 20, for some examples). But in the New Law, Christ teaches forgiveness for all sins and love for our enemies. Christ, however, was not applying the moral law to social policy. So when taking the common good into consideration, the Church has always taught that states have a moral right to use the death penalty to defend innocent people from criminals who are proven threats to society.

Times change, however, and the prisons of modern societies keep dangerous criminals safely locked away for life if necessary. Thus Pope John Paul II said that moral reasons for using the death penalty "are very rare, if not practically non-existent"[2] (*CCC*, 2267). Imprisoning the offender to protect society is a better witness to the value of life. Given this current reality, bishops in the United States and other countries have called for an end to the death penalty.

Many Christians, past and present, have renounced violence completely, even in legitimate self-defense. Their extraordinary witness has inspired Christians and non-Christians to take more seriously God's call to be peacemakers.

War

Moral law requires that all citizens and all nations do everything they can to avoid war. Pope Paul VI, frustrated by modern warfare, affirmed this teaching when he called for "War no more; no more war!" in a speech to the United Nations assembly. Our reason and the Law of Love tell us that it makes more sense to resolve conflicts without using violence in our homes, our communities, and among nations.

The reality, however, is that war still happens, and countries have a moral right and responsibility to defend their citizens. The principles of legitimate self-defense are just as applicable for nations as they are for individuals. War must be a last resort whenever there is a conflict between nations. To help states determine when war is justified, the Church developed criteria that must be met for a war to be morally permissible. States that ignore or violate these criteria are committing crimes against humanity. The criteria for a **just war** are the following:

- *Just cause* You must have a just cause, that is, you are using war to prevent or correct a grave, public evil.
- *Comparative justice* The good you achieve through war must far outweigh the resulting loss of life and disruption to society that will occur.
- *Legitimate authority* Only duly constituted public authority may use deadly force or wage war.
- *Probability of success* War may not be used in a futile cause or in a case where disproportionate measures—for example, using nuclear or biological weapons resulting in a massive loss of life—are required to achieve success.
- *Proportionality* The overall destruction expected from the use of force must be outweighed by the good to be achieved. In particular, the loss of civilian life must be avoided at all costs.
- *Last resort* Force may be used only after all peaceful alternatives have been seriously tried and exhausted.

If any of these conditions are not met, the war cannot be considered just, and believers should not participate. Christians have differing perspectives on this. Public authorities have the right to call citizens into military service for legitimate self-defense. For some Christians, answering this call and fighting in a just war fulfills a moral duty. However, other Christians take Christ's command to love our enemies so seriously that they cannot in conscience fight in any war.

just war
War involves many evils, no matter the circumstances. A war is only just and permissible when it meets strict criteria in protecting citizens from an unjust aggressor.

© Wally McNamee/CORBIS

The Gospel calls all Christians to be peacemakers. How can you promote peace and support nonviolent conflict resolution in your school and community?

The Church asks all governments not to force these conscientious objectors to serve as soldiers and to provide alternative ways for them to serve the needs of their country.

Because one of the criteria for a just war is to avoid harm to noncombatants, many people question whether a just war is possible in modern times. The use of nuclear, biological, and chemical weapons kills soldiers and civilians alike. After war is over, mines and biological contaminants are left behind, infecting, injuring, and killing innocent people, which are most often children. Even without a war, the world's buildup of weapons causes more harm than good. The enormous sums of money spent creating weapons keep us from using those resources to provide basic human rights to the neediest of people. Popes since Paul VI have consistently called for an end to the race to build and stockpile new and ever more dangerous kinds of weapons. ✝

Pray It!

A Prayer for Peace

The Church celebrates the Solemnity of Mary, the Mother of God, on January 1. This is the same day we celebrate the World Day of Peace. In his World Day of Peace homily on January 1, 2002, Pope John Paul II said, "If Jesus is Peace, Mary is the Mother of Peace, Mother of the Prince of Peace." He prayed the following prayer for peace at the end of his homily.

Hail, holy Mother,
Virgin Daughter of Zion,
how deeply must your Mother's heart suffer for this bloodshed!

The child you embrace has a name that is dear to the peoples of biblical religion: "Jesus," which means "God saves." . . . In the face of the newborn Messiah, we recognize the face of all your children, who suffer from being despised and exploited. We recognize especially the faces of your children, to whatever race, nation or culture they may belong.

For them, O Mary, for their future, we ask you to move hearts hardened by hatred so that they may open to love and so that revenge may finally give way to forgiveness.

Obtain for us, O Mother, that the truth of this affirmation—*No peace without justice, no justice without forgiveness*—be engraved on every heart. Thus the human family will be able to find the true peace that flows from the union of justice and mercy.

Holy Mother, Mother of the Prince of Peace, help us!
Mother of Humanity and Queen of Peace, pray for us!

^{Article}
41 Personal Health

How's your health? Taking care of your health is a moral issue related to the Fifth Commandment, "You shall not kill." This Commandment also requires that we not cause harm to ourselves. Here's a short questionnaire to assess how you are doing in this area:

© Justin Sneddon/istockphoto.com

- Do you eat a healthy diet, with lots of fruit and vegetables, and avoid too much fat, sugar, and salt?

- Do you get regular exercise, at least 30 minutes or more a day?

- Do you maintain a healthy weight (being too underweight is just as unhealthy as being too overweight)?

- Do you get enough sleep (at least eight to ten hours a night are needed for most teens)?

- Are you tobacco, alcohol, and drug free?

- Are you a safe driver, obeying speed laws and never talking on your phone or texting while driving?

If you can honestly answer yes to all these questions, congratulations! If you have to answer no to two or more, you probably need to take better care of your health, one of the most important gifts God has given you.

Bigger is not always better when it comes to food. What are some other messages in our society that work against maintaining a healthy lifestyle?

Moral Issues Regarding Health

You will not find any explicit revelations in Scripture or Tradition telling you to exercise daily or giving the requirements for a healthy diet. What you will find are teachings about the sacredness of our bodies and the importance of treating our bodies reverently. Psalm 139 praises God for the wonder of our bodies:

> You formed my innermost being;
> you knit me in my mother's womb.
> I praise you, so wonderfully you made me;
> wonderful are your works!
>
> (Verses 13–14)

The Body, Mind, Soul Connection

Is there a health connection between our body, mind, and soul? Scientific studies have already shown a connection between body and mind; for example, people with healthy lifestyles have better cognitive (brain) functioning. Is there a similar connection between a healthy body and a healthy soul? This has turned out to be a difficult question to answer because there is no scientific way to measure the health of a person's soul. So researchers look to external signs that indicate people's religiosity, things like whether they attend religious services and whether they pray or meditate. They have found some interesting correlations, including these:

- Hospitalized people who never attend church have an average stay of three times longer than people who attend regularly.
- Elderly people who never attend church have a stroke rate double that of people who attend regularly.
- In one national study, people who scored high on religious indicators had a 40 percent lower death rate from heart disease and cancer.

Now these studies tend to be controversial and by themselves cannot prove a direct correlation between people's faith and how physically healthy they are. But they do tend to support a central truth of our faith: Our body and soul are bound together in this life to form a unique human person. It only makes sense that what is good for one is probably good for the other.

The wonderful works the psalmist is talking about are all of us. Saint Paul reinforces the importance of our bodies when he tells the Corinthians, "Do you not know that your body is a temple of the holy Spirit within you, whom you have from God, and that you are not your own?" (1 Corinthians 6:19). And the *Catechism of the Catholic Church* instructs us: "Life and physical health are precious gifts entrusted to us by God. We must take reasonable care of them, taking into account the needs of others and the common good" (2288).

Our motive or intention for taking care of ourselves is important. Some people's primary motive for living a healthy lifestyle is to look attractive. But the primary reason to live a healthy lifestyle is to take good care of the bodies and minds God has given to us. When our focus for eating a healthy diet is on how we look, it can easily lead to a skewed perspective and even result in eating disorders like bulimia and anorexia. Remember, having the correct intention for acting morally is as important as the act itself.

Behaviors that directly put our health in danger, such as the abusive and illegal use of alcohol, tobacco, or drugs, are a particularly serious moral concern. These behaviors are a temptation many people face, but they are a particularly dangerous temptation for teens. A young person's maturing body and mind is particularly at risk with the use of these substances, making a young person more vulnerable to addiction and poor decision making. Teens using alcohol and drugs are more likely to be victims of violence, to be sexually active, to have lower grades, and to be victims in car accidents. The best moral decision you can make is to avoid alcohol and drugs completely.

The Challenge of a Healthy Lifestyle

We all know the importance of caring for our health by eating nutritious foods, leading physically active lifestyles, getting plenty of exercise, avoiding health hazards such as cigarettes and alcohol and other drugs, and making moral choices regarding sexuality. Yet it can be a challenge to always choose what is moral and healthy. Many factors affect why maintaining a healthy lifestyle is such a challenge in our culture. Here are a few of those factors. You can probably name more.

- We are bombarded with ads for fast food, which is typically high in fat, sugar, and salt.
- Teens are often affirmed and encouraged to fill up their lives with so many activities that their sleep time is affected.
- Some movies and TV shows glamorize lifestyles filled with alcohol, drugs, and dangerous driving and make these unhealthy practices seem attractive.
- The explosion of electronic-based entertainment—television, computers, video games, cell phones, movies—discourages more physically active forms of entertainment.
- We live in a culture that expects instant results, but it takes time for new, healthy habits to show their effects. When people do not see results right away, they tend to go back to their old habits.

These factors are powerful but do not have to control our choices. Living a healthy lifestyle is a spiritual discipline. If you are having difficulty with living a healthy lifestyle, you can start by asking God in prayer to give you the desire to change and to give you the strength you need to persevere. Ask family and friends to support you; we are more able to keep our commitments when we work at these commitments with other people. Finally, if you find yourself slipping back into unhealthy habits, don't give up. You are building a lifestyle for a lifetime, and God will be with you with each new commitment. ✝

Live It!

Students Describe the Effects of a Healthy Lifestyle

This student describes a change he made for his personal health:

Recently I made the best decision I have ever made in my life; I decided to be healthier. Before this decision I stayed up very late at night, never ate regular meals, and didn't exercise. I felt like I was losing control of myself, and my friends started telling me that I needed to take better care of "me." I realized that caring for my health was more important than being able to do whatever I wanted whenever I wanted. It was hard to change my old habits. But I started to eat regular meals, eating more fruit and vegetables and less fast foods. I started to exercise regularly. And guess what? I'm feeling stronger and happier every day. I feel like the luckiest person in the world; I now understand how to love myself.

This student tells how she helped a friend make an important change in her life:

A friend I have known for years was living a very unhealthy lifestyle. She would go to bed at 4 a.m. and get up at 7 a.m. She was overweight, hated exercising, and snacked at night. So I talked to her and challenged her to live a healthier lifestyle. My friend told me she would like to change but didn't know how. A few other friends and I offered to help her, and she said she would give it a try. Working together with us, she really changed her life! Now she goes to bed at 11 p.m. and gets up at 6 a.m. We play sports together, and she eats three nutritious meals a day. She doesn't snack after 7 p.m. She has a sunny disposition, and the fatigue and depression we used to see in her are completely gone.

© nullplus/istockphoto.com

Living a healthy lifestyle is a spiritual discipline. It requires making good choices, personal commitment, and ongoing practice. But the benefits to our body, mind, and spirit are well worth it.

Review

1. Why is human life qualitatively different from the lives of all other creatures?

2. How does Jesus' teaching on the sanctity of human life go beyond just condemning murder?

3. Give two reasons used to justify abortions and then state the Church's arguments against them.

4. When is genetic engineering morally permissible?

5. Why is euthanasia a serious offense against the Fifth Commandment?

6. Why is suicide wrong?

7. Why are Christians called to be peacemakers?

8. Give four criteria that are necessary for a just war.

9. Why do we have a moral obligation to take care of our physical health?

10. What are some of the challenges people face in maintaining a healthy lifestyle?

Part 2

The Sixth and Ninth Commandments: Respecting Sexuality

Closely connected to God's gift of life is his gift of sexuality. Human sexuality gives human beings the power to bring new life into the world, but it isn't just about our physical bodies; it affects the whole person, influencing our relationships with all people. Sexuality underlies our capacity to enter into loving and caring relationships and calls us to form bonds of friendship with others. For those called to Marriage, it provides the power to procreate and bring new life into the world.

God created the two sexes to be equal in dignity yet unique in some of their physical, emotional, and even spiritual characteristics. These differences make men and women complementary creatures, uniquely suited to loving each other intimately and raising a family together: "That is why a man leaves his father and mother and clings to his wife, and the two of them become one body" (Genesis 2:24).

When it is used immorally, sexuality also has great power to harm people and relationships. Two Commandments forbid its misuse: the Sixth Commandment, "You shall not commit adultery," and the Ninth Commandment, "You shall not covet your neighbor's wife." These Commandments call us to purity of heart by cultivating the virtue of chastity in our lives. By mastering our sexual passions and avoiding sexual sin, we will know the happiness that comes from being in relationships of true love and faithfulness.

The articles in this part address the following topics:

- Article 42: Sexuality, Sharing in God's Life-Giving Power (page 205)

- Article 43: Chastity, the Key to Sexual Integrity (page 209)

- Article 44: Sins against Chastity (page 213)

- Article 45: The Christian Vision of Marriage and Sexuality (page 217)

- Article 46: Sins against the Dignity of Sexuality within Marriage (page 222)

42 Sexuality, Sharing in God's Life-Giving Power

In a series of 129 general addresses delivered from September 1979 to November 1984, Pope John Paul II gave the world a wonderful gift: his teaching on sexuality, Marriage, and the family. He called this teaching the "theology of the body" because as he stated in one of his addresses: "The body, and it alone, is capable of making visible what is invisible: the spiritual and divine. It was created to transfer into the visible reality of the world the mystery hidden since time immemorial in God, and thus be a sign of it" (February 20, 1980).

nuptial
Something related to marriage or a marriage ceremony.

generative
As a theological term, something related to the power of producing new life.

Supporting his teaching with truths drawn from Scripture and Tradition, John Paul II shows how our bodies reveal to us the nature of God. He taught that our bodies have a **nuptial** and a **generative** meaning, that is, they reveal that human beings are called to participate in God's love and life. It is precisely with and through our bodies and our sexuality that we participate in God's plan of salvation. This article draws on John Paul II's theology of the body to understand the purpose of the gift of sexuality.

The Image of God

Our sexuality is a sign of God's own nature. This isn't to say that God is a male or female creature like us. But consider the obvious purpose of the two sexes. Men and women are naturally drawn into relationship with each other—a relationship whose deepest expression is the intimate love between a wife and husband. This visible reality—expressed as physical, emotional, and spiritual union—reveals to us an invisible reality, the nature of God himself. The union of man and woman is an image of the communion of the Father, Son, and Holy Spirit, the primary communion of love that all other earthly communions share in. This truth is revealed in the first biblical account of creation:

> God created man in his image;
>> in the divine image he created him;
>> male and female he created them.
>> (Genesis 1:27)

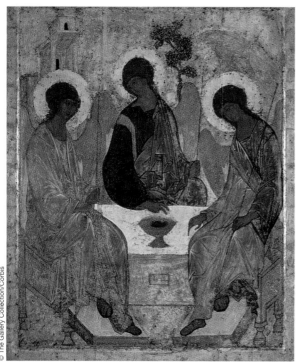

© The Gallery Collection/Corbis

This famous icon depicts the Three Persons of the Trinity as angelic beings. God the Father is on the left, Jesus Christ in the center, and the Holy Spirit on the right. Notice how their heads are inclined toward each other as a sign of respect and communion.

Notice the parallelism in this poetic verse. "God created man in his image" is the same as "male and female he created them." The two genders, male and female, are necessary parts of being made in God's image. Men and women are both necessary in God's plan, and men and women are both equal in dignity in his sight. He created men and women with the need to be in relationship with each other. Why? God wanted to make it clear that we are not meant to be alone, that we are created to be in loving communion with one another and also with the Holy Trinity. The second biblical account of creation emphasizes this truth. In this account the first man is lonely; he is meant to be in relationship with others, but the animals are not his true companions. So God says: "It is not good for the man to be alone. I will make a suitable partner for him" (Genesis 2:18). He makes a woman to be the man's partner, a true soul mate made from the man's own rib, equal to the man but unique in her own right.

The fact that men and women were made to be in relationship with each other does not mean that God calls every person to Marriage. Some people are called by God to remain unmarried for the sake of the Kingdom of God (see Jesus' words in Matthew 19:10–12). But whether married or unmarried, all people benefit from healthy relationships with people of the other sex. Priests affirm the importance that good friendships with women play in their lives. Religious sisters will say the same about male friends. The important role that sexuality plays in our lives does not require marriage or the physical act of having sex.

Man and Woman as the Image of God

You can find John Paul II's talks on the theology of the body through an Internet search. They are worth your time to study, but be warned, they are not easy reading. The Pope used technical philosophical and theological language and concepts. Here is a portion of the Pope's talk on November 14, 1979, on how the relationship of man and woman reflects the divine communion:

> In the first chapter (of Genesis), the narrative of the creation of man affirms directly, right from the beginning, that man was created in the image of God as male and female. The narrative of the second chapter, on the other hand, does not speak of the "image of God." But in its own way it reveals that the complete and definitive creation of "man" (subjected first to the experience of original solitude) is expressed in giving life to that *communio personarum* that man and woman form. . . .
>
> We can then deduce that man became the "image and likeness" of God not only through his own humanity, but also through the communion of persons which man and woman form right from the beginning. . . . Man becomes the image of God not so much in the moment of solitude as in the moment of communion. Right "from the beginning," he is not only an image in which the solitude of a person who rules the world is reflected, but also, and essentially, an image of an inscrutable divine communion of persons.

Participating in God's Love and Life

Our sexuality is not just an image of the divine communion of the Holy Trinity; it is also a call to share in God's love and his life-giving power. The theology of the body calls this the nuptial and the generative meanings of the body.

The word *nuptial* means "related to Marriage." When John Paul II says that our bodies have a nuptial meaning, he is saying that the gift of sexuality orients men and women to join together in Marriage, to "become one body" (Genesis 2:24). In Marriage a man and a woman commit to loving each other completely and without conditions—in essence to love each other as God loves. Whether we are married or not, however, it is right to say that our sexuality is a call to share God's love with others. Through our physical bodies, we share God's love with others through our words, our actions, and our touch.

The word *generative* means "related to producing new life." When John Paul II says that our bodies have a generative meaning, he is saying that the gift of sexuality is also oriented toward bringing new life into the world. God tells the first man and woman, "Be fertile and multiply; fill the earth and subdue it" (Genesis 1:28). God is the author of all life, but he shares that ability to bring new life into the world with his creatures. In Marriage a man and a woman participate in God's life-giving power by bringing children into the world. Whether or not God calls us to have children of our own, the gift of sexuality calls us to support the gift of life. We can do this by loving and caring for all the children God brings into our lives. And just as important, we can help others to accept God's invitation to eternal life by sharing the Gospel message with them.

To summarize, our sexuality and sexual identity as male or female is a great and wonderful gift, one we must gratefully and happily embrace. Both men and women reflect the image of God, especially when we are in loving relationships with other people. Our sexuality calls us to share God's love with others. It also calls us to share in his life-giving power, whether it is through bringing children into the world or by helping others answer our heavenly Father's invitation to know the fullness of life that comes through faith in his Son, Jesus Christ. ✝

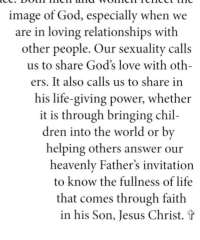

The theology of the body teaches us that our sexuality draws us into loving communion with each other and calls us to support the gift of life.

Article 43 Chastity, the Key to Sexual Integrity

chastity
The virtue by which people are able successfully and healthfully to integrate their sexuality into their total person; recognized as one of the fruits of the Holy Spirit. Also, one of the vows of religious life.

When you hear the word **chastity**, what image comes to your mind? Some people think of chastity as something practiced by uptight, unhappy individuals who are afraid of their sexuality. But this image is not true chastity. Chaste people deeply appreciate the gift of their sexuality and resist temptations to use that gift in ways that demean or hurt themselves or others. They are serene and happy people because they are using God's gift for the purposes he intended, and they do not have to worry about the harm to body and soul that sexual sin leaves in its wake.

Both the Sixth and Ninth Commandments, "You shall not commit adultery" and "You shall not covet your neighbor's wife," call all people to live chaste lives. Yes, even married people must practice chastity. More will be said specifically about the call to chastity within Marriage in student book article 45, "The Christian Vision of Marriage and Sexuality." This article considers the general vocation to chastity that all people are called to.

Integration and Self-Control

Chastity is the moral virtue of living a life of sexual integrity. *Integrity* comes from the root word *integer*, meaning "whole." To be a person of integrity means that that there is nothing that divides you; your inner life and your outer life are united. Thus a chaste person's thoughts, words, and actions all reflect God's purpose for the gift of sexuality. For example, a chaste man will not flatter a woman who is not his wife with the secret intention of seducing her into having sex with him. A chaste woman will not flirt with a man who is not her husband in any way that suggests she is sexually interested in him. Chaste men and women will not dress in ways that are intended to provoke sexual arousal in others. All these actions cause sexual disintegration and can open the doors to sexual sin.

Jesus is our model for living a chaste life. In the Sermon on the Mount he teaches us this: "You have heard that it was said, 'You shall not commit adultery.' But I say to you, everyone who looks at a woman with lust has already committed adultery with her in his heart" (Matthew 5:27–28).

The Media and Chastity

During your lifetime dozens of studies have explored the effect of media exposure on sexual values and practices. The results of these studies are not always consistent, nor are their findings always conclusive. However, most studies agree on these main points:

- The amount of sexual images and sexual content in movies, popular music, and television has increased dramatically in the last thirty years, and the images and content have gotten more sexually explicit. Sexual activities occurring between unmarried people occur four to five times more often in popular media than sexual activity between husbands and wives. Popular media rarely portray the negative consequences of such immoral sexual behavior.

- Cable television and high-speed Internet service have made soft- and hard-core pornography available in the majority of homes in the United States. This is a special concern for teen chastity because two-thirds of teens have televisions and one-third of teens have computers in their private rooms.

- Although this differs person by person, in general the more sexually explicit media teens watch or listen to, they more likely they are to be involved in sexual activity. However, this also depends on the sexual values teens learn from their parents.

These studies make it clear that living a chaste life is more difficult today because of the popular media. Chaste people must be critical in their use of popular media, recognizing when immoral activity is falsely portrayed as something good and lacking any negative consequences.

lust

Intense and uncontrolled desire for sexual pleasure. It is one of the seven capital sins.

Jesus faithfully followed this teaching on chastity in his own life. The Gospels give witness that he lived a life of sexual integrity. He had deep and loving relationships with both men and women, yet never once did he commit a sexual sin or even hold **lust** for another person in his heart. We know this because sexual purity was so important in his culture that had he sinned even once his followers would have left him. They certainly would not have risked their lives for him as they did when they continued his mission after Pentecost.

God gives us the help we need to live chaste lives; the Holy Spirit enables us to follow Christ's example through the grace of Baptism. But this takes practice and self-control. We live in a sex-obsessed culture that sends us dozens of messages every day that tell us it is okay to act on our sexual impulses. People of all ages experience pressure to be sexually active outside of marriage, and this pressure can be intense for young adults because of their changing bodies and developing sexual identities. To resist these temptations, we must be vigilant in mastering our sexual passions (see the sidebar "Ten Ways to Practice Chastity" on page 212). As any honest adult will tell you, this is a lifelong task, so don't be fooled into thinking that once you are past your teenage years, you will not have any more sexual temptations to face!

© Leonid and Anna Dedukh/shutterstock.com

Businesses often use human sexuality for advertising purposes in subtle and sometimes not-so-subtle ways. Why does "sex sell"?

Purity of Heart

Jesus proclaims in the sixth beatitude, "Blessed are the pure of heart, for they shall see God." In this beatitude he teaches that living the virtue of chastity requires maintaining purity of heart through the practice of modesty. The *Catechism of the Catholic Church (CCC)* refers to the heart as the seat of moral personality. Our heart "enables us to see *according to God;* . . . [Purity of heart] lets us perceive the human body—ours and our neighbor's—as a temple of the Holy Spirit, a manifestation of divine beauty" (*CCC,* 2519). Having a pure heart is the opposite of having a lustful heart.

The Temple in Jerusalem, described in the Old Testament, was a magnificent structure, but its most sacred room was deep within. Only one person, the high priest, could enter the holy of holies—the innermost sacred room. He could do this only after going through ritual purification. Our bodies are magnificent temples too, temples of the Holy Spirit. We too must protect our sacred inner space, our heart, from contamination by impure influences.

The virtue of modesty is one special way we protect our sacred, intimate center. We don't tell just anybody our most private secrets; we should not let just anybody see or touch our sacred places. Modesty requires patience in responding to our sexual desires. It requires that we maintain decency in

temperance
The cardinal virtue by which one moderates his or her appetites and passions to achieve balance in the use of created goods.

concupiscence
The tendency of all human beings toward sin, as a result of Original Sin.

our words and actions toward others. It requires discretion in what we wear, what we listen to, and what we watch so that we do not unnecessarily arouse our own sexual desires or the sexual desires of other people. Chastity and modesty are both virtues related to the cardinal virtue of **temperance**, meaning they are virtues through which we curb our lust to maintain the right balance in using God's gifts.

The road to chaste living may seem difficult at times, but it is well worth the effort. Can you imagine brides or grooms wishing they had had sexual partners other than their beloved? The kind of discipline required for sexual abstinence before marriage is good practice for the lifelong commitment you will make in whatever vocation God calls you to. Rather than seeing chastity as a burden, consider the freedom it gives: freedom from worry about pregnancy, freedom from disease, and freedom from the emotional wounds that result from sexual sin. Chastity provides the freedom to be sexually healthy and whole, according to God's design. ✝

Live It!

Ten Ways to Practice Chastity

1. Pray. Thank God for the gift of sexuality and ask for the strength to live a life of chastity.
2. Seek out a parent or another adult you can talk to when you have questions about sexuality.
3. Focus on making friends—not romances—with people of the other sex.
4. Turn a critical eye toward media messages that use sex to sell products.
5. Remind yourself that your value does not depend on whether and how much you date.
6. Stay away from drugs and alcohol. Impaired judgment on a date can lead to trouble.
7. If you are on a date and things get out of hand, call a friend or a parent for a ride home.
8. If you have a boyfriend or a girlfriend, communicate openly and set boundaries about touching.
9. Remember that more teenagers are *not* having sex than are having sex.
10. Make a vow—a nonnegotiable commitment—to avoid intimate sexual activity until you get married.

Promoting and encouraging chastity is very important in societies where sins against chastity are commonplace.

© Jacques M. Chenet/CORBIS

Article 44 Sins against Chastity

The Ninth Commandment, "You shall not covet your neighbor's wife," warns us against the dangers of lust and carnal **concupiscence**. Concupiscence is any desire for pleasure or sensual experience that is against reason and the moral law. Concupiscence is one of the consequences of Original Sin, and it makes us more inclined to give in to sinful temptations. Carnal concupiscence is the desire for sexual experiences that are morally wrong. Men and women tend to experience carnal concupiscence differently. Perhaps you have heard this saying: "Men use love to pursue sex, and women use sex to pursue love." Although such generalities are never completely true, it is true that men are more drawn to the pleasurable aspects of sexual acts, and women are more drawn to the relational aspects of sexual acts.

The Sixth and Ninth Commandments teach that sexual intercourse is only morally permissible between a husband and wife. This is because our bodies themselves are visible signs that our sexuality is oriented toward sharing in God's love and in his power of creating life. Sexual intercourse is the ultimate physical expression of our sexuality, the fullest expression of love that brings new life into the world. The

fornication

Sexual intercourse between a man and a woman who are not married. It is morally wrong to engage in intercourse before Marriage, a sin against the Sixth Commandment.

prostitution

The act of providing sexual services in exchange for money, drugs, or other goods. It is a serious social evil and a sin against the Sixth Commandment.

power of the love shared during sexual intercourse and the nurturing of the children that are the natural result of sexual intercourse require the commitment of Marriage. Because of this, any form of intimate sexual activity outside of Marriage is a sin against chastity.

Fornication and Prostitution

The most direct sin against chastity is **fornication**. Fornication is a biblical term that refers to having sexual intercourse outside of Marriage. This includes living together before Marriage. People you know, even friends, may believe that casual sex is no big deal. But it is a serious moral wrong. The physical consequences of fornication are often unwanted pregnancies and sexually transmitted diseases. There are also emotional consequences; premarital sex often leads to broken hearts and feelings of shame and betrayal. Finally, spiritual consequences lead us to feel separated and alienated from God. The consequences of the sin of fornication leave people wounded in body and spirit.

Gossip and the media may cause you to think that everybody is sexually active, but the reality is that more and more teenagers are questioning the wisdom of sex without the commitment of Marriage. Recent studies show that the majority of teens who have had sex say they wish they had waited. That message is gaining in popularity. Between 1995 and 2005, the percentage of high school students who have had sex dropped from 53 percent to 46 percent.

Another form of fornication, **prostitution**, is a serious societal sin. The prostitute and the person paying for the sex are treating the prostitute's body as a thing to be used rather than as a temple of the Holy Spirit. The evil of prostitution is even greater when it involves children or teens, or when people are forced or sold into prostitution.

© annedde/istockphoto.com

Why are pornography and prostitution serious sins against the Sixth and Ninth Commandments? What do these sins imply about the dignity and value of a person and his or her body?

Masturbation and Pornography

Masturbation, genital activity alone or with another person that does not result in sexual intercourse, is also a sin against chastity. Masturbation is all about self-pleasure without sharing life or real love. So are other forms of genital sexual activity that stop short of sexual intercourse, such as petting or oral sex. They are forms of exploitation and are not appropriate sexual expressions for unmarried people. Like fornication, these activities can also result in disease and emotional wounds that can prevent true intimacy in future relationships.

masturbation

Self-manipulation of one's sexual organs for the purpose of erotic pleasure or to achieve orgasm. It is a sin because the act cannot result in the creation of new life and because God created sexuality not for self-gratification but to unify a husband and wife in Marriage.

pornography

A written description or visual portrayal of a person or action that is created or viewed with the intention of stimulating sexual feelings. Creating or using pornography is a sin against the Sixth and Ninth Commandments.

© James Blinn/shutterstock.com

An offense against the Sixth and Ninth Commandments that is growing in our time is **pornography**. The Internet has made this evil more accessible to people of all ages. Pornography is dangerous because it violates human dignity. It takes the gift of sexuality and makes it an object to be exploited and abused. Even though the models and actors may agree to participate in the creation of pornography, there is nothing right and everything wrong with viewing pornographic images. The chemistry in men's brains makes them particularly susceptible to the temptation of pornography and can make viewing pornography very addictive. The use of pornography leads to a serious lack of reverence for the gift of sexuality and in some cases has been linked to violent sexual acts, especially toward women.

Homosexuality

Homosexuality is an especially challenging sexual issue. For reasons that are still unclear, some people experience a strong sexual attraction toward persons of the same sex. For most homosexual people, this same-sex attraction is deep seated and not freely chosen. Although today there is generally a greater social acceptance of people with a homosexual orientation, this has not always been true; homosexual men and women have been ridiculed, ostracized, and even

The Darkness Is Passing

The second and third chapters of the First Letter of John contain a beautiful section on the moral life, with this hopeful beginning:

> My children, I am writing this to you so that you may not commit sin. But if anyone does sin, we have an Advocate with the Father, Jesus Christ the righteous one. (2:1)

The chapter goes on to give this warning:

> Do not love the world or the things of the world. If anyone loves the world, the love of the Father is not in him. For all that is in the world, sensual lust, enticement for the eyes, and a pretentious life, is not from the Father but is from the world. Yet the world and its enticement are passing away. But whoever does the will of God remains forever. (Verses 15–17)

In this context the "world" is anything that leads us away from the love of God. The letter describes these temptations as the desires caused by concupiscence: "sensual lust, enticement for the eyes, and a pretentious (proud and selfish) life." These promises of false happiness do not last; pursuing them will not satisfy us because they are not of God.

Even though he is writing about sin, the author is positive and hopeful. Several times he reminds the reader that if we keep Christ's Commandments we will conquer evil and live in communion with the Holy Trinity. Here is one example:

> Let what you heard from the beginning remain in you. If what you heard from the beginning remains in you, then you will remain in the Son and in the Father. And this is the promise that he made us: eternal life. (Verses 24–25)

Take time to read these chapters or even the whole letter. It is a wonderful inspiration to live Christ's Commandments.

attacked and killed. The Catholic Church affirms that people with a homosexual orientation are children of God and must be treated with respect, compassion, and sensitivity. It is a grave moral offense to discriminate, act violently toward, make jokes about, or look down on them.

Although the Church is clear about accepting our homosexual brothers and sisters—that is, gay men and lesbian women—as part of the Body of Christ, homosexual acts are against natural law because they do not allow for the possibility of life. For those who realize they are sexually attracted to people of the same sex, avoiding genital sexual expression can be a cross to bear, requiring self-mastery over their sexual desires. An active prayer life and support from others within the faith community can help men and women with homosexual orientations to accept the gift of their sexuality through deepening friendships that are a sign of Christian love. ✟

Article 45 The Christian Vision of Marriage and Sexuality

In the Sacrament of Matrimony, a husband and wife make sacred vows to love and cherish each other until the end of their lives. This Sacrament calls a husband and wife to share God's love with each other, with their children, and with the wider community. The faithful love of couples who have been married for many years is a beautiful and inspiring witness to the love of God. Consider the couples you know who have been married for many years; how have they been a witness to the love of God? How have they been a blessing in the lives of other people?

In student book article 42, "Sexuality, Sharing in God's Life-Giving Power," we considered how the theology of the body reveals that the gift of sexuality is a call to share God's love and life with others. This article looks more closely at what this means for those called to the vocation of Marriage.

The Purpose of Marital Sex

Recall that in his teaching on the theology of the body, Pope John Paul II says that our sexuality has both a nuptial and a generative meaning. These are sometimes also called the

Annulments

In *God's* plan marriages are meant to last forever, but what happens when a marriage doesn't? When a couple divorces, the marriage is dissolved in the eyes of the state but not the Church. Divorced people remain full members of the Church but are not permitted to remarry as long as their original spouse is alive. Remember Jesus' words: "But I say to you, whoever divorces his wife (unless the marriage is unlawful) causes her to commit adultery, and whoever marries a divorced woman commits adultery" (Matthew 5:32). There is an exception to this, however. In some cases the married couple never truly achieves a sacramental or covenantal bond. Church officials can declare such marriages null (meaning that a sacramental Marriage never existed), and the two former spouses are free to marry again. This declaration, called an **annulment**, is not a statement about the validity of the civil bond that existed or the legitimacy of the children born to the couple during their marriage.

Those who remarry without annulling an earlier marriage are excluded from receiving Holy Communion but are not separated from the Church. "They should be encouraged to listen to the Word of God, to attend the Sacrifice of the Mass, to persevere in prayer, to contribute to works of charity and to community efforts for justice, to bring up their children in the Christian faith, to cultivate the spirit and practice of penance and thus implore, day by day, God's grace"[3] (*CCC*, 1651).

annulment
The declaration by the Church that a marriage is null and void, that is, it never existed as a sacramental union. Catholics who divorce must have the marriage annulled by the Church to be free to marry once again in the Church.

"unitive" and "procreative" ends of sexual intercourse. The nuptial meaning calls wives and husbands into intimate, loving communion; they are called to completely share themselves with each other, with total openness and honesty. Sexual intercourse is the most intense physical expression of that communion; it is literally two bodies joined together as one, bringing joy and pleasure to their union. But this physical union is also a visible sign of the emotional and spiritual union that is taking place. In fact, God has designed the physical act of sexual intercourse to release hormones that intensify and solidify the commitment that a wife and husband have for each other. (This is another reason that premarital sex is wrong, because people who engage in premarital sex must ignore their body's call to committed love.)

The committed love between a husband and wife is meant to be faithful and life-long, just as Christ's love for the Church is faithful until the end of time.

© Rene Jansa/shutterstock.com

The nakedness that a husband and wife share during sexual intercourse is a visible sign of the nakedness of mind and heart that they share. In strong marriages there are no secrets; husbands and wives are spiritually one in body, mind, and heart. This unity helps them to grow in their love for each other, their love for God, their love for their children, and their love for their neighbors. Through the grace of the Sacrament of Matrimony, the Holy Spirit empowers them to be faithful and committed in their love, so they can be the very image of the love of Jesus Christ. The Letter to the Ephesians gives a biblical example of this call: "Husbands, love your wives, even as Christ loved the church" (5:25, see 5:21–33 for the complete teaching).

The committed love between a wife and husband is meant to be faithful and lifelong, just as Christ's love for the Church is faithful until the end of time. Adultery, polygamy, and divorce have no place in God's plan for married love. Adultery and polygamy harm the unity of marriage, and divorce separates what God has joined together. In the Sermon on the Mount, Christ emphasizes the permanence of Marriage:

> It was also said, "Whoever divorces his wife must give her a bill of divorce." But I say to you, whoever divorces his wife (unless the marriage is unlawful) causes her to commit adultery, and whoever marries a divorced woman commits adultery. (Matthew 5:31–32, see also 19:3–9)

God intends Marriage to be a faithful, lifelong, loving union, a union that also has the purpose of bringing new life into the world. Through the Sacrament of Matrimony, Christian spouses receive a special grace from Christ that enables them to perfect their love, strengthen their indissoluble unity, and welcome and educate their children.

The Openness to Life

The generative meaning of the gift of sexuality calls husbands and wives to be open to new life. The physical union they share during sexual intercourse has the purpose of bringing children into the world. Just as God's love brings all created things into existence, the love of a husband and wife bring new human life into existence. A husband and wife are called to be open to sharing in God's power to bring life into the world whenever they have sexual intercourse. Bringing children into the world is an awesome gift and calling; it is a gift not to be taken lightly and without the complete commitment to raising a family. (This is another reason that premarital sex is wrong, because it risks bringing children into the world without the commitment to raising a family.)

God's will is that children are brought into the world through the faithful and intimate love shared between a husband and wife.

© gabyjalbert/istockphoto.com

For a married couple, eliminating the possibility of pregnancy while having sexual intercourse is a rejection of their call to share in God's power to bring life into the world. The refusal of fertility has no place in God's plan for marriage because it turns the couple away from the greatest gift of marriage, the child. Although the Church recognizes that couples should act responsibly in having children, the spacing of children should be accomplished through a method such as natural family planning (NFP), which emphasizes the union of the couple and their openness to life. NFP teaches married couples how to recognize the wife's fertile periods and practice chaste abstinence during those times to avoid pregnancy. All methods of **contraception**, including the use of chemicals, the use of barrier methods such as condoms and diaphragms, and surgical sterilization are morally wrong.

The gift of sexuality as expressed in Marriage has a twofold end: to deepen the joyful, loving union of the spouses and to bring new life into the world. These two purposes are both necessary and should not be separated, especially during the act of sexual intercourse. To do so will have negative effects on the couple's relationship and their spiritual life. When separating these purposes through practices such as

contraception
The deliberate attempt to interfere with the creation of new life as a result of sexual intercourse. It is morally wrong because a married couple must remain open to procreation whenever they engage in sexual intercourse.

Pray It!

Prayer for Married Couples

This prayer is adapted from the prayers said at Masses celebrated in honor of husbands and wives on wedding anniversaries. You can pray it for all married couples or for a particular couple.

O God,
Creator of all things,
who in the beginning made man and woman
that they might form the marriage bond,
bless and strengthen all married couples,
that they may show forth an ever more perfect image
of the union of Christ with his Church.
Sustain them in communion of spirit amid toil and joy,
increase, we pray, and purify their love
so that together with their children they may rejoice
in the sanctification they bring to each other.
We ask this through Christ our Lord. Amen.
                                    (Roman Missal)

artificial contraception becomes widespread in society, it will have negative effects on the future of family life itself. ✞

adultery
Sexual activity between two persons, at least one of whom is married to another. Prohibited by the Sixth Commandment.

polygamy
Having more than one spouse, an act contrary to the dignity of Marriage.

Article 46 Sins against the Dignity of Sexuality within Marriage

The Sixth Commandment clearly forbids adultery, but as we have seen in regard to other Commandments, the New Law of Christ broadens our understanding of the moral law, helping us to see how the intent of the original Commandment applies to other thoughts and actions. When applying the New Law to sexuality within Marriage, anything that contradicts the twin purposes of sexual intercourse—sharing in God's faithful love and sharing in God's power to create new life—is a serious offense against the moral law.

Sins against Fidelity

Adultery, which occurs when a married person has sex with someone who is not his or her spouse, is a serious sin against the faithful, committed love that God intends to exist between a husband and wife. Adultery causes serious emotional and spiritual harm to everyone involved: the married couple, their family, the other person involved in the adulterous relationship, and even the wider community. A married

Catholic Wisdom

Society and Marriage

*T*he *Pastoral Constitution on the Church in the Modern World* (*Gaudium et Spes*, 1965) has a powerful section on Marriage and the family. The section ends with a call to society to protect Marriage and the family. Here is part of that section:

Thus the family, in which the various generations come together and help one another grow wiser and harmonize personal rights with the other requirements of social life, is the foundation of society. All those, therefore, who exercise influence over communities and social groups should work efficiently for the welfare of marriage and the family. Public authority should regard it as a sacred duty to recognize, protect and promote their authentic nature, to shield public morality and to favor the prosperity of home life. The right of parents to beget and educate their children in the bosom of the family must be safeguarded. (52)

relationship is based in trust and faithfulness, and when one of the spouses is sexually unfaithful, the trust in the relationship is extremely difficult to regain. This is why Jesus condemns even the desire for adultery (see Matthew 5:28). No intentions or circumstances can make adultery morally right. **Polygamy**, the practice of being married to more than one person, is in essence another form of adultery and is also condemned by the moral law.

The harmful effects of divorce go beyond the husband and wife and touch many lives. Who are some of the people affected when a married couple divorces?

Divorce is another serious offense against the dignity of Marriage. Article 45, "The Christian Vision of Marriage and Sexuality," discusses Jesus' condemnation of divorce. Here is another example from Matthew's Gospel of his strong teaching against this sin:

> Some Pharisees approached him, and tested him, saying, "Is it lawful for a man to divorce his wife for any cause whatever?" He said in reply, "Have you not read that from the beginning the Creator 'made them male and female' and said, 'For this reason a man shall leave his father and mother and be joined to his wife, and the two shall become one flesh'? So they are no longer two, but one flesh. Therefore, what God has joined together, no human being must separate." They said to him, "Then why did Moses command that the man give the woman a bill of divorce and dismiss (her)?" He said to them, "Because of the hardness of your hearts Moses allowed you to divorce your wives, but from the beginning it was not so. I say to you, whoever divorces his wife (unless the marriage is unlawful) and marries another commits adultery." (19:3–9)

in vitro fertilization

The fertilization of a woman's ovum (egg) with a man's sperm outside her body. The fertilized egg is transferred to the woman's uterus. The Church considers the process to be a moral violation of the dignity of procreation.

artificial insemination

The process by which a man's sperm and a woman's egg are united in a manner other than natural sexual intercourse. In the narrowest sense, it means injecting sperm into a woman's cervical canal. The procedure is morally wrong because it separates intercourse from the act of procreation.

surrogate motherhood

A medical process in which a woman becomes pregnant through artificial means and delivers a child for someone else. She may or may not be the child's biological mother. The procedure is morally wrong because it separates intercourse from the act of procreation and pregnancy.

As you can see from this passage, divorce was relatively easy in Jesus' time, at least it was not hard for a husband to divorce his wife. Jesus protects the dignity of Marriage and also the equal dignity of the sexes by insisting that in God's plan of creation, a husband and wife are permanently bonded in Marriage.

Cohabitation, or living together before Marriage, is also a sin against the dignity of Marriage because the couple lives together as if they were married, without the complete commitment of a sacramental Marriage. Living together, even if the intention is a trial marriage, is not the same as a permanent commitment. Studies have shown that couples who lived together before marriage experience a higher rate of divorce than couples who did not live together. When couples decide to experience the pleasure of sex without the lifelong vow, it is too easy to give up on each other and to walk away from the relationship. Having sex is not difficult to learn; there is no need to "try it out." When a woman and man are called by God to Marriage, when they work at nurturing their relationship before the Marriage (without having sex), and when they make a complete commitment to God and each other to be faithful for life, they will experience all the joys and be prepared to deal with all the challenges that marriage brings.

Sins against Natural Conception

Article 45, "The Christian Vision of Marriage and Sexuality," discusses how the use of artificial contraceptives is wrong because the husband and wife must remain open to the possibility of children in every act of sexual intercourse. However, the

How would you explain to a friend why artificial means of conceiving a child—such as in vitro fertilization and artificial insemination— are against the will of God?

© istockphoto.com

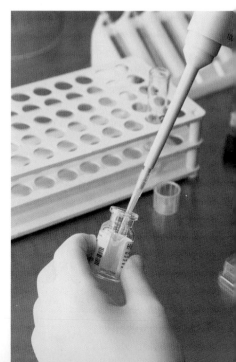

dignity of sexuality requires that children also be created naturally. Children must be the outcome of the loving union of a husband and wife in sexual intercourse and not conceived through some artificial means of conception. Thus **in vitro fertilization**, which is creating a fertilized ovum in a laboratory and then implanting it in the wife's womb, is morally wrong. So is **artificial insemination**, which is a fertility technique that artificially implants sperm in a woman's womb. The use of **surrogate motherhood**—which is placing a fertilized ovum in another woman's womb, letting the baby grow inside her, and after birth giving the newborn infant to

Humanae Vitae **and** Donum Vitae

Two Church documents guide us in understanding the purpose of sexuality within Marriage and the sins against its dignity. *On Human Life* (*Humanae Vitae*) is a papal encyclical written by Pope Paul VI in 1968. This important encyclical discusses the purpose of sexuality within Marriage and upholds the Church's constant teaching prohibiting contraception. The opening paragraphs of the encyclical state:

> The transmission of human life is a most serious role in which married people collaborate freely and responsibly with God the Creator. It has always been a source of great joy to them, even though it sometimes entails many difficulties and hardships.
>
> The fulfillment of this duty has always posed problems to the conscience of married people, but the recent course of human society and the concomitant changes have provoked new questions. The Church cannot ignore these questions, for they concern matters intimately connected with the life and happiness of human beings. (1)

The *Instruction on Respect for Human Life in Its Origin and on the Dignity of Procreation (Donum Vitae)* was published by the Doctrine of the Congregation of the Faith in 1987. It addresses new questions regarding artificial conception. Its opening sentence is a clear statement of its purpose:

> The gift of life which God the Creator and Father has entrusted to man calls him to appreciate the inestimable value of what he has been given and to take responsibility for it: this fundamental principle must be placed at the centre of one's reflection in order to clarify and solve the moral problems raised by artificial interventions on life as it originates and on the processes of procreation.

the baby's biological mother and father—is a serious moral offense. Likewise human cloning is a grave moral offense.

The emotional pain and suffering of married couples who are unable to conceive children through natural means is very real. Because of this, some people see these prohibitions against artificially induced pregnancy as unnecessary or even cruel. The Body of Christ, though, has great sympathy for husbands and wives who struggle with infertility. The Church encourages and supports research and medical treatments that increase their chances of naturally conceiving. But we must uphold the dignity of sexuality within Marriage through the creation of children as God intended. As stated previously with other moral issues, good intentions cannot make an immoral act moral. ✝

Review

1. How is the gift of sexuality a reflection of the image of God?

2. Explain the two basic meanings of *sexuality,* according to the theology of the body.

3. Give a definition of a chaste person.

4. How can a person maintain purity of heart?

5. Define *fornication* and explain why it is a sin.

6. Why is pornography a dangerous sexual sin?

7. Explain the twofold meaning and purpose of *marital sexuality.*

8. Why are artificial means of contraception wrong?

9. Who is harmed by adultery?

10. Name three artificial means of conception and explain why they are wrong.

Making Moral Choices

Part 1

Gifts and Guides

This final section considers the following practical questions about the moral life:

- How does a moral person live?
- What are the gifts God gives us to live a moral life?
- What guides us in making good moral decisions?
- What happens when we miss the mark and we sin?
- How do we practice forgiveness and reconciliation?

The short answer to these questions is that through the Catholic faith God has given us an abundance of resources to strengthen and guide us. Being Catholic is like being at a free gourmet restaurant for moral living. In the Catholic faith, we find the best of all that we need: moral principles, the theological virtues, the Commandments, the Beatitudes, Jesus' life and his teachings, and two thousand years of wisdom and reflection on moral issues and principles. We have moral support from parents, priests, youth leaders, teachers, counselors, and peers who share our values. Grace, the cardinal virtues, and the Sacraments are the gifts that help us to put all this wisdom into action. Conscience guides us in making reasoned, moral judgments about how to act. We truly have everything we need to live a holy, happy, and healthy life.

The articles in this part address the following topics:

Article 47 Called to Be Holy

There was a young woman who loved art. As a child she drew picture after picture, which her parents proudly displayed in the family's kitchen and den. She worked hard in high school to get accepted into a college with a prestigious art program. She labored diligently to learn new and varied techniques for painting and sculpting. She spent long hours into the night painting the same image over and over to get the brush strokes just right. Finally, she graduated with honors, ready to begin her lifelong dream. She got a job as a commercial designer to pay her bills. But she also set up her own home studio where she could work on the art she really wanted to create.

However, she had a problem. Every time she started a project in her home studio, she rarely got further than her initial sketches. Or if she did start a painting, she would get halfway through, get disgusted with her work, and toss it out. After months of this, she made a lunch appointment with an art teacher she greatly respected. During lunch she explained her difficulty. "What are you thinking about while you are painting?" the teacher asked. "I'm thinking about the technique I'm using and how I'm not getting it right," she replied.

"What gave you the desire to create art?" the teacher asked. "Try to remember what made you want to be an artist in the first place."

The woman replied, "I just loved making beautiful things."

"Then forget the techniques," said the teacher, "and just focus on making something beautiful. You've learned the techniques, and they are a part of you. Trust that they will work."

You can probably guess the end of the story. The artist focused on making something beautiful and trusted the techniques she had learned to create it. Her passion returned, and now she couldn't paint and sculpt fast enough.

Our moral life is like this. If you forget the goal of Christian morality you can study moral theologians, papal documents, and the *Catechism of the Catholic Church*, learn everything there is to know about Christian morality, and still struggle to live a good moral life. We must never forget that the goal of Christian morality is to live a holy life, a life that is purified from sin and darkness by our commitment to live as true followers of Christ. This is what motivates the saints to put into daily practice the moral principles and teachings taught by the Church. When we pursue this goal as all the great saints have before us, in whatever vocation God calls us to, we shall be passionate about living the moral life.

Disciples of Christ

The primary role and description of a Christian is that he or she is a disciple of Christ. And what is the primary characteristic of being a disciple? Jesus gives us the answer in the Gospel of John: "This is how all will know that you are my disciples, if you have love for one another" (13:35). Jesus teaches us, his disciples, the New Law, the Law of Love. He teaches us that the Old Law was meant for one thing, to teach us how to love. The moral life, discipleship, and love are all connected; they are all different ways of expressing the same reality. And that reality is that God created us to be a holy people in full communion with the Father, Son, and Holy Spirit, and with one another.

Here is a great mystery of the Christian life: Human beings do not create love; we simply tap into and share God's love. We must live in Christ so that he can live in us. We cannot be holy on our own power. We need God's love working in us and through us. The First Letter of John contains a beautiful expression of this truth.

> In this is love: not that we have loved God, but that he loved us and sent his Son as expiation for our sins. Beloved, if God so loved us, we also must love one another. No one has ever seen God. Yet, if we love one another, God remains in us, and his love is brought to perfection in us. This is how we know that we remain in him and he in us, that he has given us of his Spirit. . . . We know that we love the children of God when we love God and obey his commandments. For the love of God is this, that we keep his commandments. And his commandments are not burdensome. (4:10–13, 5:2–3)

Letting God's love fill us and flow through us is the only way that human beings will overcome sin and grow in holiness. It is the reason for which we were created and how we find our ultimate fulfillment and happiness.

The Ability to Love Is within Us

Saint Basil the Great is a Doctor of the Church who lived from 330 to 379 in Asia Minor. His writings have greatly influenced Christian doctrine. In this selection Basil talks about the spark of divine love that lives within us.

First, let me say that we have already received from God the ability to fulfill all his commands. We have no reason to resent them, as if something beyond our capacity were being asked of us. We have no reason either to be angry, as if we had to pay back more than we had received. When we use this ability in a right and fitting way, we lead a life of virtue and holiness. But if we misuse it, we fall into sin.

This is the definition of sin: the misuse of a power given us by God for doing good, a use contrary to God's commandments. On the other hand, the virtue that God asks of us is the use of the same powers based on a good conscience in accordance with God's commands.

Since this is so, we can say the same about love. Since we received a command to love God, we possess from the first moment of our existence an innate power and ability to love. The proof of this is not to be sought outside ourselves, but each one can learn this from himself and in himself. *(Detailed Rules for Monks)*

© Gene Plaisted

Vocation and Holiness

On our journey to holiness, we all have the same destination, but we can take different paths, or vocations, to get there. In the most general sense, a vocation is the call from God to share his love with others and grow in holiness. All

Christians share this common vocational call, grounded in the Sacraments of Baptism, the Eucharist, and Confirmation. Living that call happens in a variety of ways; these ways are responses to specific needs, to different states of life, and even to different temperaments. We must listen in prayer to how God is calling us to live our baptismal vocation and seek out opportunities to answer that call. The following are some examples of opportunities that are worth consideration:

There are many ways we can live out the vocational call that we receive through the Sacraments of Baptism, the Eucharist, and Confirmation. What vocational options are you most interested in?

- *A meaningful job* The most common calling is to share God's love with the world through employment that contributes to the good of society. Teachers, accountants, authors, medical workers, businesspeople, factory workers, media providers, support staff, managers, farmers, food service workers, and so many others share God's love by providing important goods and services with a joyful and caring attitude.

© Lorraine Swanson/istockphoto.com

- *Volunteer work* Society is full of special needs that require the response of dedicated volunteers. Volunteering to visit people who are sick and homebound, to provide meals and hospitality for people who are homeless and hungry, to help raise money for important charities, to work for pro-life issues, and to help build homes for needy families are some ways that people share God's love through volunteer work and organizations. If you are attracted to one of these needs more than others, it is probably a sign that God is calling you to volunteer to help with that need.

- *Service to the Church* The Church needs people to help in a variety of ministries, whether as a volunteer or a full-time lay ecclesial minister. God might be calling you to help in outreach ministry, catechetical ministry, or liturgical ministry.

- *Missionary activity* God calls some people to travel to foreign lands to share his love with people who have little knowledge or experience of Christians and Christianity.

This usually requires a commitment of several years or more.

- *Religious movements* Many different religious movements associated with the Church encourage and support our call to share God's love with others. For example, Catholic Charismatic Renewal focuses on the Gifts of the Holy Spirit. Communion and Liberation is a movement whose purpose is growth in Christian maturity and collaboration with the mission of Christ in all walks of life. Many other movements and programs like Teens Encounter Christ, Cursillo, LifeTeen, and religious Third Orders can help you to grow in holiness.

Vocation in the more specific sense is a lifelong commitment to live a holy life as an ordained minister, as a consecrated religious, in Christian Marriage, or in the dedicated single life. Although the baptismal vocational opportunities mentioned previously can and probably will change over a person's lifetime, the vocations of Marriage, the priesthood, the diaconate, religious life (brothers and sisters), and consecrated virgins are stable and lifelong. These vocations invite us into significant and life-changing encounters with God. Living them faithfully purifies us of selfishness, dishonesty, envy, conceit, and lust. They offer us profound ways of receiving and sharing God's love with spouses, family, religious communities, and the People of God. They challenge us to put our complete trust in God's saving power.

The vocation to the priesthood can be lived out in many ways: priests can be missionaries, they can teach in schools and universities, they can be chaplains in the military and in hospitals, and they can be parish pastors.

© Sébastien Cailleux/Sygma/Corbis

Many people believe that Christian morality is simply a big list of fun things that you are forbidden to do. But this is not what Christian morality is at all. Yes, God's Law forbids us from doing things that appear to be fun but in reality are harmful to us and others. But Christian morality is so much more than that; it is nothing less than the call to be perfect in holiness (see Matthew 5:48) as disciples of Christ. It is the way we invite God's love to live in us and through us. It is the way we grow in our communion with God and with one another. It leads us to true and eternal happiness. If people really understood what Christian morality truly was, how could anyone help but try her or his best to live it? ✝

grace

The free and undeserved gift of God's loving and active presence in the universe and in our lives, empowering us to respond to his call and to live as his adopted sons and daughters. Grace restores our loving communion with the Holy Trinity, lost through sin.

Article 48 Grace

During struggles with powerful moral temptations, some people find themselves asking, "Why is God doing this to me?" They might even feel that God is letting them be tempted beyond their ability to resist the temptation. Scripture and Tradition reveal otherwise. First, they teach that God is never the source of temptation. The Letter of James says: "No one experiencing temptation should say, 'I am being tempted by God'; for God is not subject to temptation to evil, and he himself tempts no one. Rather, each person is tempted when he is lured and enticed by his own desire" (1:13–14). The author of James tells us that we are tempted not by God but by our own passions and desires, the lingering effects of concupiscence.

Second, Scripture and Tradition reveal that God provides the means to resist every temptation or difficulty we face. We read the following in the First Letter to the Corinthians: "No trial has come to you but what is human. God is faithful and will not let you be tried beyond your strength; but with the trial he will also provide a way out, so that you may be able to bear it" (10:13). What Saint Paul is saying is that God gives us the **grace** we need to resist moral temptations and live the Commandments of the moral law. Grace comes from the Greek word *charis,* which can also mean "favor," "talent," or "gift." Theologically defined, grace is the free and undeserved gift of God's loving and active presence in the universe and in our lives, empowering us to respond to his call and to live

The Gifts of the Holy Spirit

The Gifts of the Holy Spirit are related to grace because they are also unmerited spiritual gifts bestowed on us by the Holy Spirit at Baptism and increased in us at Confirmation. Jesus possessed these gifts in their fullness. There are traditionally seven of these gifts, based on Isaiah 11:1–3:

- *Wisdom* Through wisdom, the wonders of nature, every event in history, and all the ups and downs of our lives take on deeper meaning and purpose. The wise person sees where the Holy Spirit is at work and is able to share that insight with others.

- *Understanding* The gift of understanding is the ability to comprehend how a person must live his or her life as a follower of Jesus. Through the gift of understanding, Christians realize that the Gospel tells them not just who Jesus is but also who *we* are.

- *Right judgment* Sometimes called counsel, the gift of right judgment is the ability to know the difference between right and wrong and then to choose what is good. It helps us to act on and live out what Jesus has taught.

- *Courage* Sometimes called fortitude, the gift of courage enables us to take risks and to overcome fear as we try to live out the Gospel of Jesus.

- *Knowledge* The gift of knowledge is the ability to comprehend the basic meaning and message of Jesus. Jesus revealed the will of God, his Father, and taught people what they need to know to achieve fullness of life and ultimately salvation.

- *Reverence* Sometimes called piety, the gift of reverence gives Christians a deep sense of respect for God. Through the gift of reverence, we can come before God with the openness and trust of small children, totally dependent on the One who created us.

- *Wonder and awe* The gift of wonder and awe in the presence of God is sometimes translated as "the fear of the Lord." Though we can approach God with the trust of little children, we are also often aware of his total majesty, unlimited power, and desire for justice.

as his adopted sons and daughters. Grace restores our loving communion with the Holy Trinity, lost through sin.

Grace is God's initiative in preparing us for salvation. It is at work in our soul to help us realize that we need to respond in faith to God's invitation to be in relationship with him. Grace does not take away human freedom but helps us to use our freedom in responding to God's offer of friendship and salvation. In a real sense, God's grace is the source of our freedom; it enables our free response and perfects it.

Although all three Divine Persons of the Trinity confer grace, the work of grace is often associated with the Third Person of the Trinity, the Holy Spirit. The *Catechism of the Catholic Church* talks about the Holy Spirit's infusing grace in our souls and that "grace includes the gifts that the Spirit grants us to associate us with his work, to enable us to collaborate in the salvation of others and in the growth of the Body of Christ, the Church" (2003).

© Alinari Archives/CORBIS

This famous painting by Raphael covers a wall in a room of the Vatican Museum. Can you see the Three Persons of the Trinity depicted? What is their relationship to the Eucharist depicted on the altar below?

Kinds of Grace

Article 4, "Justification and Sanctification," discussed how God's grace frees us from sin and sanctifies us, that is, it makes us holy. We call this kind of grace **sanctifying grace**. Through our Baptism, the Holy Spirit gives us sanctifying grace to heal our wounded soul and make us whole again. He confers on us the righteousness of God by uniting us to the Passion and Resurrection of Jesus Christ. Sanctifying grace make us sharers in God's own life and love. It is also called deifying grace or habitual grace because it is always at work within us, disposing us to live and act in accord with God's will.

There is nothing we human beings can do to merit the initial movements of grace in our lives, which causes our awareness of the need for God and leads to conversion. But once we have responded with faith to the Holy Spirit's initial promptings, we can merit for ourselves and other people all the graces needed to sustain our earthly life and to attain eternal life. The *Catechism of the Catholic Church (CCC)* identifies three kinds of these graces: **actual graces, sacramental graces,** and **special graces** (see 2000–2004).

Actual grace is the work of God in our lives, either preparing us for conversion or helping in our sanctification. An example of actual grace might be a person finding just the right Scripture passage that moves her to talk to a priest about joining the Church. Or it might come in the form of a friend who just happens to be there right when you need someone's support in making an important moral decision. Actual grace is the strength the Holy Spirit gives us to make it through the grief of losing a loved one. It is important to ask God in prayer for what we need to follow his will because he will always provide the grace we need.

Sacramental graces are the special gifts we receive through the Seven Sacraments. The Sacraments are effective signs, that is, they make the spiritual realities they symbolize present at the time and place they are celebrated. For example, in the Eucharist we receive the grace of being spiritually nourished by Christ's Word and with his Body and Blood. In the Sacrament of Confirmation, we receive the grace of being strengthened so we are better able to participate in the

sanctifying grace
A supernatural gift of God by which our sins are forgiven and we are made holy. It restores our communion with God.

actual graces
God's interventions and support for us in the everyday moments of our lives. Actual graces are important for conversion and for continuing growth in holiness.

sacramental graces
The gifts proper to each of the Seven Sacraments.

special graces
Gifts intended for the common good of the Church, also called charisms.

Catholic Wisdom

The Fruits of the Holy Spirit

The fruits of the Holy Spirit are the good qualities formed in us by the Holy Spirit as we grow in holiness. These qualities are perfected in us through God's grace active in our lives and virtuous living. The Tradition of the Church lists twelve fruits, an expanded version of Saint Paul's list in Galatians 5:22–23. The twelve fruits are these:

- charity
- joy
- peace
- patience
- kindness
- goodness
- generosity
- gentleness
- faithfulness
- modesty
- self-control
- chastity

Can you match each of the Seven Sacraments to their depictions in this stained-glass window? Can you describe the sacramental grace we receive in each Sacrament?

© Gene Plaisted

Church's mission. In the Sacrament of Anointing of the Sick, we receive the grace of being healed—spiritually, physically, or both.

Special graces, also called charisms, are given to us to build up the Church. Saint Paul teaches about these gifts in his letters, especially in his First Letter to the Corinthians:

> There are different kinds of spiritual gifts but the same Spirit; there are different forms of service but the same Lord; there are different workings but the same God who produces all of them in everyone. To each individual the manifestation of the Spirit is given for some benefit. To one is given through the Spirit the expression of wisdom; to another the expression of knowledge according to the same Spirit; to another faith by the same Spirit; to another gifts of healing by the one Spirit; to another mighty deeds; to another prophecy; to another discernment of spirits; to another varieties of tongues; to another interpretation of tongues. (12:4–10)

What special grace has God given to you for the good of the Body of Christ?

For Christian morality, tuning in to grace is crucial. Grace is the help God gives us to respond to our vocation to be his adopted daughters and sons. Without any effort on our part, grace connects us to the divine life of the Trinity. Through grace God's infinite love is there before we realize it, preparing us and inviting us to respond to the invitation to love him back. Although we don't earn grace by being good, grace helps us to be good. When we are grace filled, we are at our best, living holy and happy lives. ✝

Article 49 The Cardinal Virtues

Though grace is a free gift that helps us to live morally, virtues are moral guides that we need to develop by working at them. Virtues harness the power of grace within us. They are habits that firmly direct us in making good moral decisions. Like mastering skills in any sport, virtues capitalize on the abilities God has already placed within us. For example, most people have the physical potential to shoot a basket, to dribble a soccer ball, or to master a swimming stroke. When athletes first learn to do these things, someone had to show them the technique. As they practiced the technique, the skill became more natural, and they were able to play the

Other Virtues

The word *cardinal* is derived from the Latin *cardo*, meaning "pivot," something on which many other things depend. Thus the cardinal virtues of justice, prudence, temperance, and fortitude are the primary virtues on which many other virtues depend. If we develop these four good habits in our lives, many other virtuous habits are possible. For example, if we develop the virtue of temperance, it is easier to develop the virtues of patience and living a healthy lifestyle.

The following are some examples of virtues: compassion, honesty, chastity, charity, caring for the earth, caring for our bodies, expressing gratitude, and respecting life. The life of Christian virtue is an ongoing journey. Do you notice that when you practice a good habit it becomes easier to do other good things and to avoid bad habits?

© William Walsh/istockphoto.com

cardinal virtues
Based on the Latin word for "pivot," four virtues that are viewed as pivotal or essential for full Christian living: prudence, justice, fortitude, and temperance.

prudence
The cardinal virtue by which a person is inclined toward choosing the moral good and avoiding evil; sometimes called the rudder virtue because it helps steer the person through complex moral situations.

game without having to be preoccupied with the basic skills required.

People develop human virtues in a similar way. Everyone has the moral potential to live a virtuous life. But most people benefit from having these virtues explained to them and being shown how to live them out in daily life. Then the more we intentionally "practice" these virtues, the more they will become part of us, and we will naturally apply them to moral decisions we face. This article looks at the human virtues called the cardinal virtues and the next article considers the theological virtues.

Prudence, Temperance, Justice, and Fortitude

Human virtues are the virtues we develop by our own effort with the help of God's grace. They guide our intellect and our will in controlling our passions and in making good moral choices based on reason and faith. Four virtues play a pivotal role and accordingly are called **cardinal virtues**. They are prudence, justice, temperance, and fortitude. Every human virtue can be grouped around the cardinal virtues. As you develop the cardinal virtues in your life, you become

a person of moral character. To have character means that you do the right thing, even under difficult circumstances.

Prudence is the opposite of being impulsive. Acting impulsively is okay for a two-year-old. It may even be appropriate for a grown person in certain settings that call for creativity or spontaneity. But making moral decisions impulsively will get you into trouble. Prudence directs you to approach moral problems thoughtfully and objectively. Also called wise judgment, prudence relies heavily on our reason. In fact, Saint Thomas Aquinas called it "right reason in action"[1] (*CCC*, 1806). Prudence helps you to stop and think before you act.

Justice is the virtue concerned with giving both God and neighbor what is their due. It is the habit of taking into account the needs of others as much as your own needs. It takes determination and dedication to be a just person. Remember that God takes justice a step further than simple fairness. Fairness is doing an equal share of work; justice is

justice
The cardinal virtue concerned with the rights and duties within relationships; the commitment, as well as the actions and attitudes that flow from the commitment, to ensure that all persons—particularly those who are poor and oppressed—receive what is due them.

Pray It!

Prayer for a Virtuous Life

Good and gracious God,

When I feel the lure of excess
and crave too much of a good thing,
help me to develop temperance,
the self-control that gives my life balance and wholeness.

When I feel driven to act on impulse,
give me prudence,
the wisdom to stop and think before I act.

When I find that I am preoccupied with myself,
my own wants and worries,
help me to see others with eyes of compassion
and to reach out to them with loving justice.

When I face obstacles to living morally
that tempt me to move away from you,
give me fortitude,
the courage to overcome the temptation. Amen.

This painting by Raphael depicts the cardinal virtues. They are represented by four women: fortitude is holding an oak branch, prudence is looking in a mirror, temperance is holding reins, and justice is by herself, holding a sword.

© Brian Singer-Towns/Saint Mary's Press

temperance

The cardinal virtue by which one moderates his or her appetites and passions to achieve balance in the use of created goods.

fortitude

Also called strength or courage, the cardinal virtue that enables one to maintain sound moral judgment and behavior in the face of difficulties and challenges; one of the four cardinal virtues.

doing more because someone else can't. Justice is about loving and serving poor people and even loving your enemies.

Temperance is about balance in your life. You know that stress, greed, or sickness can come from too much of a good thing. The pleasures in life must be balanced with moderation. Too much play isn't good; neither is all work and no play. Exercise is good for our bodies; too much can lead to an obsession. Food is another good we must learn to balance. Healthy food nourishes our bodies and gives us pleasure, but too much food leads to obesity and too little food can lead to eating disorders. The virtue of temperance is about self-control and balance in all areas of our lives.

Fortitude is the moral virtue that strengthens us to overcome obstacles to living morally. It is easy to be good when we have no strong temptation in our lives. When you are not feeling the ecstasy of being in love, the Church's teaching on premarital sex makes perfect sense. If you are not angry, nonviolence is a worthy ideal. But when you are in the heat of any moment, whether it is sexual passion, anger, or some other strong feeling, fortitude gives you strength to overcome the temptation to ignore the moral law. It is the habit of doing the right thing even though part of you wants to do the wrong thing. Fortitude is also called moral courage or moral strength.

We must work hard to develop the cardinal virtues so that they become habitual ways of thinking and acting. We do this through education in morality and by deliberately making prudent, just, temperate, and courageous moral decisions. We have to persevere in this even when it is a struggle. The good news is that God is with us in our efforts to live virtuous lives. With God guiding our efforts through divine grace, the cardinal virtues will bring our moral lives to a higher level of integrity. ☦

Article 50 The Theological Virtues

Human virtues are habits that guide us in choosing good moral actions. But faith, hope, and love—the theological virtues—are different. They are the foundation from which all human virtues flow. They are the source of energy for perfecting our relationship with God. *Theological* means "of the study of God." These virtues are theological because in accepting them and using them, we are drawn into deeper knowledge of and relationship with the Holy Trinity. Faith, hope, and love flow from God and back to him, providing a sort of "power loop" of divine energy that we can tap into through our faith. They give life and meaning to all the other virtues.

This tomb carving is a representation of the theological virtues: faith, hope, and love. Can you determine which figure represents which virtue?

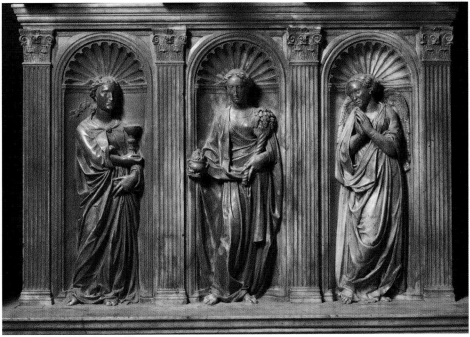

faith

In general, the belief in the existence of God. For Christians, the gift of God by which one freely accepts God's full Revelation in Jesus Christ. It is a matter of both the head (acceptance of God's revealed truth) and the heart (love of God and neighbor as a response to God's first loving us); also, one of the three theological virtues.

hope

The theological virtue by which we trust in the promise of God and expect from him both eternal life and the grace we need to attain it; the conviction that God's grace is at work in the world and that the Kingdom of God established by and through Jesus Christ is becoming realized through the workings of the Holy Spirit among us.

Through the virtues of faith, hope, and love, we grow in our understanding of God and we deepen our relationship with him.

Faith, Hope, and Love

Faith is belief in God. It is both a gift and a response. Faith is the gift of God inviting us to believe in him, never forcing our acceptance. Faith is also our response—we accept or reject the offer. Our belief in God affects every dimension of our lives; we can't just say we believe in God and leave it at that. As disciples of Christ, we must live our faith, confidently professing it and spreading it to others.

Hope in God is closely connected to our faith. It enables us to keep our eyes on the prize of Heaven and eternal life. It inspires us in this life, helping us to overcome discouragement. Even when a situation seems hopeless, maintaining our hope in God helps us to remember our ultimate destiny and gets us through difficulties. Hope, working together with faith and love, gives us confidence to live the higher purpose of our lives.

And then there is **love**, also called charity. This is the greatest of all the theological virtues. Love is the virtue that gives life to the Commandment to love God above all things, and our neighbor as ourself. "Beloved, let us love one another, because love is of God; everyone who loves is begotten by God and knows God. Whoever is without love does

© zbindere/istockphoto.com

The Centrality of the Theological Virtues

Since the beginning of Christianity, the greatest teachers among the Church Fathers have affirmed the centrality of faith, hope, and love in the life of the Christian. Saint Paul in his First Letter to the Corinthians (AD 55) summarizes his teaching on the importance of love with the simple but profound sentence:

> So faith, hope, and love remain, these three; but the greatest of these is love. (13:13)

Saint Augustine in his *Explanations of the Psalms* (AD 400) teaches that unlike most every other thing, the theological virtues cannot be taken from us:

> What are you going to give (to God), that you did not receive from him? . . . He gave you faith, hope, and love: these you can offer to him, these you can sacrifice. But plainly, everything else can be taken from you against your will by an enemy; but these cannot be taken from you unless you are willing. (55, 19)

Saint Gregory I in his *Homilies on Ezekiel* (AD 593) teaches why the theological virtues are always in us:

> In the hearts of the saints, the Holy Spirit, in respect to some virtues, remains always, but in respect to other virtues he comes only to go away again, and he goes away only to come again. For in faith, hope, and love, and in other virtues without which it is not possible to attain our heavenly homeland . . . he does not desert the hearts of the perfect. (1, 5, 11)

not know God, for God is love" (1 John 4:7–8). More than a feeling—even though feelings of love are wonderful—love is an attitude. At times we must go beyond feelings and will ourselves to love others. Love like this is possible because of God, and it makes all things possible.

The theological virtues are the foundation of Christian morality; they give the Christian moral life its unique character. God has implanted these virtues in our hearts, and we just need to draw upon their power. We do this through faith and prayer and especially the reception of the Eucharist and the Sacrament of Penance and Reconciliation. ✝

love

The human longing for God and a selfless commitment to supporting the dignity and humanity of all people simply because they are created in God's image. Also called charity, it is one of the three theological virtues.

Article 51 The Sacraments

"The moral life is spiritual worship" (*CCC*, 2031). What does the Church mean by this statement? It means that our worship of God is not limited to our liturgical celebrations. We also worship him by living a virtuous life. Saint Paul points to this in his Letter to the Romans, "I urge you therefore, brothers, by the mercies of God, to offer your bodies as a living sacrifice, holy and pleasing to God, your spiritual worship" (12:1). In other words, we offer God our praise, adoration, and sacrifice by living his Law of Love in our daily lives.

When it comes to our worship of God, the Seven Sacraments entrusted to the Church by Christ hold the highest place of honor. These "efficacious signs of grace" (*CCC*, 1131) were instituted by Christ to lead us to his Father by the power of the Holy Spirit. The visible rites by which the Sacraments are celebrated make present the grace which they signify in those people who receive them with faith and the proper disposition. The Sacraments are necessary for our salvation; they are necessary for us to live a moral life; they are necessary for us to grow in holiness. Our Christian moral life is nourished and strengthened by the liturgy and the celebration of the Sacraments. In this article we look at how each of the Seven Sacraments offers us the grace and strength to live a moral life.

How is living a good, moral life a way of worshipping God?

© Aldo Murillo/istockphoto.com

The Seven Sacraments and Morality

The Seven Sacraments help us to remember that Christ, whom we encounter through the life of the Church, is the Sacrament of salvation. Through the Sacraments we remember the life, ministry, and message of Jesus, and we celebrate his risen presence and saving power as it is made real in our lives. Here is a brief summary of each Sacrament and its connection to the moral life.

- *Baptism* Through the sanctifying grace received at Baptism we are welcomed into the Christian community, our sins—Original and personal—are forgiven, and we are spiritually reborn as a child of God. Our Baptism is the beginning of our Christian moral journey, and through it we receive the grace we need to turn our lives toward God and be faithful to his Commandments.

- *Confirmation* Through Confirmation the grace received at Baptism is perfected, strengthening our bond with the Church and enriching our lives with an outpouring of the Holy Spirit. We experience a growth in the Gifts of the Spirit to help us to live virtuous lives in loving service to others in the name of Christ.

- *Eucharist* The Eucharist is the source and summit of the moral life. Listening to the Word of God and receiving the Body and Blood of Christ nourishes and strengthens us to resist temptation and to make the sacrifices needed to share Christ's love and justice with the world. And we also bring our efforts at living virtuously to the Eucharist and offer them to God the Father in union with the sacrifice of Jesus, his Son.

This cross is decorated with a sculpture of Christ standing in a chalice. What is the symbolic meaning of this image? How is the Eucharist connected to living a moral life?

© Elio Ciol/CORBIS

- *Penance and Reconciliation* We will not be perfect in all our moral choices. Through the Sacrament of Penance and Reconciliation we receive the grace of God's forgiveness, cleansing us from our sin and releasing us from shame and guilt. The Sacrament reconciles us with God and with the Church. The next part of this book looks more deeply at the role forgiveness and reconciliation play in the moral life.

- *Anointing of the Sick* Through the grace received in the Sacrament of Anointing of the Sick, our suffering is united with Christ's Passion. We regain mental and physical health if that is God's will, and we are prepared for our death if that be his will. The Sacrament strengthens us to continue living virtuously even amid illness and physical suffering.

- *Matrimony* The grace received in the Sacrament of Matrimony helps a husband and wife to live the vocation of Christian marriage virtuously. It helps them to be faithful to each other in marriage and to be open to the gift of children. The Sacrament helps them to guide and educate their children to follow God's Commandments.

- *Holy Orders* The grace received in the Sacrament of Holy Orders helps bishops, priests, and deacons to live their clerical vocations virtuously. It enables them to live chastely and to love and serve God's people with all their heart and soul. The Sacrament helps them to be an example of moral living for the People of God and to guide his people into holiness.

The Power of Christ's Passion

This quote on the power of the Sacraments is from the writings of Saint Thomas Aquinas, the great theologian of the Middle Ages and a Doctor of the Church.

> Christ's good is communicated to all Christians, even as the power in the head is shared by all the members. This communication is effected by the sacraments of the Church, in which the power of Christ's Passion operates, the effect of which is the bestowal of grace for the remission of sins. (*Expositio in symbolum apostolicum*)

If we truly wish to live virtuous lives, we must participate in the sacramental life of the Church. Christ gave these Sacraments to the Church for our benefit, as an aid to living a holy life. If we desire and are open to the graces they provide, our moral journey will greatly benefit. ✝

Article 52 The Role of Conscience

God has given us several guides to assist us in moral living. We have his Revelation, transmitted through Scripture and Tradition and authentically interpreted and taught by the Magisterium, to teach us moral truth. We have natural law, the God-given ability that enables us to understand what to do and what to avoid. We have the witness of the saints, who inspire us by their heroic moral virtues. We have parents, friends, and trustworthy leaders who point us to the right moral choices. We have been referring to these moral guides throughout this book, and they are all important. However, these guides will fail to direct and influence our lives if we choose to ignore them. In order to live as God calls us to, we must allow these guides—especially natural law and God's Revelation transmitted through Scripture and Tradition and taught by the Magisterium—to form our conscience, and we must learn how to listen to and follow our conscience.

Conscience is at work through all stages of moral decision making. It helps people recognize that a particular choice or action has moral consequences to consider. For example, conscience will probably not be concerned about choosing what shirt or blouse to wear to school. But if that shirt or blouse conveys a verbal or nonverbal message of some kind our conscience will prompt us to consider the impact of that message on others. Conscience is also at work when people are making a moral decision. It helps them to apply reason in judging the most moral course of action in a particular situation. Finally, conscience makes a judgment about the moral correctness of specific act. If the act is

Our conscience is at work in all the stages of moral decision making. Our conscience's ultimate purpose is to make a judgment about the moral correctness of a specific act.

© DSGpro/istockphoto.com

yet to be performed, conscience will give moral certainty about the right choice to make. If the act has already been performed, we experience the inner peace that comes from having done the right thing or the guilt that comes from having acted immorally. A guilty conscience prompts us to take responsibility for our sinful actions and seek forgiveness and make reparation for any harm we have caused.

Conscience is not the moral opinion of the majority because large groups of people can often be wrong. Conscience is not just a feeling because feelings about moral decisions can change, but what is morally right stays the same. Conscience is not a little voice in your head telling you what to do (although some people might describe it that way). "A voice in your head" sounds like something outside of us is trying to intrude on our freedom. But conscience is not something foreign to us; it is part of us. The *Catechism* describes it as "a judgment of reason by which the human person recognizes the moral quality of a concrete act" (1796). Thus the quality of our conscience depends largely on how well we use our reason to understand Divine Law and whether we follow the moral judgments made based on reason and Divine Law. Let's look more closely at both of these conditions.

Conscience Formation

To use reason well in making moral judgments we must educate ourselves about Divine Law. This process is also called conscience formation. A well-formed conscience will lead you to make the right moral judgment, in keeping with God's Commandments. It is principled, honest, and truthful. Because a well-formed conscience is so important to our moral life, we have a serious obligation to educate our conscience well. Here are some proven ways to form your conscience:

- Study the doctrine of the Church to learn the moral truth revealed by God. Reading this textbook is a good start. However, our education in faith is a lifelong process that you must continue, especially as you encounter complex moral issues that this book could only briefly describe.
- Read and reflect on the Word of God in Scripture. God's Word is a "light for [our] path" (Psalm 119:105), and the

Facing the FACTS: A Moral Decision-Making Process

When facing a moral decision, having a process that takes into account the core principles of moral decision making can be helpful. Although there is no official process, some unofficial ones provide handy checklists you can use. This one uses an acronym: FACTS.

- *F*ind the facts. Identify the three elements of the moral decision: the object, the intention, and the circumstances. Be clear about what you are deciding, what your true intention is in making the decision, and what circumstances are affecting your freedom in making the decision.

- *A*ssess the alternatives. Consider all the possible actions that could be taken in responding to this situation. Do not leave any choice out because it seems too challenging.

- *C*onsider the consequences. For each alternative action identified, evaluate how that action would affect your relationships with God, with other people, and with yourself. Which action leads to the truest sharing of God's love?

- *T*hink about God's teachings. Be sure your conscience is properly formed before making this decision. What does God's revealed truth teach about this moral situation? How do the Ten Commandments and Christ's Law of Love apply?

- *S*eek spiritual support. As you consider your choice, ask the Holy Spirit for the gifts you need to make a good decision. Seek the wisdom of trusted spiritual mentors. Once your conscience is certain, draw strength from the Eucharist to carry out your decision.

more time we spend with it in study and prayer the more it influences our daily life and practice.

- Examine the moral choices you have made at the end of every day or every week. The more you practice identifying your good and bad decisions the more trained your conscience becomes at recognizing sinful choices before you make them.

- Read the lives of the saints and other holy people, both ancient and modern. Their stories of moral courage and integrity will inspire you in forming and following your conscience.

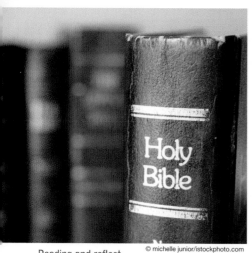
© michelle junior/istockphoto.com

Reading and reflecting on Holy Scripture are important ways of forming our conscience. What are some other important ways of properly forming our conscience?

- Receive the Sacraments of the Eucharist and Penance and Reconciliation regularly. The graces you receive from these Sacraments will strengthen your desire to seek moral truth and to follow it.

With a well-formed conscience, we are better prepared to respond to moral situations. When our conscience has been educated in the moral virtues, making good moral decisions comes more naturally. When our conscience has developed a habit of making good moral decisions in small matters we are better prepared to make good decisions in more serious matters. When our conscience is regularly exercised, we are better prepared to make a good moral decision in situations that call for a quick decision.

Obeying Your Conscience

When it comes to following our conscience there is one essential rule to follow: We must always obey the judgment of a certain conscience. When our conscience has been properly prepared and we are certain about the morally right course of action to take, then we must take that action. To do otherwise would be a sin. This doesn't mean that following our conscience will always be easy. There are times in most people's lives when they wish they did not have to follow their conscience. Following your conscience might mean sacrificing popularity, material wealth, or even your own safety (remember the martyrs). Christ himself faced these challenges but stayed true to his conscience despite them. So must we.

Keep in mind that a certain conscience is not always a correct conscience. When faced with a moral decision, conscience can make either a right judgment in keeping with reason and Divine Law or it can make an erroneous judgment that is not in keeping with reason and Divine Law. Occasionally someone's conscience can be erroneous through no fault of the person. Consider this example. A trusted tax authority tells someone that it is legal to take a certain tax credit and the person takes it. However, it turns out that the tax credit does not apply to that person and taking it is actually illegal. But the person taking the credit did not commit a sin because his conscience was in error through no fault of his own. Should he find out later that the tax credit was not legal, he would be morally responsible for correcting the mistake.

culpable
To be guilty of wrong-doing.

Most of the time, though, we are at least partially responsible for any sin committed due to an erroneous judgment by our conscience. This is because in most cases we could have prevented the ignorance that caused our conscience to make the wrong judgment. This ignorance might happen because we never took the time to study the teachings of the Gospel, or because we rejected the Church's moral authority, or because we let ourselves be influenced by the bad example of other people. It could also happen because we let our conscience become dulled by sinful habits

Live It!

Teens' Experience in Following Their Conscience

Teens are aware of the role that conscience plays in their lives. In describing how they experience their conscience some teens say it as an inner voice, while others describe it as a feeling in their gut. One student explains it like this: "When I do something that is wrong, or even think about doing something that is wrong, I get a sick feeling in my stomach. It is really important that I listen to that feeling because it is God's way of telling me what is right."

When asked why it is important to follow our conscience, one teen explained her own experience this way: "I know when I am not following my conscience because I start feeling less happy," says one student. Another says, "Following your conscience is important so that you can feel good about yourself and be proud of yourself before God. If I don't follow my conscience I feel shameful and don't like myself."

The teens we asked also showed deep insight in identifying the people or sources who have been important in forming their consciences. The most frequently mentioned sources are

- parents
- the Bible
- religion classes
- real-life experiences

How do you experience your conscience speaking to you? Who or what do you turn to in forming your conscience?

or vices. When our conscience leads us into erroneous moral judgments because of these things we are still **culpable** for the sins we commit.

Our conscience is the greatest guide God has given us for living the moral life. It is the law that he has inscribed on our hearts (see Jeremiah 31:33). Properly formed it will faithfully direct us on our journey to holiness. Using it only requires that we take the time to be still, turn inward, reflect on our life, and listen for the interior voice directing us on how best to love God, love our neighbor, and love ourselves. ☩

Review

1. What is the primary characteristic of being a disciple of Jesus Christ?

2. Describe four different opportunities that Christians have to live their baptismal vocation.

3. Define grace.

4. Name three kinds of grace and give an example for each kind.

5. What are the four cardinal virtues, and why are they important for living a moral life?

6. How are the theological virtues different from the cardinal virtues?

7. What does it mean to say, "The moral life is spiritual worship"?

8. Choose three Sacraments and explain how the graces of each Sacrament are connected to living a moral life.

9. Why is a well-formed conscience important in Christian morality?

10. Describe three things that you can do to form your conscience.

Part 2

Forgiveness and Reconciliation

Corrie ten Boom belonged to a Dutch family who were part of the Dutch resistance during World War II. In her book *The Hiding Place,* she tells how her family created a small secret closet that could hide up to six people, and they used it to hide Jewish people during Nazi searches. Her family was betrayed and sent to concentration camps, where her father and sister later died. Eventually Corrie was freed. Years later, after speaking about forgiveness at a Church service, she met a German man whom she recognized as a guard at the concentration camp where her father had died. He thanked her for her message and held out his hand to shake hers. Corrie was so filled with anger that she could not bring herself to shake his hand. Recognizing her difficulty in extending forgiveness, Corrie said a prayer, asking Jesus to forgive him. As she then shook his hand, she had an extraordinary feeling and something like an electric current went down her arm and into the man. Suddenly she was filled with love for the man, a love that did not come from her. She realized that along with the command to forgive your enemies, Jesus also gives the love itself.

The articles in this final part consider more closely the powerful role forgiveness plays in Christian morality. The Gospel calls us to both seek forgiveness and give forgiveness. We can seek forgiveness and reconciliation with God and the Church through the Sacrament of Penance and Reconciliation. We may also have to seek forgiveness from the people our sin has hurt and make reparation for the harm we have caused them. Granting forgiveness to others who have harmed us is just as important and possibly even more difficult. But until we have forgiven those who have hurt us, we cannot experience the fullness of God's forgiveness for ourselves.

The articles in this part address the following topics:

53 The Gospel Call to Forgiveness

His only crime was calling for people to be faithful to their religious heritage and calling for justice for the poor. He was arrested by the leaders of his religion and brought before them, accused of crimes against their religion—in a secret hearing in the middle of the night! Those religious leaders brought him before their local governor and falsely accused him of planning a rebellion against the government. The governor, despite having no personal knowledge of the man and calling for no other witnesses, had him publicly humiliated and brutally whipped. When this punishment wasn't enough to placate the religious leaders, the governor ordered the man to be crucified—a torturous, prolonged death meant to discourage anyone else from committing the same crimes.

Despite all this—the unjust accusations, the secret trials, the brutal treatment, the torturous death—the man forgave his executioners while hanging on the cross. He prayed, "Father, forgive them, they know not what they do" (Luke 23:34). The man, of course, is Jesus Christ, the Son of God. Throughout his earthly ministry, he preached about the importance of forgiveness, and he lived what he preached right up until the end of his earthly life.

From his agony on the cross, Jesus forgives those who crucified him. In what other ways did he teach us about the importance of forgiveness?

Contrast the value that Jesus placed on forgiveness with the value placed on revenge portrayed by many heroes in books and movies. The basic action book or film plot goes like this: The hero gets falsely accused or someone close to the hero gets hurt or killed or abducted by villains. The hero vows to get revenge and tracks the evil people down. After overcoming many obstacles and dangers, the hero confronts the villains, brutalizes them, and very often kills them—the more violent and bloody the better—and the reader or the audience erupts into cheers.

Let's be honest, sometimes revenge seems so satisfying and so right. So why doesn't Jesus endorse it? Why did he preach exactly the opposite? Why was he so emphatic that we must seek and grant forgiveness?

Seeking Forgiveness

Recall a spiritual truth discussed in article 11, "Sin in the New Testament": Every human being except Jesus and his mother, Mary, is guilty of sin and subject to death because of this. What is even more unfortunate than being guilty of sin is denying our sinfulness. Denying our sin is easy to do; whether the cause is pride or shame, we find it hard to admit to God, ourselves, and other people that we have missed the mark. This denial is tragic because we cannot ask for forgiveness until we admit that we are sinners. And only by seeking God's forgiveness will we find the healing we need to repair the damage to heart and soul caused by our sin.

This is why Jesus has such high praise for those who acknowledge their sin and seek forgiveness. The Gospel of Luke tells about a time when Jesus is invited to the house of a Pharisee for dinner (see 7:36–50). While at dinner a woman, who is a known sinner, comes into the house and bathes Jesus' feet with her tears, wipes them with her hair, and rubs them with ointment. Her wordless actions express her deep sorrow for her sins and the desire to be forgiven. The Pharisee is shocked that Jesus allows this sinful woman to even touch him. After telling a parable about debtors whose debts were forgiven, Jesus concludes by telling the Pharisee, "So I tell you, her many sins have been forgiven; hence, she has shown great love. But the one to whom little is forgiven, loves little" (7:47). In praising the woman, Jesus makes a connection between forgiveness and love. Those who admit their sin and seek forgiveness experience an increase of love in their hearts: love for God, love for themselves, and love for others.

The Gospel of Christ calls us to seek forgiveness. We see this call expressed at the beginning of the Church. After receiving the Holy Spirit at Pentecost, Peter speaks to the crowds and shares the Good News of Jesus' life, death, and Resurrection (see Acts of the Apostles 2:14–39). Afterward the crowds ask Peter and the other Apostles how they should respond. Peter says, "Repent and be baptized, every one of

Judging Other People

Jesus Christ commands us to be forgiving people. But does that also mean that we should overlook the wrong things that other people do? What right do we have to tell friends who are shoplifting, or drinking underage, or involved in premarital sex that their actions are sinful? Didn't Jesus himself say, "Stop judging, that you may not be judged" (Matthew 7:1)?

The truth is that we cannot ignore the sinful acts of others. Caring for others means we want the best for them, and that means a life free from sin. We would warn our friends if their reckless driving endangers their physical well-being. It is even more important to warn friends about the danger of sinful acts that endanger their spiritual well-being, their full communion with God in this life and the next. Sin is real and its negative effects are real; encouraging others to avoid sin is truly an act of love.

There is an old saying, "love the sinner, hate the sin" (see how Jesus treats the woman caught in adultery, John 8:1–11). This is what Jesus meant when he said, "Stop judging." He meant never stop loving someone because of their sinful acts. When we take the difficult step of warning another person that something they are doing is objectively wrong, we must always do it with an attitude of loving concern. We should pledge our support and friendship and never condemn the person or threaten to stop caring for him or her.

We live in a culture that says we should be tolerant of other people, no matter what they do. But tolerance is not a higher value than the Law of Christ. Being tolerant of sinful actions only leads to pain, chaos, and the spread of evil. We must always remind one another of the eternal truth revealed by Christ; this is not being intolerant or judgmental.

you, in the name of Jesus Christ for the forgiveness of your sins; and you will receive the gift of the holy Spirit" (2:38). The same is true for us today. Those who are unbaptized must seek forgiveness through the Sacrament of Baptism, and those who are baptized who have committed serious sin must seek forgiveness through the Sacrament of Penance and Reconciliation. When we do this, God's love will heal our wounded souls and fill our empty hearts.

Giving Forgiveness

Forgiveness has another crucial side. We must not only seek forgiveness from God and others but also be willing to forgive those who have sinned against us. These two sides of forgiveness are spiritually inseparable. Jesus teaches this truth several times in the Gospels. Consider the parable of the unforgiving servant in the Gospel of Matthew. In this parable a king forgives a large debt owed to him by one of his servants. But then this servant goes out and has a fellow servant who owes him a much smaller amount thrown into prison. When the king finds out about this, he angrily summons the first servant before him. "You wicked servant!" says the king. "I forgave you your entire debt because you begged me to. Should you not have had pity on your fellow servant, as I had pity on you?" (18:32–33).

Jesus' point in telling the parable is this: We are like the first servant; through the forgiveness of our sins, God has erased the huge debt caused by our sin. Without God's forgiveness, all sin leads to eternal death and separation from God. How then can we not be merciful and forgive those who have sinned against us? Jesus makes this point in teaching his disciples the Lord's Prayer: "And forgive us our sins / for we ourselves forgive everyone in debt to us" (Luke 11:4). In still another

Asking for forgiveness requires honesty and humility. Giving forgiveness requires trust, courage, and humility. Which is more challenging for you: to ask for forgiveness or to forgive someone who has hurt you?

© Ryan Lane/istockphoto.com

Catholic Wisdom

The Saints on Forgiveness

"No one heals himself by wounding another." (Saint Ambrose)

"There are many kinds of alms the giving of which helps us to obtain pardon for our sins; but none is greater than that by which we forgive from our heart a sin that someone has committed against us." (Saint Augustine)

"The saints rejoiced at injuries and persecutions, because in forgiving them they had something to present to God when they prayed to him." (Saint Teresa of Ávila)

reconciliation

The process of restoring broken relationships with God, with the Church, and with people who were directly offended by our sins.

place, he says: "Stop judging and you will not be judged. Stop condemning and you will not be condemned. Forgive and you will be forgiven" (Luke 6:37). All these teachings of Jesus lead to one inescapable conclusion: God's forgiveness of our sins depends on whether we forgive other people's sins against us. Put another way, it is a sin to withhold our forgiveness from someone who sincerely asks us for it. ✝

Article 54 Seeking Forgiveness and Reconciliation

The movie *The Mission* (Warner Home Video, 1992) is a powerful story about forgiveness and **reconciliation**. The movie is set during a time when Spanish Jesuit missionaries are establishing missions in the South American jungle to evangelize the native people living there. Part of the story is centered on a mercenary and slave trader named Mendoza who kills his brother in a jealous rage. Overcome with guilt and remorse, he seeks forgiveness from God and from the native people he had previously enslaved. In a powerful scene, Mendoza does penance by climbing a treacherous waterfall, weighed down by the former tools of his trade, his weapons and armor. When he finally reaches the top, the native warriors have to choose between killing this former enemy and forgiving him. They choose to forgive him, and in a symbolic act cut off his armor and weapons and throw them over the waterfall. Having received the forgiveness of God and of the people he had sinned against, God's love fills Mendoza's heart and he joins the Jesuit order and becomes a missionary, serving the native people.

Seeking forgiveness and reconciliation may indeed involve dramatic moments such as those portrayed in *The Mission*. But for faithful

Movies like *The Mission* emphasize the importance of forgiveness on our journey toward God. What other movies have you seen in which forgiveness is an important theme?

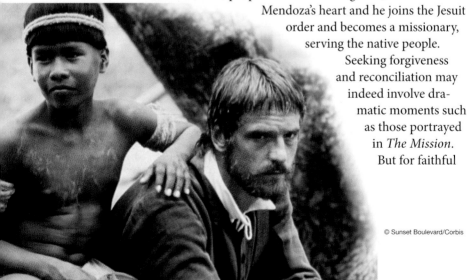

Christians, it often involves offenses much less serious than slave trading, sins such as white lies, gossip, cheating, and minor envies. But just because these sins may be less serious does not mean that they are harmless to our spiritual health. Venial sins that go unconfessed can easily become vices

Conducting an Examination of Conscience

A regular examination of conscience is a good way to see if our conscience is prompting us to seek forgiveness. Here is a simple one based on the two Great Commandments.

Love of God

- Is there anything that I am allowing to take God's place in my life?
- Do I pray regularly, and when I do pray, do I give my full attention to my prayer?
- Do I attend Mass and receive the Eucharist every week? Do I keep Sunday holy?
- Am I making a good effort to grow in my relationship with God by receiving the Sacrament of Penance and Reconciliation, spiritual reading, retreats, and other spiritual practices?
- Am I always reverent to God in my words and actions?

Love of Neighbor

- Have I treated anyone with disrespect, especially my parents, brothers and sisters, teachers, and other people in authority?
- Have I obeyed the rules and laws of my school, state, and country?
- Have I harmed another person intentionally or through my careless actions? Have I been unkind or cruel to others in thought, word, or deed?
- Have I harmed another person's dignity by engaging in gossip or spreading demeaning stories about the person?
- Have I protected my chastity at all times? Have I viewed pornography, engaged in lustful thoughts, or been sexually active in any way outside of marriage?
- Have I been truthful in all situations calling for the truth? Have I cheated or been dishonest in any way?
- Have I been envious of someone else in any way?
- Have I participated in or supported another person's sinful actions?
- Have I been of service to others who I was in a position to help? Have I reached out in some way to people in need?
- Have I encouraged others to avoid sin?

contrition
To have hatred for our sin and a commitment not to sin again.

and lead to more serious sin. We must not wait until habits of unrepented sin lead us to commit a sin so serious that it causes a complete breakdown of our relationship with God and the people we love, as it did for Mendoza.

If we humans have the tendency to deny our sinfulness, what breaks through the denial and prompts us to seek forgiveness and reconciliation? It is the voice of conscience, that inner guide God has placed in every human heart. If our conscience is dull and poorly formed, it may take the impact of a serious sin for us to hear its call to repentance. That is why we must be attentive to our conscience and see that it is properly formed (see article 52, "The Role of Conscience"). Two good ways to be attentive to our conscience is through a regular examination of conscience and by regular reception of the Sacraments of the Eucharist and of Penance and Reconciliation.

Seeking Forgiveness from God

Our relationship with God suffers when we are in a state of unrepented sin. If the sins are venial sins, our relationship with God has been weakened but has not been broken. When we realize that we are guilty of a venial sin, we should confess it to God in prayer and ask for his forgiveness with a commitment not to sin again. Recognizing and turning away from our sin and committing not to sin again is called **contrition**, and having a contrite heart is essential when asking God for forgiveness. Venial sins do not require that we receive the Sacrament of Penance and Reconciliation, but it is strongly recommended that we also confess our minor faults in the Sacrament.

When we commit a mortal sin, our relationship with God is ruptured because we have intentionally turned away from God through a conscious and willful choice to disobey his Commandments. Once we realize that we have committed a mortal sin and are contrite, we should ask for God's forgiveness in our private prayer and then confess our sins and receive absolution in the Sacrament of Penance and Reconciliation as soon as we can. When we are guilty of mortal sin, receiving the Sacrament is the sure way of reconciliation with God and with the Church.

It is natural to wonder, "Why do I have to confess my sins to a priest?" This question has many possible answers, but let's consider two important reasons. First, the priest is the visible sign of the presence of Christ himself. Christ shares the power to forgive sins with the bishops of the Church (see John 20:23), and priests—and only priests—share the bishops' power to forgive sins. So when the priest absolves us from our sins in the Sacrament of Penance and Reconciliation, it is Christ himself who is forgiving us. Second, because human beings are creatures with bodies and souls, all the Sacraments have both physical and spiritual realities. The visible, physical elements of the Sacraments signify the spiritual realities made present through the visible rites and the power of Christ and the Holy Spirit. In the Sacrament of Penance and Reconciliation, the physical elements include the confession of the person's sins to the priest and the priest laying hands on the person while saying

Pray It!

Act of Contrition

An Act of Contrition is a prayer expressing our remorse for the sins we have committed and our resolve to keep from repeating these sins in the future. The following Acts of Contrition may be said during the Sacrament of Penance and Reconciliation, but we can also pray them whenever we are aware of the presence of sin in our lives.

My God,
I am sorry for my sins with all my heart.
In choosing to do wrong and failing to do good,
I have sinned against you whom I should love above all things.
I firmly intend, with your help, to do penance,
to sin no more, and to avoid whatever leads me to sin.
Our Savior Jesus Christ suffered and died for us.
In his name, my God, have mercy. Amen.

Lord Jesus, Son of God,
have mercy on me, a sinner. Amen.

Lord Jesus,
you chose to be called the friend of sinners.
By your saving death and Resurrection, free me from my sins.
May your peace take root in my heart
and bring forth a harvest of love, holiness, and truth. Amen.

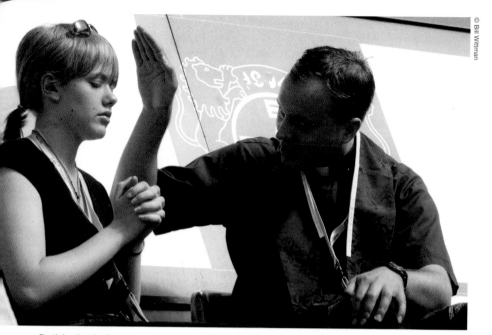

© Bill Wittman

Participating in the Sacrament of Penance and Reconciliation must be a regular part of our spiritual life. Through this Sacrament we come to know the healing and forgiving love of God.

the words of **absolution**. The physical act of telling your sins to the priest and then the extension of the priest's hands over your head while you hear the words of forgiveness "in the name of the Father, and of the Son, and of the Holy Spirit" is a profound part of the healing process. This is because, through the action of the Holy Spirit, the visible elements communicate and put us in touch with the spiritual reality of God's forgiveness of our sins.

Seeking Forgiveness from Others

Receiving absolution takes away our sin but does not repair the harm caused to other people or even the harm we may have caused ourselves. So after confessing our sin, we must still seek to repair the harm caused by our sin and to grow in moral virtue, especially the virtue needed to avoid the same sin in the future. In the Sacrament of Penance and Reconciliation, the priest directs us to perform certain acts to satisfy this need. This satisfaction is called our **penance**. The penance assigned by the priest confessor could be prayer, a spiritual discipline, or acts intended to heal our relationships with the people who were harmed by our sins.

The penance we receive from the priest is not the only way we can seek forgiveness from others and make reparation for our sin. In fact, after we realize that we have directly sinned against another person and are truly sorry for the harm we have caused, we can express our sorrow to the person as soon as is reasonable. When making our apology, we must exercise the virtues of prudence and humility. For example, we should apologize in person rather than through a text message. This could be misunderstood to mean that our apology isn't sincere. Instead we should apologize when we have privacy and time to talk. We will want to make the apology as positive as possible and not compound the hurt by having it appear insincere or poorly thought out. If necessary, we can seek advice from a trusted friend or counselor about how best to express our sorrow and ask for forgiveness.

Keep in mind that we may also need to make reparation in some concrete ways. If we steal something, we need to return it or make some other compensation of equal value. If we harm someone's reputation, we can set the record straight by telling people we were wrong in what we said about the person. If we are unsure about how to make reparation, we can also ask the person we have sinned against how we might compensate for our offense. We are not required, however, to make amends in any way that would harm ourself or another person.

absolution

An essential part of the Sacrament of Penance and Reconciliation in which the priest pardons the sins of the person confessing, in the name of God and the Church.

penance

In general, an attitude of the heart in which one experiences regrets for past sin and commits to a change in behaviors or attitudes. In the Sacrament of Penance and Reconciliation, the priest assigns penitents a penance to help them make amends for their sins. Particular acts of penance may include spiritual disciplines such as prayers or fasting.

© Peter Bernik/shutterstock.com

When we seek forgiveness from another person, our apology must be sincere. If we are not sincere, what is the likely or probable result?

Expressing our sorrow for our sins to the people we have hurt and making reparation for the damage caused by our sin is part of the healing process. We cannot control whether the other person chooses to forgive us. We can only do our best to express our sorrow and leave the rest to the work of the Spirit; some healing takes a great deal of time. We will get better at expressing our sorrow with practice; let us not compound our sin by being too proud to ask for forgiveness. ✝

Article 55 Granting Forgiveness

On October 2, 2006, an Amish community experienced the unthinkable. A man entered an Amish schoolhouse in Nickel Mines, Pennsylvania. He took ten young girls, ages six to thirteen years old, hostage. Police arrived and within minutes the man had shot all ten girls and then shot and killed himself. Five of the girls died, and the other five were severely injured.

Then something happened that many people considered miraculous and some others considered foolish. The people in the Amish community refused to condemn the killer and reached out in compassion to his family. On the day of the shooting, one Amish grandfather was heard to say, "We must not think evil of this man." Amish neighbors comforted the killer's widow, parents, and parents-in-law and explicitly offered them forgiveness. Members of the community attended the killer's funeral and set up a charitable fund for his family.

This Amish community took Jesus' words on forgiveness seriously. They have given us a powerful example of the importance of forgiving others. This doesn't mean that they didn't experience extreme pain and grief, quite the contrary. Said one authority on Amish faith: "The hurt is very great. But they don't balance the hurt with hate." Another counselor made the point that because the Amish can express their forgiveness, and because they do not seek revenge, they are better able to concentrate on their own healing.

© JASON REED/Reuters/Corbis

The Effects of Failing to Forgive

When we refuse to forgive others who have sinned against us, we hang on to resentments and the feelings of pain, sadness, and anger that accompany them. We may wish to harm the other person in retaliation. But the saints and spiritual leaders teach that it is important to forgive people who have hurt us even if they have not asked for our forgiveness. "Remember," someone once said, "that reconciliation takes two, but forgiveness only requires one." We saw Jesus practicing this on the cross; he forgave the people who crucified him before they even asked for forgiveness. So why should we forgive someone who has hurt us, even if the person has not asked us for forgiveness?

The answer of many authorities—both spiritual and medical—is because when we hold on to past hurts and refuse to forgive, we only continue to suffer ourselves. Medical researchers have traced the lack of forgiveness to physical conditions such as higher blood pressure, depression, anxiety, chronic pain, and higher risk of alcohol and substance

After the tragic murder of five young girls in 2006, the Amish community of Nickel Mines, Pennsylvania, showed the world the true meaning of forgiveness.

"Forgive Them Anyway"

This simple but profound reflection is associated with Blessed Mother Teresa of Calcutta and is based on a reflection written for students by Kent Keith. It goes to the heart of why we must forgive and love others, even if our love is not returned.

The Paradoxical Commandments

1. People are illogical, unreasonable, and self-centered. Forgive them anyway.
2. If you do good, people will accuse you of selfish, ulterior motives. Do good anyway.
3. If you are successful, you will win false friends and true enemies. Succeed anyway.
4. The good you do today will be forgotten tomorrow. Do good anyway.
5. Honesty and frankness make you vulnerable. Be honest and frank anyway.
6. The biggest men and women with the biggest ideas can be shot down by fearful people. Think big anyway.
7. People favor underdogs but follow only top dogs. Fight for a few underdogs anyway.
8. What you spend years building may be destroyed overnight. Build anyway.
9. People really need help but may attack you if you do help them. Help people anyway.
10. Give the world the best you have and you'll get kicked in the teeth. Give the world the best you have anyway.

abuse. When someone sins against us, we often experience psychological and spiritual trauma. The more serious this trauma is, the more potentially damaging is the physical suffering we experience when that hurt goes unhealed.

However, the most important reason for forgiving others is because it is crucial to our spiritual well-being. Holding on to resentments and thoughts of revenge damages our relationship with God. When we live with anger and hate, we cannot be in full communion with God, who is all-loving. Article 53, "The Gospel Call to Forgiveness," discusses how Jesus made the connection between divine forgiveness and our forgiveness of others. God does not withhold forgiveness from us, but when we refuse to forgive others, we prevent ourselves from accepting his forgiving love. In a sense, when we withhold forgiveness from those who have hurt us, we are choosing our own spiritual suffering.

The process of forgiveness and reconciliation is often a difficult one. Our hurt and resentment can make forgiveness nearly impossible. We can move forward only with the help of God.

From Hurt and Resentment to Forgiveness and Healing

In general, our culture is not a forgiving culture. This might be one reason that forgiving people who have hurt us seems like a foreign concept to many people. When true forgiveness is practiced, as it was in the case of the Amish community in Pennsylvania, some people find it difficult to believe it is even real. Although it is sometimes hard to understand and sometimes even harder to live, true forgiveness should be the norm for Christians, as Christ commands. When you find it hard to practice forgiveness— whether the hurt is great or small—here are some suggestions to move forward:

© Igor Balasanov/istockphoto.com

- Do not think of yourself as a victim. Do not let the person who has hurt you continue to control your life. You are a beloved child of God who has God's grace to strengthen you. Do the right thing—forgive and move on.

- Allow yourself to feel the pain of being hurt. Some people never get to forgiveness because they will not admit to being hurt. This is especially true for men.

- Make a decision to forgive. Forgiveness is not a feeling; it is a choice. You do not need to wait until you stop hurting to forgive.

- Do not wait for the person to change or to come to you and ask for forgiveness. Doing so only continues to put you in the role of the victim. In prayer, ask for the Holy Spirit's grace to strengthen you and guide you. Pray for the willingness to forgive when you find yourself not wanting to forgive someone. ✝

Live It!

Teens Discuss the Importance of Forgiveness

Teens agree that one of life's greatest challenges is forgiving someone who has hurt us. This is especially true when it comes to friends and family. We expect our friends and family to be faithful and loving, so when they are unfaithful or unloving the hurt can be profound. One student told a story about a friend who spread some unflattering rumors about her. When she confronted her friend initially, her friend denied spreading the rumors. Days passed and other friends were taking sides and not talking to one another. The student realized she would have to take the first step to try to mend the situation. So she talked to her friend heart to heart and they were able to reconcile. Her conclusion: "Forgiving my friend was the best decision I've ever made because it made our relationship stronger and healthier."

Students also realize that they are only hurting themselves by refusing to forgive. Another student told the story of how a friend's father deeply hurt the family through his sins of adultery and physical abuse. The friend was very angry and depressed because of her father's actions and told the student that she was never going to forgive her father. Several months after this conversation, the friend told the student that she had decided to forgive her father. She said that her father had repented of his sins and that the family decided to give him one more chance. But even if he doesn't change, the friend said, I have to forgive him so that I can free myself of my anger and move on.

The stories of forgiveness told by these teens show the importance of God's gifts of faith, hope, and love. What role has forgiveness played in your life? Is there someone whom you need to forgive?

Review

1. Why is it so important that we ask for God's forgiveness of our sins?

2. Give two examples from the Gospels in which Jesus teaches about the importance of forgiving those who have sinned against us.

3. How must we ask God's forgiveness for mortal sins?

4. What are some things to keep in mind when seeking forgiveness from other people?

5. What is the potential effect on ourselves when we fail to forgive others? What is the potential effect on ourselves when we extend forgiveness to others?

6. What are some things people can do to start the process of forgiveness?

Glossary

A

abortion The deliberate termination of a pregnancy by killing the unborn child. It is a grave sin and a crime against human life. *(page 187)*

absolution An essential part of the Sacrament of Penance and Reconciliation in which the priest pardons the sins of the person confessing, in the name of God and the Church. *(page 264)*

actual graces God's interventions and support for us in the everyday moments of our lives. Actual graces are important for conversion and for continuing growth in holiness. *(page 237)*

adulation Excessive flattery, praise, or admiration for another person. *(page 150)*

adultery Sexual activity between two persons, at least one of whom is married to another. Prohibited by the Sixth Commandment. *(page 222)*

almsgiving Freely giving money or material goods to a person who is needy, often by giving to a group or organization that serves poor people. It may be an act of penance or of Christian charity. *(page 179)*

annulment The declaration by the Church that a marriage is null and void, that is, it never existed as a sacramental union. Catholics who divorce must have the marriage annulled by the Church to be free to marry once again in the Church. *(page 218)*

artificial insemination The process by which a man's sperm and a woman's egg are united in a manner other than natural sexual intercourse. In the narrowest sense, it means injecting sperm into a woman's cervical canal. The procedure is morally wrong because it separates intercourse from the act of procreation. *(page 225)*

Asherah (also called Astarte or Ashtoreth) The Canaanite goddess of love and fertility, often represented by a serpent and worshipped in sacred groves. She was considered a false god by the Israelites but also worshipped by them when they fell away from the one true God. *(page 83)*

atheist; atheism One who denies the existence of God; the denial of the existence of God. *(page 88)*

B

Baal The Canaanite god of rain and vegetation, often represented by a bull and worshipped in the "high places." He was considered a false god by the Israelites but worshipped by them when they fell away from the one, true God. *(page 83)*

beatitude Our vocation as Christians, the goal of our existence. It is true blessedness or happiness which we experience partially here on earth and perfectly in Heaven. *(page 19)*

blasphemy Speaking, acting, or thinking about God, Jesus Christ, the Virgin Mary, or the saints in a way that is irreverent, mocking, or offensive. It is a sin against the Second Commandment. *(page 99)*

C

calumny Ruining the reputation of another person by lying or spreading rumors. It is also called slander and is a sin against the Eighth Commandment. *(page 149)*

canon law The name given to the official body of laws which provide good order in the visible body of the Church. *(page 46)*

capital sins Seven sins that are particularly harmful because they lead to and reinforce other sins and vices. The seven are traditionally called pride, covetousness (greed), envy, anger (wrath), gluttony, lust, and sloth. *(page 68)*

cardinal virtues Based on the Latin word for "pivot," four virtues that are viewed as pivotal or essential for full Christian living: prudence, justice, fortitude, and temperance. *(page 240)*

catechism A popular summary, usually in book form, of Catholic doctrine about faith and morals and commonly intended for use within formal programs of catechesis. *(page 39)*

catechist A person called by God to the ministry of the education and formation of Christians by teaching others the essentials of Christian doctrine and forming them as disciples of Jesus Christ. *(page 126)*

chastity The virtue by which people are able successfully and healthfully to integrate their sexuality into their total person; recognized as one of the fruits of the Holy Spirit. Also, one of the vows of the consecrated life. *(page 209)*

circumstances The specific conditions or facts affecting a moral decision. Circumstances can increase or decrease the goodness or evil of an action. *(page 64)*

civil authorities Leaders of public groups that are not religious institutions, particularly government leaders. *(page 130)*

civil disobedience Deliberate refusal to obey an immoral demand from civil authority or an immoral civil law. *(page 134)*

common good Social conditions that allow for all citizens of the earth, individuals and families, to meet basic needs and achieve fulfillment. *(page 71)*

commutative justice This type of justice calls for fairness in agreements and contracts between individuals. It is an equal exchange of goods, money, or services. *(page 161)*

conciliar Something connected with an official council of the Church, normally an Ecumenical Council such as the Second Vatican Council. *(page 164)*

concupiscence The tendency of all human beings toward sin, as a result of Original Sin. *(page 16, 213)*

conscience The "interior voice" of a person, a God-given sense of the law of God. Moral conscience leads people to understand themselves as responsible for their actions, and prompts them to do good and avoid evil. To make good judgments, one needs to have a well-formed conscience. *(page 143)*

contraception The deliberate attempt to interfere with the creation of new life as a result of sexual intercourse. It is morally wrong because a married couple must remain open to procreation whenever they engage in sexual intercourse. *(page 221)*

contrition To have hatred for our sin and a commitment not to sin again. *(page 262)*

corporal works of mercy Charitable actions that respond to people's physical needs and show respect for human dignity. The traditional list of seven works includes feeding the hungry, giving drink to the thirsty, clothing the naked, sheltering the homeless, visiting the sick, visiting prisoners, and burying the dead. *(page 163)*

covenant A solemn agreement between human beings or between God and a human being in which mutual commitments are made. *(page 95)*

culpable To be guilty of wrongdoing. *(page 254)*

D

Decalogue The Ten Commandments. *(page 37)*

detraction Unnecessarily revealing something about another person that is true but is harmful to his or her reputation. It is a sin against the Eighth Commandment. *(page 149)*

divination The practice of seeking power or knowledge through supernatural means apart from the one, true God; a sin against the First Commandment. *(page 87)*

E

envy Resentment or sadness because of another person's good fortune. It is one of the capital sins and contrary to the Tenth Commandment. *(page 172)*

eschatology The area of Christian faith having to do with the last things: the Last Judgment, the particular judgment, the resurrection of the body, Heaven, Hell, and Purgatory. *(page 114)*

Eternal Law The order in creation that reflects God's will and purpose; it is eternal because it is always true and never changes. All other types of law have their basis in Eternal Law and are only true if they reflect the truth of Eternal Law. *(page 30)*

euthanasia A direct action, or a deliberate lack of action, that causes the death of a person who is handicapped, sick, or dying. Euthanasia is a violation of the Fifth Commandment against killing. *(page 191)*

evangelical counsels To go beyond the minimum rules of life required by God (such as the Ten Commandments and the Precepts of the Church) and strive for spiritual perfection through a life marked by a commitment to chastity, poverty, and obedience. *(page 81)*

examination of conscience Prayerful reflection on, and assessment of, one's words, attitudes, and actions in light of the Gospel of Jesus; more specifically, the conscious moral evaluation of one's life in preparation for reception of the Sacrament of Penance and Reconciliation. *(page 100)*

excommunication A severe penalty the Church imposes on a Catholic who has committed a grave sin or offense against canon law in which the person is banned from celebrating or receiving the Sacraments. The Church imposes excommunication in the hope that the sinner will repent and be reconciled with God and the Church. *(page 189)*

F

faith In general, the belief in the existence of God. For Christians, the gift of God by which one freely accepts full Revelation in Jesus Christ. It is a matter of both the head (acceptance of God's revealed truth) and the heart (love of God and neighbor as a response to God's first loving us); also, one of the three theological virtues. *(page 244)*

fornication Sexual intercourse between a man and a woman who are not married. It is morally wrong to engage in intercourse before marriage, a sin against the Sixth Commandment. *(page 214)*

fortitude Also called strength or courage, the cardinal virtue that enables one to maintain sound moral judgment and behavior in the face of difficulties and challenges; one of the four cardinal virtues. *(page 242)*

free will The gift from God that allows human beings to choose from among various actions, for which we are held accountable. It is the basis for moral responsibility. *(page 13)*

G

generative As a theological term, something related to the power of producing new life. *(page 205)*

grace The free and undeserved gift of God's loving and active presence in the universe and in our lives, empowering us to respond to his call and to live as his adopted sons and daughters. Grace restores our loving communion with the Holy Trinity, lost through sin. *(page 234)*

Great Commandments Jesus' summary of the entire divine Law as the love of God and the love of neighbor. *(page 42)*

greed The desire to accumulate earthly goods beyond what we need. It is one of the capital sins and contrary to the Tenth Commandment. *(page 172)*

H

heresy The conscious and deliberate rejection of a dogma of the Church. *(page 78)*

hope The theological virtue by which we trust in the promise of God and expect from God both eternal life and the grace we need to attain it; the conviction that God's grace is at work in the world and that the Kingdom of God established by and through Jesus Christ is becoming realized through the workings of the Holy Spirit among us. *(page 244)*

I

idolatry The worship of other beings, creatures, or material goods in a way that is fitting for God alone. It is a violation of the First Commandment. *(page 82)*

infallibility The Gift of the Holy Spirit to the whole Church by which the leaders of the Church—the Pope and the bishops in union with him—are protected from fundamental error when formulating a specific teaching on a matter of faith and morals. *(page 48)*

intellect The divine gift that gives us the ability to see and understand the order of things that God places within creation and to know and understand God through the created order. *(page 13)*

intention The intended outcome or goal of the person choosing the object when making a moral decision. *(page 64)*

in vitro fertilization The fertilization of a woman's ovum (egg) with a man's sperm outside her body. The fertilized egg is transferred to the woman's uterus. The Church considers the process to be a moral violation of the dignity of procreation. *(page 225)*

J

Johannine writings The Gospel of John and the three Letters of John. *(page 139)*

justice The cardinal virtue concerned with the rights and duties within relationships; the commitment, as well as the actions and attitudes that flow from the commitment, to ensure that all persons—particularly those who are poor and oppressed—receive what is due them. *(page 241)*

justification The process by which God frees us from sin and sanctifies us. *(page 23)*

just war War involves many evils, no matter the circumstances. A war is only just and permissible when it meets strict criteria in protecting citizens from an unjust aggressor. *(page 197)*

L

legitimate defense The teaching that limited violence is morally acceptable in defending yourself or your nation from an attack. *(page 195)*

love The human longing for God and a selfless commitment to supporting the dignity and humanity of all people simply because they are created in God's image. Also called "charity," it is one of the three theological virtues. *(page 244)*

lust Intense and uncontrolled desire for sexual pleasure. It is one of the seven capital sins. *(page 210)*

M

magic The belief in supernatural power that comes from a source other than God; a sin against the First Commandment. *(page 87)*

Magisterium The Church's living teaching office, which consists of all bishops, in communion with the Pope. *(page 48)*

mammon An Aramaic word meaning wealth or property. *(page 159)*

masturbation Self-manipulation of one's sexual organs for the purpose of erotic pleasure or to achieve orgasm. It is a sin because the act cannot result in the creation of new life and because God created sexuality not for self-gratification but to unify a husband and wife in Marriage. *(page 215)*

merit God's reward to those who love him and follow Christ's Law of Love. To have merit is to be justified in the sight of God, free from sin and sanctified by his grace. We do not earn merit on our own; it is a free gift from God due to the grace of Christ in us. *(page 25)*

monotheism The belief in and worship of only one God. *(page 83)*

moral law The moral law is established by God and is a rational expression of Eternal Law. Moral law reflects God's wisdom; it is the teaching that leads us to the blessed life he wants for us. *(page 30)*

mortal sin An action so contrary to the will of God that it results in a complete separation from God and his grace. As a consequence of that separation, the person is condemned to eternal death. For a sin to be a mortal sin, three conditions must be met: the act must involve grave matter, the person must have full knowledge of the evil of the act, and the person must give his or her full consent in committing the act. *(page 67)*

N

natural law The moral law that can be understood through the use of reason. It is our God-given ability to understand what it means to be in right relationship with God, other people, the world, and ourselves. The basis for natural law is our participation in God's wisdom and goodness because we are created in the divine likeness. *(page 32)*

New Law Divine Law revealed in the New Testament through the life and teaching of Jesus Christ and through the witness and teaching of the Apostles. The New Law perfects the Old Law and brings it to fulfillment. Also called the Law of Love. *(page 40)*

nuptial Something related to marriage or a marriage ceremony. *(page 205)*

O

object In moral decision making, the object is the specific thing—an act, word, or thought—that is being chosen. *(page 64)*

Old Law Divine Law revealed in the Old Testament, summarized in the Ten Commandments. Also call the Law of Moses. It contrasts with the New Law of the Gospels. *(page 37)*

original holiness The original state of human beings in their relationship with God, sharing in the divine life in full communion with him. *(page 15)*

original justice The state of complete harmony of our first parents with themselves, with each other, and with all of creation. *(page 23)*

Original Sin From the Latin *origo,* meaning "beginning" or "birth." The term has two meanings: (1) the sin of the first human beings, who disobeyed God's command by choosing to follow their own will and so lost their original holiness and became subject to death, (2) the fallen state of human nature that affects every person born into the world. *(page 15)*

P

pantheon A group of gods and goddesses worshipped by a particular people or religion. *(page 82)*

parables Stories rooted in daily life that use symbolism or allegory as a teaching tool and that usually have a surprise ending. *(page 159)*

Paschal Mystery The work of salvation accomplished by Jesus Christ mainly through his life, Passion, death, Resurrection, and Ascension. *(page 19)*

penance In general, an attitude of the heart in which one experiences regrets for past sin and commits to a change in behaviors or attitudes. In the Sacrament of Penance and Reconciliation, the priest assigns penitents a penance to help them make amends for their sins. Particular acts of penance may include spiritual disciplines such as prayers or fasting. *(page 264)*

Pentateuch A Greek word meaning "five books," referring to the first five books of the Old Testament. *(page 39)*

perjury The sin of lying while under an oath to tell the truth. It is a sin against the Second Commandment. *(page 100)*

plagiarism Copying someone else's words or ideas without permission or giving proper credit to the person. *(page 161)*

polygamy Having more than one spouse, an act contrary to the dignity of Marriage. *(page 223)*

pornography A written description or visual portrayal of a person or action that is created or viewed with the intention of stimulating sexual feelings. Creating or using pornography is a sin against the Sixth and Ninth Commandments. *(page 215)*

poverty of heart The recognition of our deep need for God and the commitment to put God above everything else in life, particularly above the accumulation of material wealth. *(page 177)*

Precepts of the Church Sometimes called the commandments of the Church, these are basic obligations for all Catholics that are dictated by the laws of the Church. *(page 46)*

profanity Speaking disrespectfully about something that is sacred or treating it with disrespect. *(page 92)*

prostitution The act of providing sexual services in exchange for money, drugs, or other goods. It is a serious social evil and a sin against the Sixth Commandment. *(page 214)*

providence The guidance, material goods, and care provided by God that is sufficient to meet our needs. *(page 174)*

prudence The cardinal virtue by which a person is inclined toward choosing the moral good and avoiding evil; sometimes called the rudder virtue because it helps steer the person through complex moral situations. *(page 241)*

R

reconciliation The process of restoring broken relationships with God, with the Church, and with people who were directly offended by our sins. *(page 260)*

reparation Making amends for something one did wrong that caused harm to another person or led to loss. *(page 143)*

S

Sabbath In the Old Testament, the "seventh day," on which God rested after the work of Creation was completed. In the Old Law, the weekly day of rest to remember God's work through private prayer and communal worship. For Catholics, Sunday, the day on which Jesus was raised, which we are to observe with participation in the Eucharist in fulfillment of the Third Commandment. *(page 104)*

sacramental graces The gifts proper to each of the Seven Sacraments. *(page 237)*

sacred The quality of being holy, worthy of respect and reverence. *(page 91)*

sacred art Art that evokes faith by turning our minds to the mystery of God, primarily through the artistic depiction of Scripture, Tradition, and the lives of Jesus, Mary, and the saints. *(page 154)*

sacrilege An offense against God. It is the abuse of a person, place, or thing dedicated to God and the worship of him. *(page 87)*

salvation history The pattern of specific salvific events in human history that reveal God's presence and saving actions. *(page 19)*

sanctify, sanctification To make holy; sanctification is the process of becoming closer to God and growing in holiness, taking on the righteousness of Jesus Christ with the gift of sanctifying grace. *(page 24)*

sanctifying grace A supernatural gift of God by which our sins are forgiven and we are made holy. It restores our communion with God. *(page 236)*

scandal An action or attitude—or the failure to act—that leads another person into sin. *(page 186)*

simony Buying or selling something spiritual, such as a grace, a Sacrament, or a relic. It violates the honor of God. *(page 88)*

sin of commission A sin that is the direct result of a freely chosen thought, word, or deed. *(page 66)*

sin of omission A sin that is the result of a failure to do something required by God's moral Law. *(page 66)*

social doctrine The body of teaching by the Church on economic and social matters that includes moral judgments and demands for action in favor of those being harmed. *(page 163)*

social justice The defense of human dignity by ensuring that essential human needs are met and that essential human rights are protected; to fight against social sin. *(page 70)*

social sin The collective effect of many personal sins over time, which corrupts society and its institutions by creating "structures of sin." *(page 70)*

solidarity Union of one's heart and mind with all people. Solidarity leads to the just distribution of material goods, creates bonds between opposing groups and nations, and leads to the spread of spiritual goods such as friendship and prayer. *(page 131)*

soul Our spiritual principle, it is immortal, and it is what makes us most like God. Our soul is created by God, and he unites it with our physical body at the moment of conception. The soul is the seat of human consciousness and freedom. *(page 12)*

special graces Gifts intended for the common good of the Church, also called charisms. *(page 237)*

state The word used in Church documents to indicate a political authority, for example, a kingdom, a nation, a country, or a state within a country. *(page 70)*

suicide Deliberately taking one's own life. It is a serious violation of the Fifth Commandment for it is God's will that we preserve our own lives. *(page 193)*

superstition Attributing to someone or something else a power that belongs to God alone and relying on such powers rather than trusting in God; a sin against the First Commandment. *(page 86)*

surrogate motherhood A medical process in which a woman becomes pregnant through artificial means and delivers a child for someone else. She may or may not be the child's biological mother. The procedure is morally wrong because it separates intercourse from the act of procreation and pregnancy. *(page 225)*

T

temperance The cardinal virtue by which one moderates his or her appetites and passions to achieve balance in the use of created goods. *(page 212, 242)*

theological virtues The name for the God-given virtues of faith, hope, and love. These virtues enable us to know God as God and lead us to union with him in mind and heart. *(page 78)*

tithe A commitment to donate a tenth or some other percentage of our income to the Church and other charitable causes. *(page 81)*

V

venerate An action that shows deep reverence for something sacred. For example, on Good Friday, individuals in the assembly venerate the cross by bowing before it or kissing it. *(page 84)*

venial sin A less serious offense against the will of God that diminishes one's personal character and weakens but does not rupture one's relationship with God. *(page 67)*

vice A practice or habit that leads a person to sin. *(page 68)*

virtue A habitual and firm disposition to do good. *(page 68)*

vocation A call from God to all members of the Church to embrace a life of holiness. Specifically, it refers to a call to live the holy life as an ordained minister, as a vowed religious (sister or brother), in a Christian Marriage, or in single life. *(page 126)*

Index

Page numbers in italics refer to illustrations.

Acknowledgments

Scripture texts used in this work are taken from the *New American Bible, revised edition* © 2010, 1991, 1986, 1970 Confraternity of Christian Doctrine, Inc., Washington, D.C. All Rights Reserved. No part of this work may be reproduced or transmitted in any form or by any means, electronic or mechanical, including photocopying, recording, or by any information storage and retrieval system, without permission in writing from the copyright owner.

The excerpts marked *Catechism* and *CCC* are from the English translation of the *Catechism of the Catholic Church* for use in the United States of America, second edition. Copyright © 1994 by the United States Catholic Conference, Inc.—Libreria Editrice Vaticana (LEV). English translation of the *Catechism of the Catholic Church: Modifications from the Editio Typica* copyright © 1997 by the United States Catholic Conference, Inc.—LEV.

The excerpts on pages 12, 59, 110, and 184 are adapted from writings by the early Church Fathers, at *www.ccel.org.*

The excerpt on pages 34–35 is from Saint Augustine, "On The Trinity," Book XIV, chapters 15 and 21, at *www.newadvent.org/fathers/130114.htm.*

The excerpts in the sidebars on pages 35 and 44 are from *God Is Love (Deus Caritas Est),* numbers 28 and 18, at *www.vatican.va/holy_father/benedict_xvi/ encyclicals/documents/hf_ben-xvi_enc_20051225_deus-caritas-est_en.html.* Copyright © 2005 LEV.

The excerpts on pages 71 and 72 and the excerpt in the sidebar on page 222 are from *Pastoral Constitution on the Church in the Modern World* (*Gaudium et Spes,* 1965), numbers 26, 26, and 52, respectively, at *www.vatican.va/archive/ hist_councils/ii_vatican_council/documents/vat-ii_cons_19651207_gaudium-et-spes_en.html.* Copyright © LEV.

The excerpt in the sidebar on page 73 is from "Meeting with the Members of Catholic Charities USA: Address of His Holiness John Paul II," number 6, at *www.vatican.va/holy_father/john_paul_ii/speeches/1987/september/documents/ hf_jp-ii_spe_19870913_organizzaz-caritative_en.html.* Copyright © 1987 LEV.

The prayers on pages 88, 134, and 221 are from *The Roman Missal* © 2010, International Commission on English in the Liturgy Corporation (ICEL). English translation prepared by the ICEL. Used with permission of the ICEL.

The prayer on page 109 is from *The Roman Missal* © 1973, ICEL. English translation prepared by the ICEL (New York: Catholic Book Publishing Company, 1985), page 208. Illustrations and arrangement copyright © 1985–1974 by the Catholic Book Publishing Company, New York. Used with permission of the ICEL.

The excerpt in the sidebar on page 114 is from "Homily of John Paul II: Mass in the Church of the Holy Sepulchre," number 4, at *www.vatican.va/holy_ father/john_paul_ii/travels/documents/hf_jp-ii_hom_20000326_holy-sepulchre_ en.html.* Copyright © 2000 LEV.

The excerpt on page 169 is from "Message of His Holiness Pope John Paul II for the Celebration of the World Day of Peace, 1990," number 8, at *www.vatican. va/holy_father/john_paul_ii/messages/peace /documents/hf_jp-ii_mes_19891208_ xxiii-world-day-for-peace_en.html.* Copyright © 1989 LEV.

or concern about, any of the information or sources listed within, please contact Saint Mary's Press.

Endnotes Cited in Quotations from the *Catechism of the Catholic Church*, Second Edition

Section 1
1. Saint Augustine, *In Jo. ev.* 72, 3: J. P. Migne, ed., Patrologia Latina (Paris: 1841–1855) 35, 1823.
2. Saint Thomas Aquinas, *Dec. præ.* I

Section 2
1. Saint John Chrysostom, *De incomprehensibili* 3, 6: J. P. Migne, ed., Patrologia Graeca (Paris: 1857–1866) 48, 725.

Section 4
1. Congregation for the Doctrine of the Faith, *Donum vitae* I, 2.
2. John Paul II, *Evangelium vitae* 56.
3. *Familiaris consortio* 84.

Section 5
1. Saint Thomas Aquinas, Summa Theologiae II–II, 47, 2.